On Core Mathematics

Grade 2

HOUGHTON MIFFLIN HARCOURT

Cover photo credit: Garry Gay/Alamy

Printed in the U.S.A.

ISBN 978-0-547-57519-3

17 0928 20 19 18 17 16

4500596547 ^ B C D E F G

Table of Contents

Operations and Algebraic Thinking

▶ **Represent and solve problems involving addition and subtraction.**

▶ **Add and subtract within 20.**

▶ **Work with equal groups of objects to gain foundations for multiplication.**

Number and Operations in Base Ten

▶ **Understand place value.**

▶ Use place value understanding and properties of operations to add and subtract.

Measurement and Data

▶ **Measure and estimate lengths in standard units.**

▶ **Relate addition and subtraction to length.**

▶ **Work with time and money.**

Represent and interpret data.

Geometry

Reason with shapes and their attributes.

Name ______________________________

COMMON CORE STANDARD CC.2.OA.1

Lesson Objective: Use bar models to represent a variety of addition and subtraction situations.

Algebra • Use Drawings to Represent Problems

You can use bar models to show problems.

There are 5 girls and 11 boys at the park.
How many more boys than girls are at the park?

How many boys? → 11

How many girls? → 5

6

Write a number sentence. 11 − 5 = 6

There are 6 more boys than girls.

Complete the bar model. Then write a number sentence to solve.

1. Nathan had 7 stamps. Then he got 9 more stamps. How many stamps does Nathan have now?

7	9

_____

_____ + _____ = _____ _____ stamps

Name ______________________

Lesson 1
CC.2.OA.1

Algebra • Use Drawings to Represent Problems

Complete the bar model. Then write a number sentence to solve.

1. Sara has 4 yellow beads and 3 green beads. How many beads does Sara have?

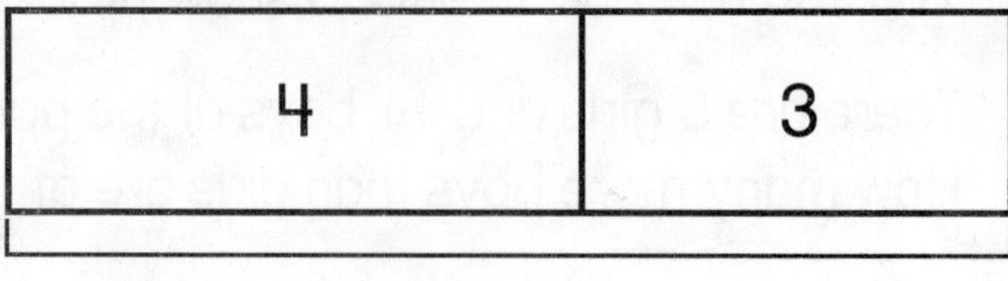

______

____

______ beads

2. Adam had 12 trucks. He gave 4 trucks to Ed. How many trucks does Adam have now?

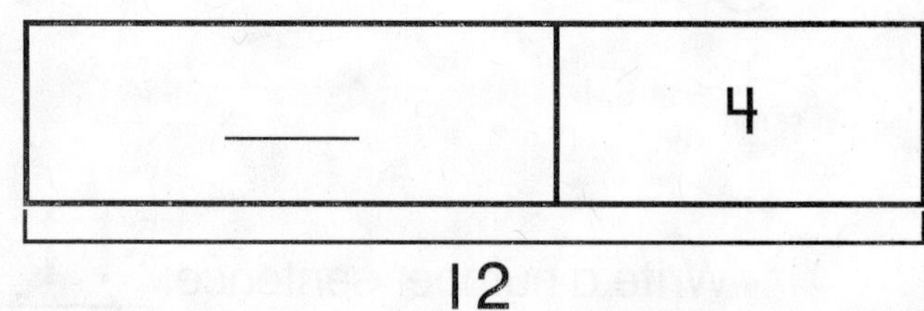

____

______ trucks

3. Grandma has 14 red roses and 7 pink roses. How many more red roses than pink roses does she have?

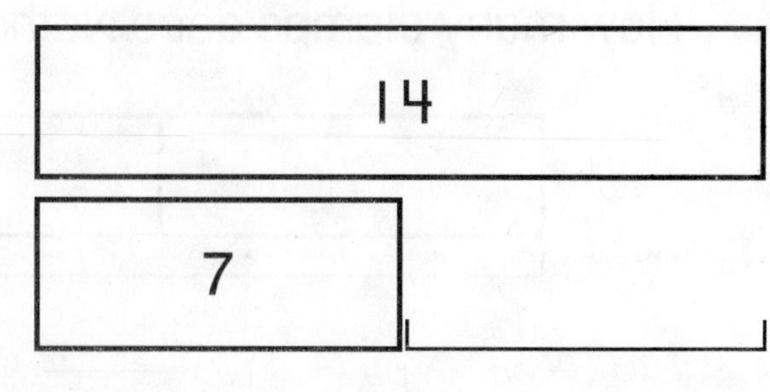

______

____

______ more red roses

Name ___________________________

Lesson 2

COMMON CORE STANDARD CC.2.OA.1

Lesson Objective: Write equations to represent and solve a variety of addition and subtraction situations.

Algebra • Use Equations to Represent Problems

Some red fish and 9 green fish are in a tank.
The tank has 14 fish. How many red fish are there?

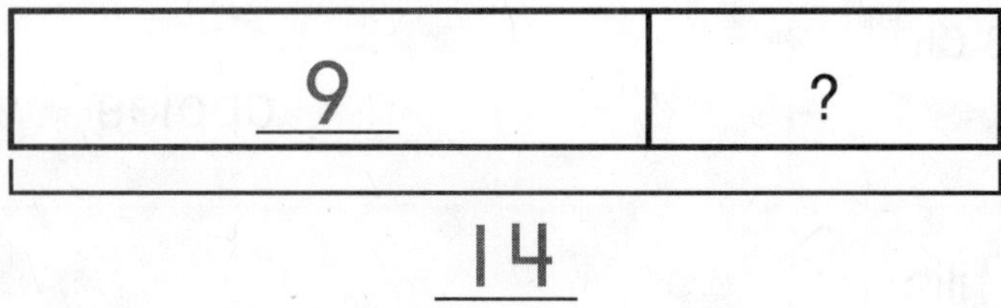

Write a number sentence.

Use a ■ for the missing number.

$14 - 9 = ■$

5 red fish in the tank.

Write a number sentence for the problem.
Use a ■ for the missing number. Then solve.

1. There are 13 trees in a park. 8 are pine trees. The rest are oak trees. How many oak trees are there?

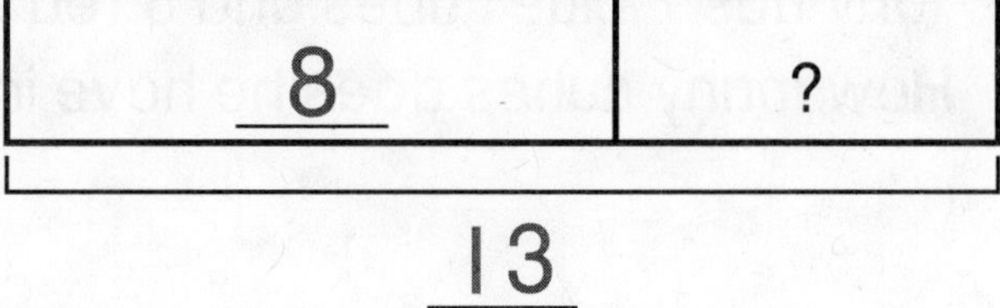

So there are ___________________

_____ oak trees

Name ______________________________

Lesson 2
CC.2.OA.1

Algebra • Use Equations to Represent Problems

Write a number sentence for the problem.
Use a ▢ for the missing number. Then solve.

1. There were 15 apples in a bowl. Dan used some apples to make a pie. Now there are 7 apples in the bowl. How many apples did Dan use?	______________________ _____ apples
2. Amy has 16 gift bags. She fills 8 gift bags with whistles. How many gift bags are not filled with whistles?	______________________ _____ gift bags
3. There were 5 dogs at the park. Then 9 more dogs joined them. How many dogs are at the park now?	______________________ _____ dogs

PROBLEM SOLVING

Write or draw to show how you solved the problem.

4. Tony has 7 blue cubes and 6 red cubes. How many cubes does he have in all?

_____ cubes

Name ______________________________

Lesson 3

COMMON CORE STANDARD CC.2.OA.1

Lesson Objective: Solve problems involving 2-digit addition by using the strategy *draw a diagram.*

Problem Solving • Addition

Hannah has 14 pencils. Juan has 13 pencils. How many pencils do they have in all?

Unlock the Problem

What do I need to find?	What information do I need to use?
how many pencils they have in all	Hannah has 14 pencils. Juan has 13 pencils.

Show how to solve the problem.

Hannah's 14 pencils	Juan's 13 pencils

? pencils in all

14 + 13 = ■

27 pencils

Solve.

1. There are 21 peanuts in a bag. 16 more peanuts are put into the bag. How many peanuts are in the bag in all?

21 peanuts	16 peanuts

______ peanuts in all

____

______ peanuts

Name ______________________________

Problem Solving • Addition

Label the bar model. Write a number sentence with a ■ for the missing number. Solve.

1. Jacob counts 37 ants on the sidewalk and 11 ants on the grass. How many ants does Jacob count?

   ____

   _____ ants

2. There are 14 bees in the hive and 17 bees in the garden. How many bees are there in all?

   ____

   _____ bees

3. There are 28 flowers in Sasha's garden. 16 flowers are yellow and the rest are white. How many white flowers are in Sasha's garden?

   ____

   _____ white flowers

Name ______________________

Lesson 4

COMMON CORE STANDARD CC.2.OA.1

Lesson Objective: Represent addition situations with number sentences using a symbol for the unknown number.

Algebra • Write Equations to Represent Addition

Sara took 16 pictures.
Then she took 17 more pictures.
How many pictures did Sara take in all?

Use a bar model to show the problem.

16 pictures	17 pictures

__?__ pictures in all

Write a number sentence. Solve.

16 + 17 = ■   __33__ pictures

Use a bar model to show the problem. Write a number sentence. Use a ■ for the missing number. Then solve.

1. Josh has 18 basketball cards and 14 baseball cards. How many cards does he have altogether?

_____ basketball cards	_____ baseball cards

_____ cards altogether

______________________   _____ cards

Name ______________________________

Algebra • Write Equations to Represent Addition

Write a number sentence for the problem. Use a ■ for the missing number. Then solve.

1. Emily and her friends went to the park. They saw 15 robins and 9 blue jays. How many birds did they see?

______________ ■

_____ birds

2. Joe has 13 fish in one tank. He has 8 fish in another tank. How many fish does Joe have?

______________ ■

_____ fish

PROBLEM SOLVING

Solve.

3. There are 21 children in Kathleen's class. 12 of the children are girls. How many children in her class are boys?

_____ boys

Name ______________________________

Lesson 5

COMMON CORE STANDARD CC.2.OA.1

Lesson Objective: Solve problems involving 2-digit subtraction by using the strategy *draw a diagram.*

Problem Solving • Subtraction

Katie had a box of 42 craft sticks. She used 26 craft sticks to make a sailboat. How many craft sticks were not used?

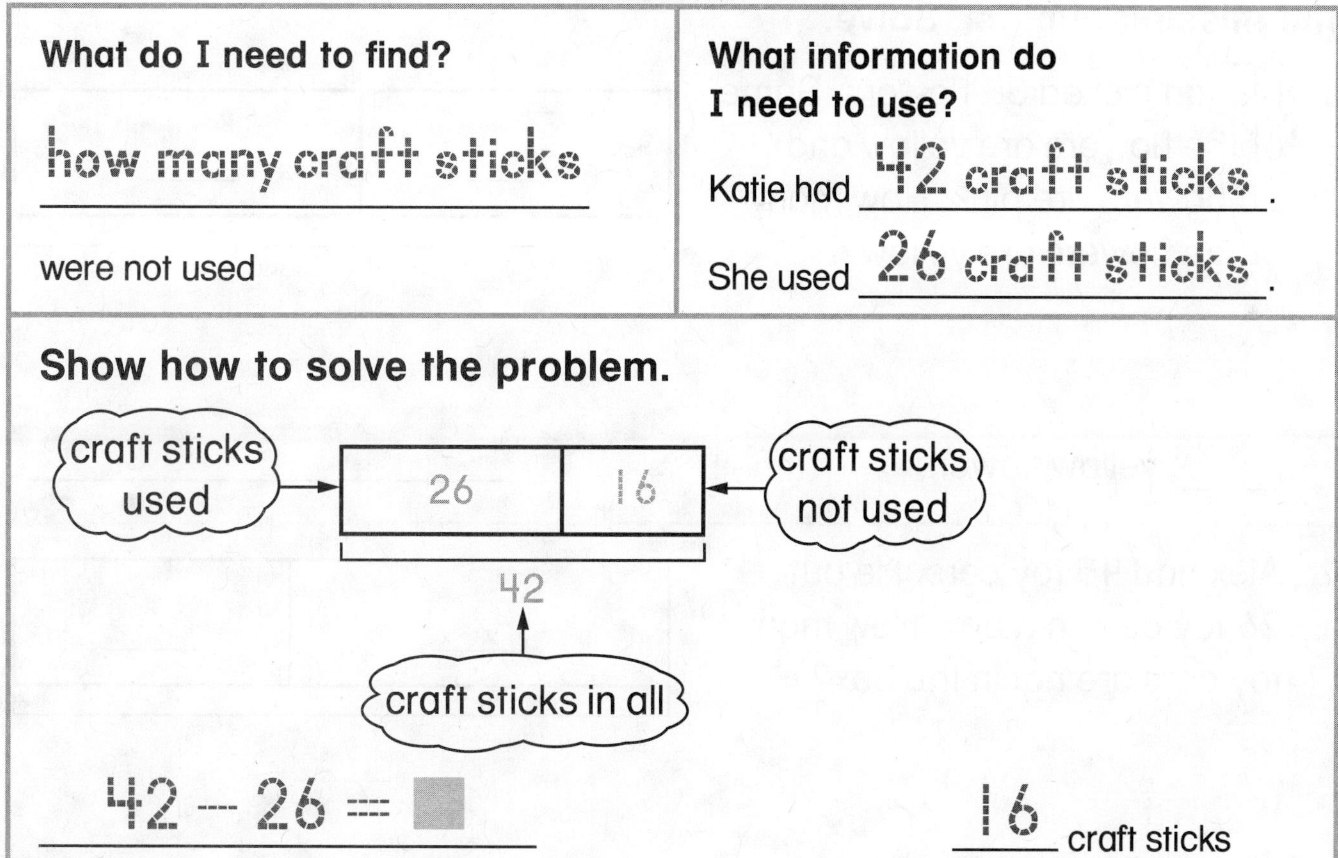

Write a number sentence with a ■ for the missing number. Solve.

1. Ms. Lee took 35 purses to the fair. She sold 14 purses. How many purses does she have left?

14	?

35

______________________ ______ purses

Name ______________________________

Problem Solving • Subtraction

Label the bar model. Write a number sentence with a ■ for the missing number. Solve.

1. Megan picked 34 flowers. Some of the flowers are yellow and 18 flowers are pink. How many of the flowers are yellow?

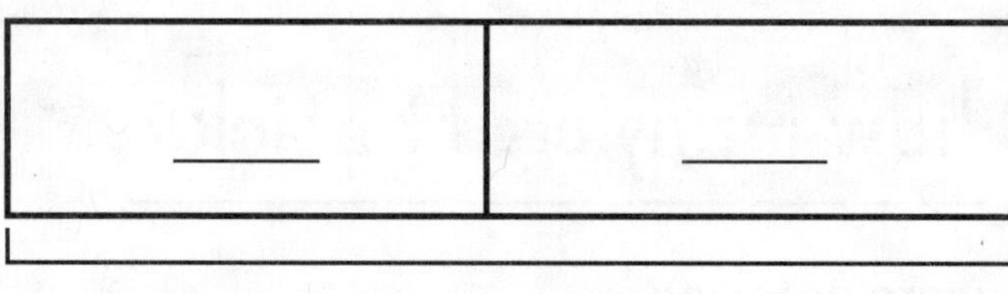

_____ yellow flowers ______________________

2. Alex had 45 toy cars. He put 26 toy cars in a box. How many toy cars are not in the box?

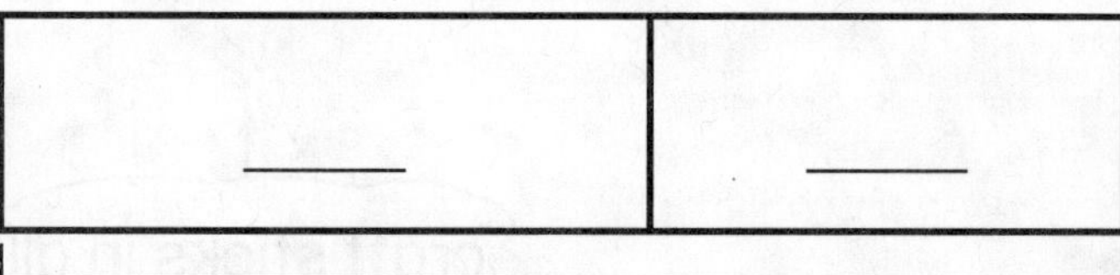

_____ toy cars ______________________

3. Mr. Kane makes 43 pizzas. 28 of the pizzas are small. The rest are large. How many pizzas are large?

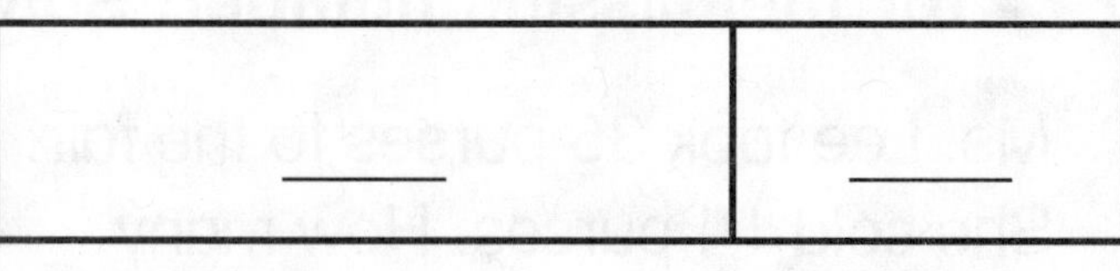

_____ large pizzas ______________________

Name ______________________

Lesson 6

COMMON CORE STANDARD CC.2.OA.1

Lesson Objective: Represent subtraction situations with number sentences using a symbol for the unknown number.

Algebra • Write Equations to Represent Subtraction

37 birds were in the trees.
13 birds flew away.
How many birds are in the trees now?

The bar model shows the problem.

37

Use the bar model to write a number sentence.

37 − 13 = ■

Subtract to find the missing part.

$$\begin{array}{r} 37 \\ -\ 13 \\ \hline 24 \end{array}$$

So, the answer is 24 birds.

Write a number sentence for the problem.
Use a ■ for the missing number. Then solve.

1. Gina has 23 pens. 15 pens are blue and the rest are red. How many pens are red?

15	?

23

______________________ ______ red pens

Name ______________________________

Algebra • Write Equations to Represent Subtraction

Write a number sentence for the problem. Use a ■ for the missing number. Then solve.

1. 29 children rode their bikes to school. After some of the children rode home, there were 8 children with bikes still at school. How many children rode their bikes home?

______________________ _____ children

2. 32 children were on the school bus. Then 24 children got off the bus. How many children were still on the bus?

______________________ _____ children

PROBLEM SOLVING

Solve. Write or draw to explain.

3. There were 21 children in the library. After 7 children left the library, how many children were still in the library?

_____ children

Name ______________________________

COMMON CORE STANDARD CC.2.OA.1

Lesson Objective: Analyze word problems to determine what operations to use to solve multistep problems.

Solve Multistep Problems

Mr. Wright had 34 blue pencils and 25 red pencils. He gave 42 pencils to students. How many pencils does he have now?

The first sentence tells you what Mr. Wright had.

and

$$\begin{array}{r} 34 \\ +\ 25 \\ \hline 59 \end{array}$$

The second sentence tells you that he gave 42 of the pencils to students.

$$\begin{array}{r} 59 \\ -\ 42 \\ \hline 17 \end{array}$$

Mr. Wright has __17__ pencils now.

Solve the problem in steps. Show what you did.

1. Kara had 37 stickers. She gave 11 stickers to Sam and 5 stickers to Jane. How many stickers does Kara have now?

_____ stickers

Name ______________________________

Solve Multistep Problems

Complete the bar models for the steps you do to solve the problem.

1. Greg has 60 building blocks. His sister gives him 17 more blocks. He uses 38 blocks to make a tower. How many blocks are not used in the tower?

______ blocks

2. Jenna has a train of 26 connecting cubes and a train of 37 connecting cubes. She gives 15 cubes to a friend. How many cubes does Jenna have now?

______ cubes

PROBLEM SOLVING

Solve. Write or draw to explain.

3. Ava has 25 books. She gives away 7 books. Then Tom gives her 12 books. How many books does Ava have now?

______ books

Name ____________________

COMMON CORE STANDARD CC.2.OA.2

Lesson Objective: Use doubles facts as a strategy for finding sums for near doubles facts.

Use Doubles Facts

Use doubles facts to help you find sums.

If you know 6 + 6, you can find 6 + 7.

6 + 6 = 12

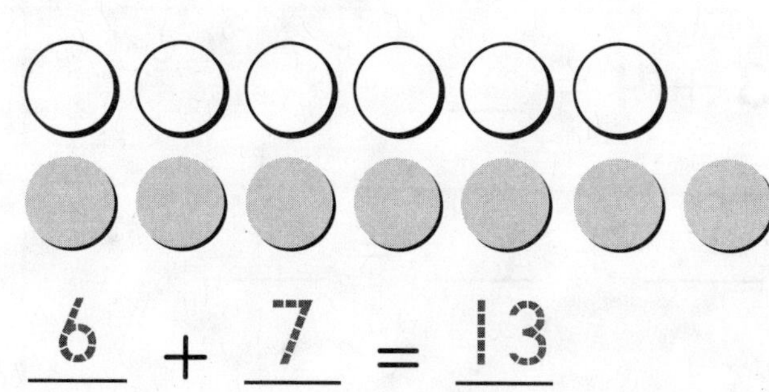

7 is 1 more than 6.
So 6 + 7 is 1 more than 6 + 6.

6 + 7 = 13

Write a doubles fact you can use to find the sum. Write the sum.

1. 4 + 5 = ____ ____ + ____ = ____

2. 5 + 6 = ____ ____ + ____ = ____

3. 7 + 8 = ____ ____ + ____ = ____

4. 8 + 9 = ____ ____ + ____ = ____

Name ____________________

Lesson 8
CC.2.OA.2

Use Doubles Facts

Write a doubles fact you can use to find the sum. Write the sum.

1. $2 + 3 =$ ____

____ + ____ = ____

2. $7 + 6 =$ ____

____ + ____ = ____

3. $3 + 4 =$ ____

____ + ____ = ____

4. $8 + 9 =$ ____

____ + ____ = ____

5. $6 + 5 =$ ____

____ + ____ = ____

6. $4 + 5 =$ ____

____ + ____ = ____

PROBLEM SOLVING 

Solve. Write or draw to explain.

7. There are 6 ants on a log. Then 7 ants crawl onto the log. How many ants are on the log now?

______ ants

Name ______________________

Lesson 9

COMMON CORE STANDARD CC.2.OA.2

Lesson Objective: Recall sums for basic facts using properties and strategies.

Practice Addition Facts

Use what you know to find sums.

Add in any order.

☆☆☆ ★★★★★

$3 + 5 = \underline{8}$

If you know 3 + 5, then you know 5 + 3.

★★★★★ ☆☆☆

$5 + 3 = \underline{8}$

Count on to add. To add 1, 2, or 3 to any number, count on from that number.

☆☆☆☆☆ ★

$5 + 1 = \underline{6}$

Write the sums.

1. $5 + 7 =$ ____ $7 + 5 =$ ____	**2.** ____ $= 5 + 1$ ____ $= 5 + 2$	**3.** $6 + 2 =$ ____ $6 + 3 =$ ____
4. ____ $= 9 + 5$ ____ $= 5 + 9$	**5.** $7 + 3 =$ ____ $3 + 7 =$ ____	**6.** $5 + 2 =$ ____ $5 + 3 =$ ____
7. ____ $= 3 + 6$ ____ $= 6 + 3$	**8.** $4 + 1 =$ ____ $1 + 4 =$ ____	**9.** $8 + 2 =$ ____ $8 + 3 =$ ____

Name ______________________

Lesson 9
CC.2.OA.2

Practice Addition Facts

Write the sums.

1. 9 + 1 = ____ 1 + 9 = ____	2. 7 + 6 = ____ 6 + 7 = ____	3. 8 + 0 = ____ 5 + 0 = ____
4. ____ = 7 + 9 ____ = 9 + 7	5. 4 + 4 = ____ 4 + 5 = ____	6. 9 + 9 = ____ 9 + 8 = ____
7. 8 + 8 = ____ 8 + 7 = ____	8. 2 + 2 = ____ 2 + 3 = ____	9. ____ = 6 + 3 ____ = 3 + 6
10. 6 + 6 = ____ 6 + 7 = ____	11. ____ = 0 + 7 ____ = 0 + 9	12. 5 + 5 = ____ 5 + 6 = ____
13. 8 + 5 = ____ 5 + 8 = ____	14. 8 + 2 = ____ 2 + 8 = ____	15. 7 + 4 = ____ 4 + 7 = ____

PROBLEM SOLVING REAL WORLD

Solve. Write or draw to explain.

16. Jason has 7 puzzles. Quincy has the same number of puzzles as Jason. How many puzzles do they have altogether?

____ puzzles

Name ______________________

Lesson 10

COMMON CORE STANDARD CC.2.OA.2

Lesson Objective: Recall sums for addition facts using the make a ten strategy.

Algebra • Make a Ten to Add

8 + 5 = ?

Step 1 Start with the greater addend.
Break apart the other addend to make a ten.

8  5

Step 2 You need to add **2** to 8 to make a ten. So, break apart 5 as **2** and 3.

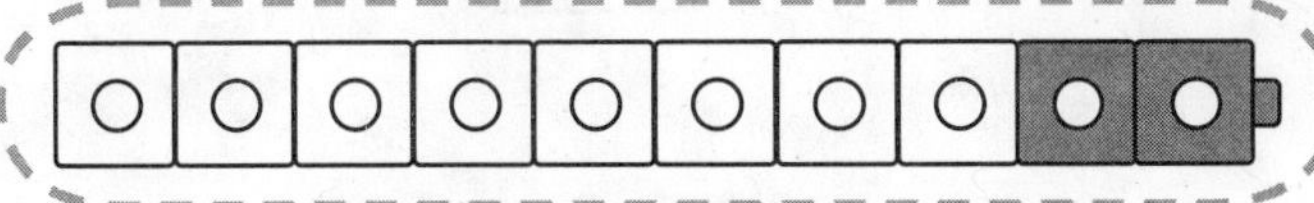

8 + 2 = 10 3

Step 3 Add on the rest to the 10. 10 + 3 = 13

Step 4 Write the sum. 8 + 5 = 13

Show how you can make a ten to find the sum. Write the sum.

1. 7 + 6 = ____
   3 3
   10 + ____ = ____

2. 9 + 2 = ____
   1 1
   10 + ____ = ____

3. 4 + 8 = ____
   2 2
   10 + ____ = ____

4. 5 + 9 = ____
   10 + ____ = ____

5. 8 + 6 = ____
   10 + ____ = ____

6. 4 + 9 = ____
   10 + ____ = ____

Name ____________________

Algebra • Make a Ten to Add

Show how you can make a ten to find the sum. Write the sum.

1. 9 + 7 = ____

   1 6

   10 + ____ = ____

2. 8 + 5 = ____

   10 + ____ = ____

3. 8 + 6 = ____

   10 + ____ = ____

4. 3 + 9 = ____

   10 + ____ = ____

5. 8 + 7 = ____

   10 + ____ = ____

6. 6 + 5 = ____

   10 + ____ = ____

7. 7 + 6 = ____

   10 + ____ = ____

8. 5 + 9 = ____

   10 + ____ = ____

PROBLEM SOLVING

Solve. Write or draw to explain.

9. There are 9 children on the bus. Then 8 more children get on the bus. How many children are on the bus now?

   ____ children

Name ______________________________

Lesson 11

COMMON CORE STANDARD CC.2.OA.2

Lesson Objective: Find sums of three addends by applying the Commutative and Associative Properties of Addition.

Algebra • Add 3 Addends

Add numbers in any order.
The sum stays the same.

1 + 4 + 6 = 11
5 + 6 = 11

1 + 4 + 6 = 11
1 + 10 = 11

1 + 4 + 6 = 11
7 + 4 = 11

Solve two ways. Circle the two addends you add first.

1. 2 + 3 + 2 = ____ 2 + 3 + 2 = ____

2. 7 + 2 + 3 = ____ 7 + 2 + 3 = ____

3. 1 + 1 + 9 = ____ 1 + 1 + 9 = ____

4. 6 + 4 + 4 = ____ 6 + 4 + 4 = ____

Name ______________________

Algebra • Add 3 Addends

Solve two ways. Circle the two addends you add first.

1. $2 + 3 + 7 =$ ____ $2 + 3 + 7 =$ ____

2. $5 + 3 + 3 =$ ____ $5 + 3 + 3 =$ ____

3. $4 + 5 + 4 =$ ____ $4 + 5 + 4 =$ ____

4. $4 + 4 + 4 =$ ____ $4 + 4 + 4 =$ ____

5.
$$\begin{array}{r} 5 \\ 4 \\ +\ 5 \\ \hline \end{array} \qquad \begin{array}{r} 5 \\ 4 \\ +\ 5 \\ \hline \end{array}$$

6.
$$\begin{array}{r} 6 \\ 3 \\ +\ 4 \\ \hline \end{array} \qquad \begin{array}{r} 6 \\ 3 \\ +\ 4 \\ \hline \end{array}$$

PROBLEM SOLVING

Choose a way to solve. Write or draw to explain.

7. Amber has 2 red crayons, 5 blue crayons, and 4 yellow crayons. How many crayons does she have in all?

____ crayons

Name ________________________

COMMON CORE STANDARD CC.2.OA.2

Lesson Objective: Use the inverse relationship of addition and subtraction to recall basic facts.

Algebra • Relate Addition and Subtraction

Use addition facts to help you subtract.

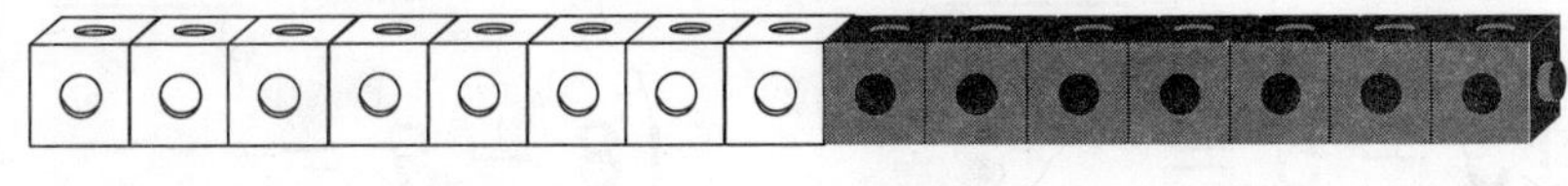

8 + 7 = 15

Think of 8 + 7 = 15 to find the difference for a related fact: 15 − 7 = ______.

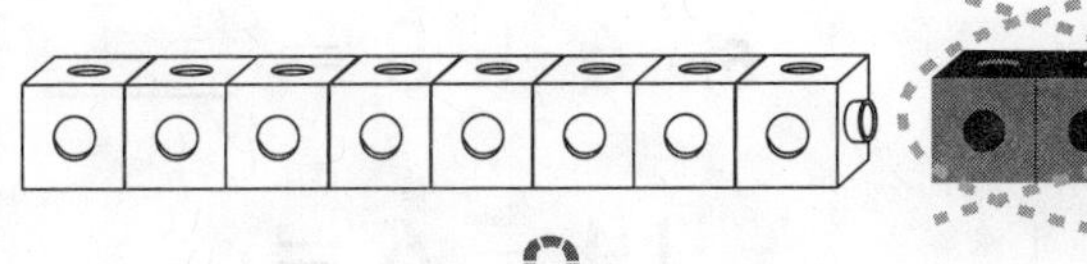

15 − 7 = 8

Write the sum and the difference for the related facts.

1. 6 + 3 = ____ 9 − 6 = ____	2. 7 + 6 = ____ 13 − 7 = ____
3. 6 + 8 = ____ 14 − 8 = ____	4. 7 + 4 = ____ 11 − 7 = ____
5. 8 + 4 = ____ 12 − 4 = ____	6. 8 + 8 = ____ 16 − 8 = ____
7. 9 + 7 = ____ 16 − 7 = ____	8. 7 + 5 = ____ 12 − 7 = ____

Name ______________________

Algebra • Relate Addition and Subtraction

Write the sum and the difference for the related facts.

1. $9 + 6 =$ ____ $15 - 6 =$ ____	2. $8 + 5 =$ ____ $13 - 5 =$ ____	3. $9 + 9 =$ ____ $18 - 9 =$ ____
4. $7 + 3 =$ ____ $10 - 3 =$ ____	5. $7 + 5 =$ ____ $12 - 5 =$ ____	6. $6 + 8 =$ ____ $14 - 6 =$ ____
7. $6 + 7 =$ ____ $13 - 6 =$ ____	8. $8 + 8 =$ ____ $16 - 8 =$ ____	9. $6 + 4 =$ ____ $10 - 4 =$ ____
10. $7 + 9 =$ ____ $16 - 9 =$ ____	11. $9 + 4 =$ ____ $13 - 9 =$ ____	12. $8 + 7 =$ ____ $15 - 7 =$ ____

PROBLEM SOLVING

Solve. Write or draw to explain.

13. There are 13 children on the bus. Then 5 children get off the bus. How many children are on the bus now?

____ children

Name ______________________

Lesson 13

COMMON CORE STANDARD CC.2.OA.2

Lesson Objective: Recall differences for basic facts using mental strategies.

Practice Subtraction Facts

Here are two ways to find differences.

10 − 3 = ?

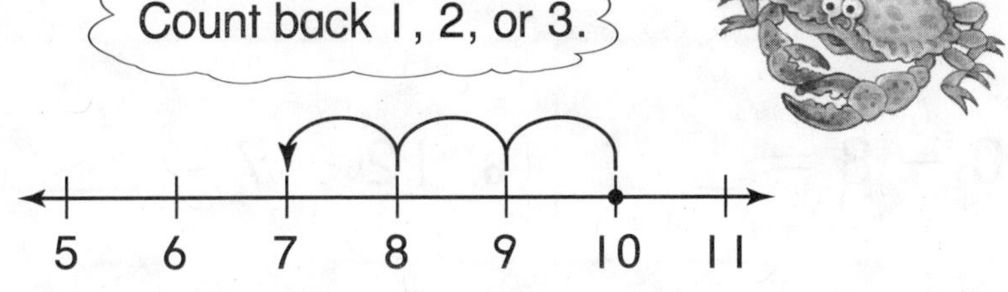

10 − 1 = 9

10 − 2 = 8

10 − 3 = 7

Think of a related addition fact.

3 + 7 = 10

so, 10 − 3 = 7

Write the difference.

1. 13 − 5 = ____	**2.** 10 − 4 = ____
3. 12 − 3 = ____	**4.** 11 − 2 = ____
5. 9 − 3 = ____	**6.** 12 − 5 = ____
7. 16 − 8 = ____	**8.** 13 − 7 = ____

Name ______________________

Practice Subtraction Facts

Write the difference.

1. $15 - 9 =$ ____	2. $10 - 2 =$ ____	3. ____ $= 13 - 5$
4. $14 - 7 =$ ____	5. $10 - 8 =$ ____	6. $12 - 7 =$ ____
7. ____ $= 10 - 3$	8. $16 - 7 =$ ____	9. $8 - 4 =$ ____
10. $11 - 5 =$ ____	11. $13 - 6 =$ ____	12. ____ $= 12 - 9$
13. $16 - 9 =$ ____	14. ____ $= 11 - 9$	15. $12 - 8 =$ ____
16. $14 - 8 =$ ____	17. $10 - 5 =$ ____	18. $12 - 5 =$ ____
19. $15 - 7 =$ ____	20. $14 - 9 =$ ____	21. $17 - 9 =$ ____

PROBLEM SOLVING

Solve. Write or draw to explain.

22. Mr. Li has 16 pencils. He gives 9 pencils to some students. How many pencils does Mr. Li have now?

____ pencils

Name ____________________

Lesson 14

COMMON CORE STANDARD CC.2.OA.2

Lesson Objective: Find differences on a number line to develop the mental strategy of decomposing to simplify facts.

Use Ten to Subtract

You can get to ten to help find differences.

13 − 7 = ?

Step 1 Start with the first number.

Step 2 Subtract ones to get to 10.

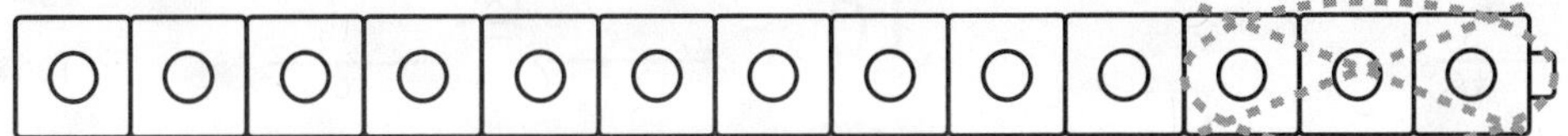

13 − 3 = 10

Step 3 Subtract the rest from the 10.

Think: I had 7. I subtracted 3 to get to 10.
Now I subtract the 4 I have left. 10 − 4 = 6

Step 4 Write the difference. 13 − 7 = 6

Show the tens fact you used. Write the difference.

1. 15 − 8 = ____
   5 3
   10 − 3 = ____

2. 12 − 4 = ____
   2 2
   10 − ____ = ____

3. 11 − 7 = ____
   10 − ____ = ____

4. 13 − 5 = ____
   10 − ____ = ____

Name ______________________

Use Ten to Subtract

Show the tens fact you used. Write the difference.

1. 14 − 6 = ____

   10 − ____ = ____

2. 12 − 7 = ____

   10 − ____ = ____

3. 13 − 7 = ____

   10 − ____ = ____

4. 15 − 8 = ____

   10 − ____ = ____

5. 11 − 7 = ____

   10 − ____ = ____

6. 14 − 5 = ____

   10 − ____ = ____

PROBLEM SOLVING REAL WORLD

Solve. Write or draw to explain.

7. Carl read 15 pages on Monday night and 9 pages on Tuesday night. How many more pages did he read on Monday night than on Tuesday night?

   ____ more pages

Name ______________________________

Lesson 15

COMMON CORE STANDARD CC.2.OA.3

Lesson Objective: Classify numbers up to 20 as even or odd.

Algebra • Even and Odd Numbers

These are even numbers.
They show pairs with no cubes left over.

4 is even. 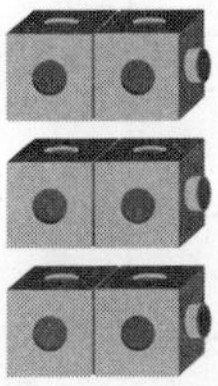 6 is even.  8 is even. 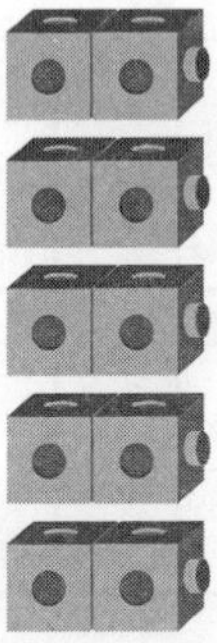 10 is even.

These are odd numbers.
They show pairs with 1 cube left over.

3 is odd.  5 is odd.  7 is odd.  9 is odd.

Count out the number of cubes.
Make pairs. Then write even or odd.

1. 15 ______	**2.** 11 ______
3. 12 ______	**4.** 13 ______
5. 16 ______	**6.** 14 ______

Name ______________________________

Lesson 15
CC.2.OA.3

Algebra • Even and Odd Numbers

Shade in the ten frames to show the number. Circle even or odd.

1. 15

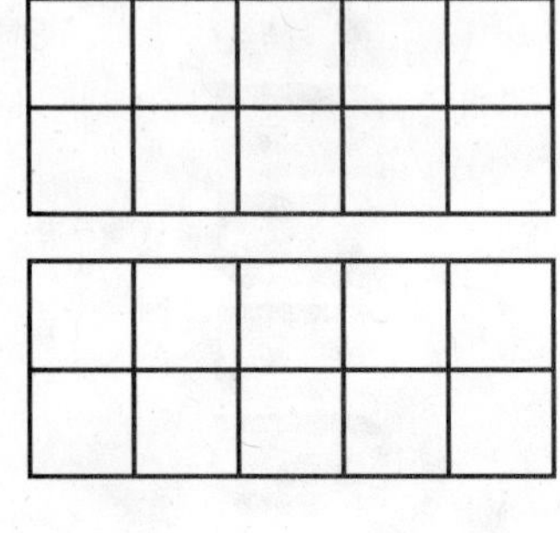

even odd

2. 18

even odd

3. 11

even odd

4. 17

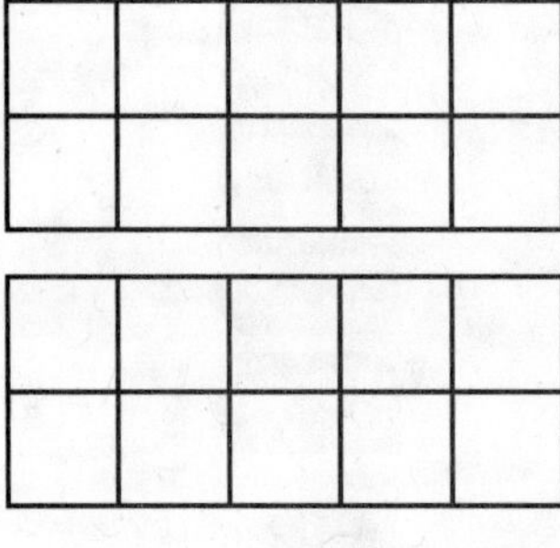

even odd

5. 13

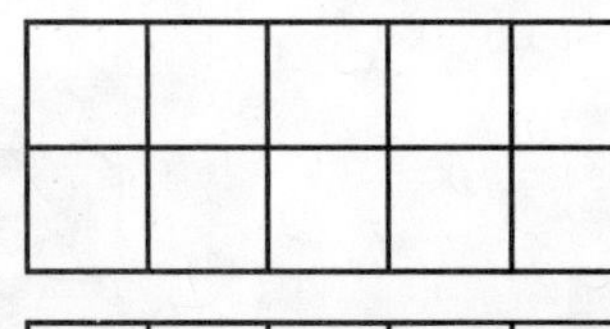

even odd

6. 20

even odd

PROBLEM SOLVING REAL WORLD

7. Mr. Dell has an odd number of sheep and an even number of cows on his farm. Circle the choice that could tell about his farm.

9 sheep and 10 cows

10 sheep and 11 cows

8 sheep and 12 cows

Name ______________________________

Lesson 16

COMMON CORE STANDARD CC.2.OA.3

Lesson Objective: Write equations with equal addends to represent even numbers.

Algebra • Represent Even Numbers

An even number of cubes will make two equal groups.

Count 8 cubes. Put the cubes into two equal groups. Do the two groups have equal numbers of cubes? To check, match one to one.

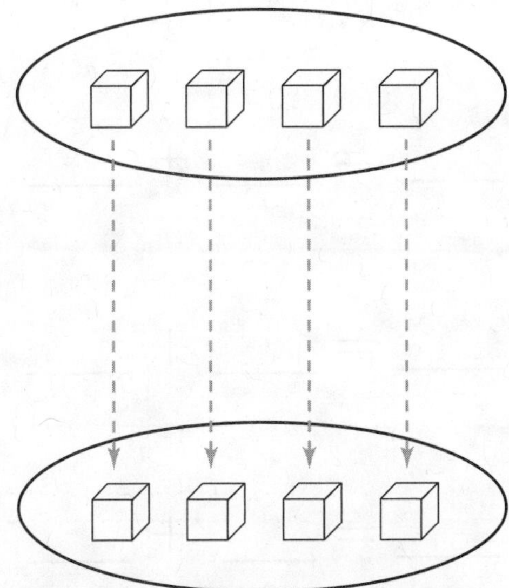

8 = 4 + 4

How many cubes are there in all? Complete the addition sentence to show the equal groups.

1. ____ = ____ + ____

2. ____ = ____ + ____

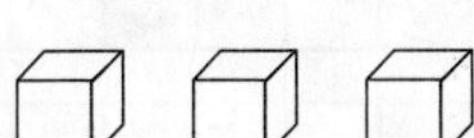

3. ____ = ____ + ____

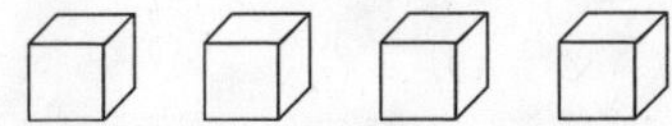

4. ____ = ____ + ____

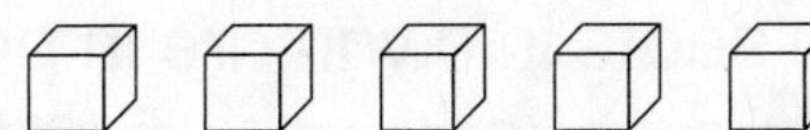

Name ______________________

Lesson 16
CC.2.OA.3

Algebra • Represent Even Numbers

Shade in the frames to show two equal groups for each number. Complete the addition sentence to show the groups.

1. 8 ____ = ____ + ____

2. 18 ____ = ____ + ____

3. 10 ____ = ____ + ____

4. 14 ____ = ____ + ____

5. 20 ____ = ____ + ____

6. 12 ____ = ____ + ____

PROBLEM SOLVING

Solve. Write or draw to explain.

7. The seats in a van are in pairs. There are 16 seats. How many pairs of seats are there?

____ pairs of seats

Name ___________________________

Lesson 17

COMMON CORE STANDARD CC.2.OA.4

Lesson Objective: Solve problems involving equal groups by using the strategy *act it out.*

Problem Solving • Equal Groups

Clarence puts grapes in 4 rows.
He puts 5 grapes in each row.
How many grapes does Clarence have?

Unlock the Problem

What do I need to find?	What information do I need to use?
how many grapes Clarence has	Clarence has 4 rows of grapes. He puts 5 grapes in each row.

Show how to solve the problem.

Clarence has 20 grapes.

Draw to show what you did.

1. Rachel puts her markers in 3 rows.
   Each row has 3 markers.
   How many markers does Rachel have?

   Rachel has _____ markers.

Name ______________________________

Problem Solving • Equal Groups

Act out the problem.
Draw to show what you did.

1. Mr. Anderson has 4 plates of cookies. There are 5 cookies on each plate. How many cookies are there in all?

_____ cookies

2. Ms. Trane puts some stickers in 3 rows. There are 2 stickers in each row. How many stickers does Ms. Trane have?

_____ stickers

3. There are 5 books in each box. How many books are in 5 boxes?

_____ books

Name ____________________

COMMON CORE STANDARD CC.2.OA.4

Lesson Objective: Write equations using repeated addition to find the total number of objects in arrays.

Algebra • Repeated Addition

Find the total number of cats.

- Circle each row.
- Count how many rows.

  3 equal rows
- Count how many in one row.

  4 cats in one row
- Write an addition sentence. Add the number of cats in each row.

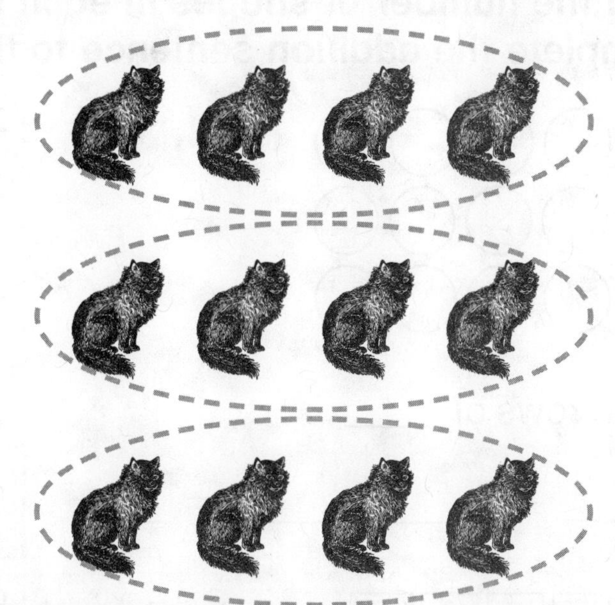

4 + 4 + 4 = 12

Find the number of shapes in each row.
Complete the addition sentence to find the total.

1. ●●●●●
   ●●●●●
   ●●●●●

   3 rows of ____

   ____ + ____ + ____ = ____

2. ✖✖✖✖
   ✖✖✖✖
   ✖✖✖✖
   ✖✖✖✖

   4 rows of ____

   ____ + ____ + ____ + ____ = ____

Name ______________________

Algebra • Repeated Addition

Find the number of shapes in each row.
Complete the addition sentence to find the total.

1. 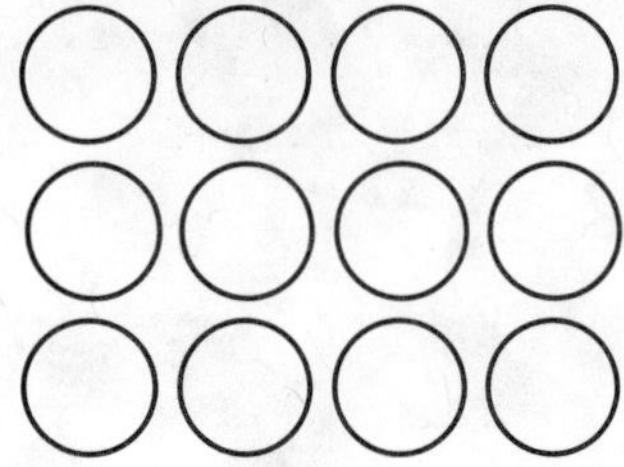

3 rows of ____

____ + ____ + ____ = ____

2. 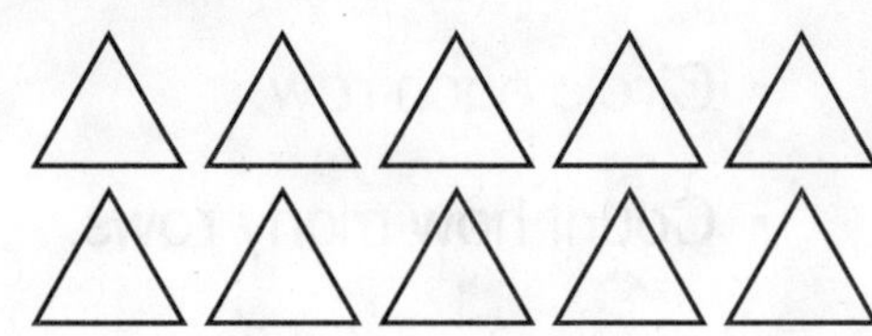

2 rows of ____

____ + ____ = ____

3. 

4 rows of ____

____ + ____ + ____ + ____ = ____

4. 

4 rows of ____

____ + ____ + ____ + ____ = ____

PROBLEM SOLVING

Solve. Write or draw to explain.

5. A classroom has 3 rows of desks. There are 5 desks in each row. How many desks are there altogether?

____ desks

Name ____________________

Lesson 19

COMMON CORE STANDARD CC.2.NBT.1

Lesson Objective: Write 3-digit numbers that are represented by groups of tens.

Explore 3-Digit Numbers

10 tens

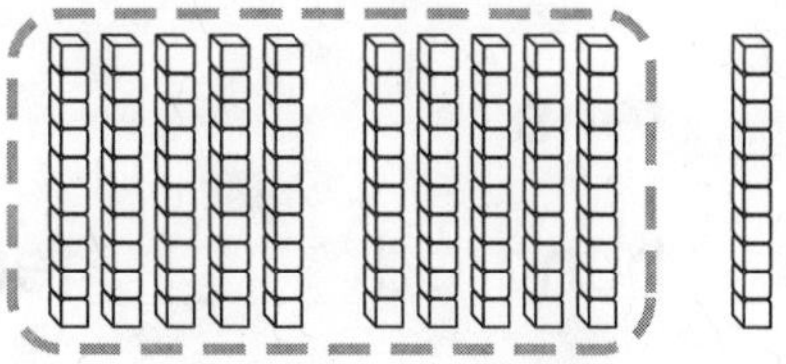

11 tens

1 hundred 1 ten

110

10 tens

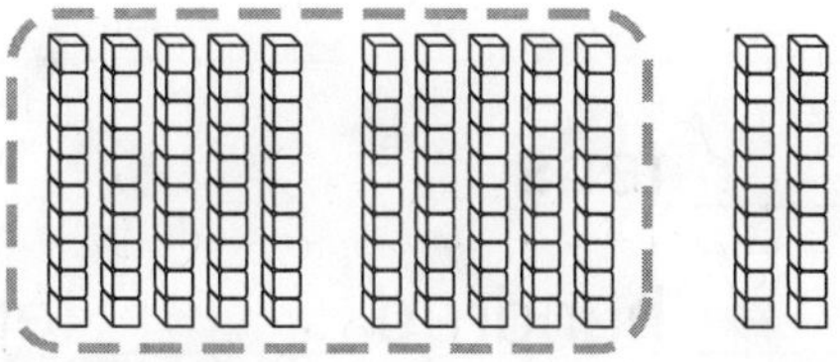

12 tens

1 hundred 2 tens

120

10 tens

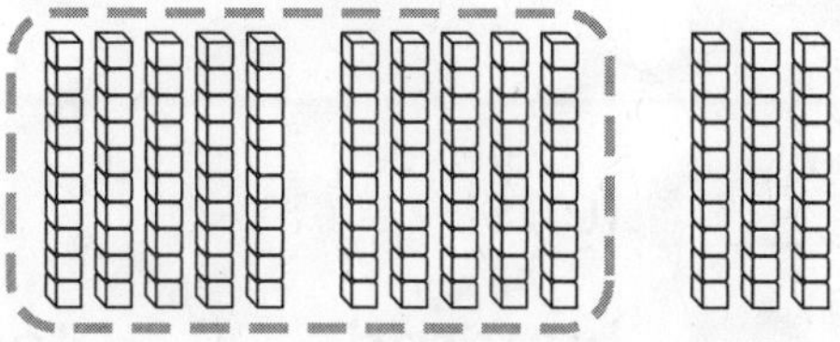

13 tens

1 hundred 3 tens

130

Circle tens to make 1 hundred. Write the number in different ways.

1. 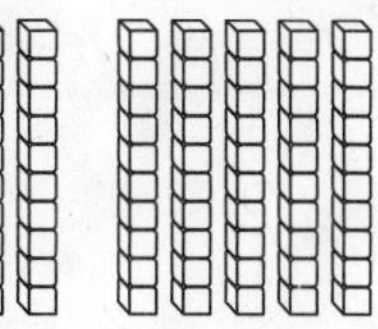 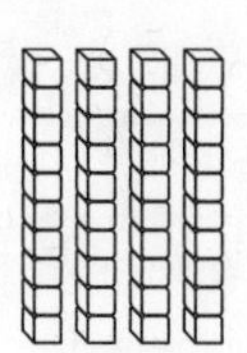 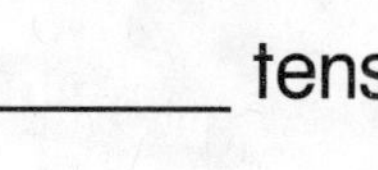

_______ tens

_______ hundred _______ tens

____

2. 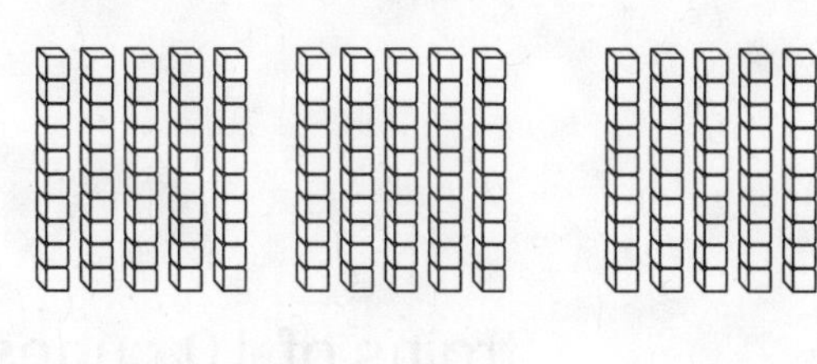

_______ tens

_______ hundred _______ tens

____

Name ______________________________

Lesson 19
CC.2.NBT.1

Explore 3-Digit Numbers

Circle tens to make 1 hundred. Write the number in different ways.

1. 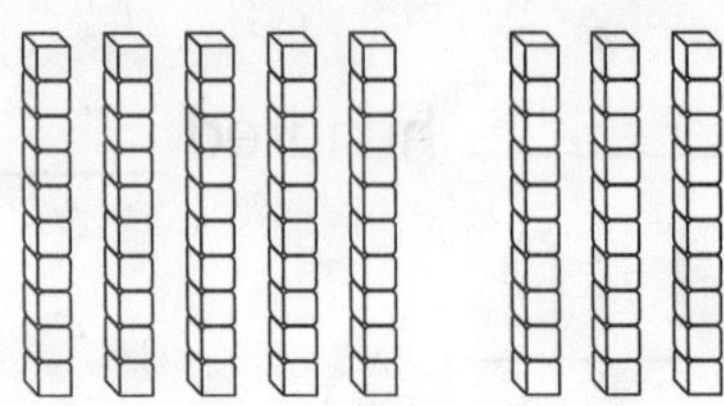

______ tens

______ hundred ______ tens

______

2. 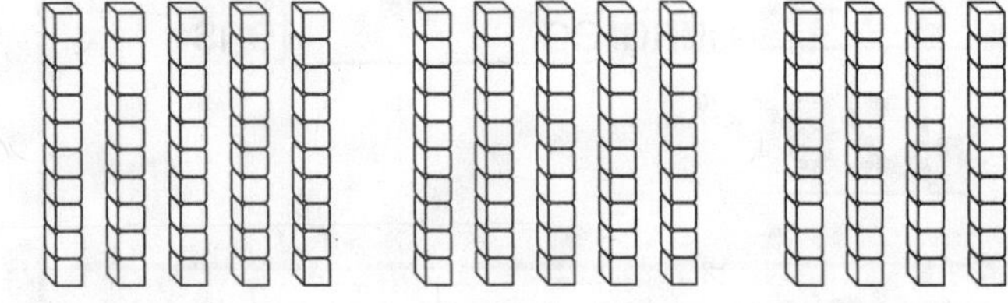

______ tens

______ hundred ______ tens

______

3. 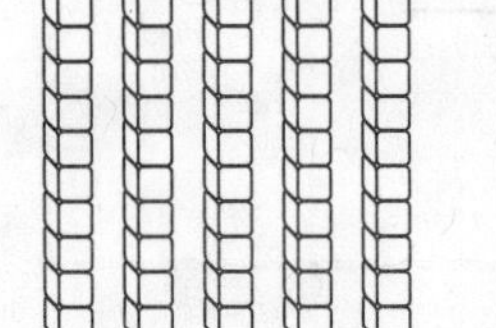

______ tens

______ hundred ______ tens

______

PROBLEM SOLVING

Solve. Write or draw to explain.

4. Millie has a box of 1 hundred cubes. She also has a bag of 70 cubes. How many trains of 10 cubes can she make?

______ trains of 10 cubes

Name ______________________________

Lesson 20

COMMON CORE STANDARD CC.2.NBT.1

Lesson Objective: Use concrete and pictorial models to represent 3-digit numbers.

Model 3-Digit Numbers

Show 243.

With blocks:

Hundreds	Tens	Ones

In a chart:

Hundreds	Tens	Ones
2	4	3

With a quick picture:

Write how many hundreds, tens, and ones. Show with ▦ ▯ ▫. Then draw a quick picture.

1. 138

Hundreds	Tens	Ones

2. 217

Hundreds	Tens	Ones

3. 352

Hundreds	Tens	Ones

4. 174

Hundreds	Tens	Ones

Name ______________________________

Model 3-Digit Numbers

Write how many hundreds, tens, and ones.
Show with [hundred block] [ten rod] [ones]. Then draw a quick picture.

1. 118

Hundreds	Tens	Ones

2. 246

Hundreds	Tens	Ones

3. 143

Hundreds	Tens	Ones

4. 237

Hundreds	Tens	Ones

PROBLEM SOLVING

5. Write the number that matches the clues.
   - My number has 2 hundreds.
   - The tens digit is 9 more than the ones digit.

   My number is ________.

Hundreds	Tens	Ones

Name ______________________________

COMMON CORE STANDARD CC.2.NBT.1

Lesson Objective: Apply place value concepts to write 3-digit numbers that are represented by pictorial models.

Hundreds, Tens, and Ones

How many are there in all?

Hundreds	Tens	Ones

3 hundreds 2 tens 5 ones

Write how many in the chart.

Hundreds	Tens	Ones
3	2	5

Write the number as hundreds plus tens plus ones.

300 + 20 + 5

3 hundreds 2 tens 5 ones is the same as 325.

Write how many hundreds, tens, and ones are in the model. Write the number in two ways.

1. 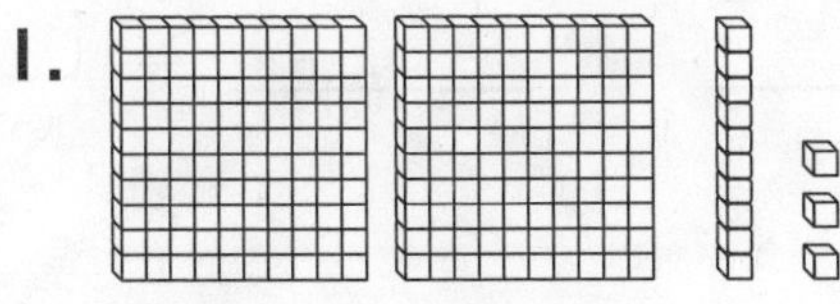

Hundreds	Tens	Ones

______

____ + ____ + ____

2. 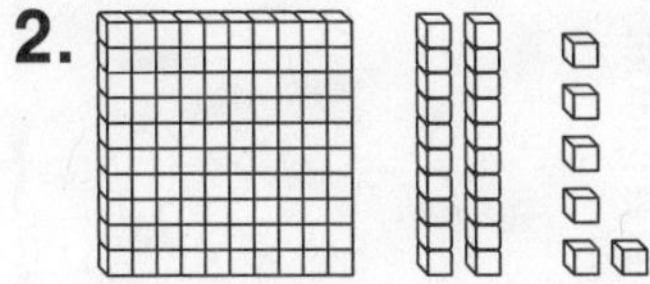

Hundreds	Tens	Ones

______

____ + ____ + ____

Name ______________________

Hundreds, Tens, and Ones

Write how many hundreds, tens, and ones are in the model. Write the number in two ways.

1. 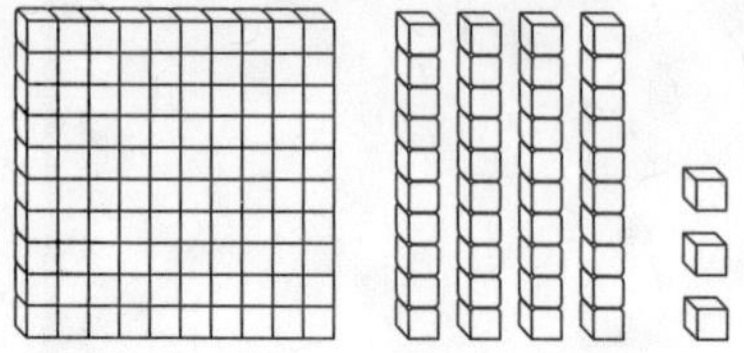

Hundreds	Tens	Ones

______

______ + ______ + ______

2. 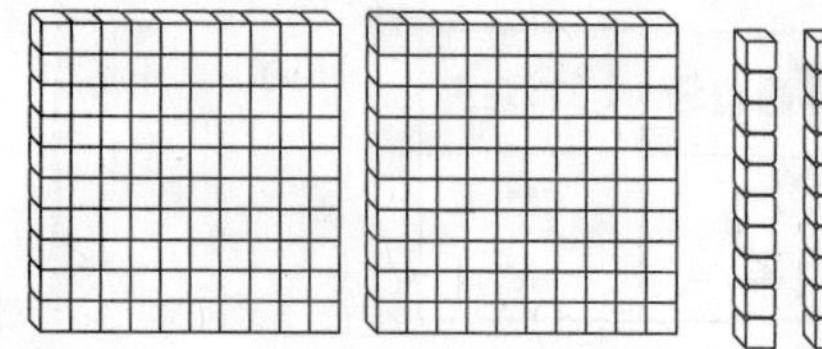

Hundreds	Tens	Ones

______

______ + ______ + ______

3. 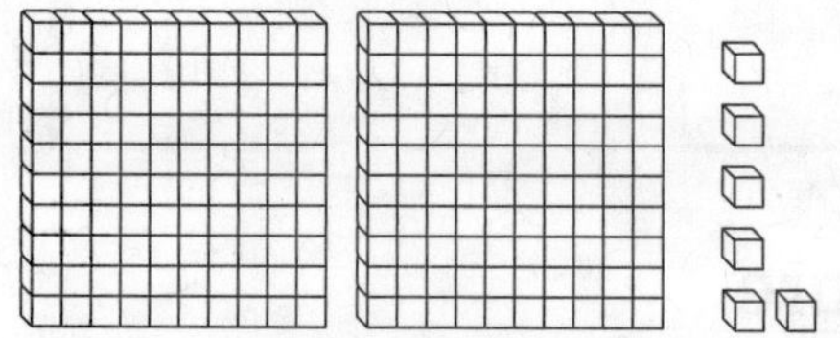

Hundreds	Tens	Ones

______

______ + ______ + ______

PROBLEM SOLVING

4. Write the number that answers the riddle.
Use the chart.
A model for my number has 6 ones blocks,
2 hundreds blocks, and 3 tens blocks.
What number am I?

Hundreds	Tens	Ones

______

Name ____________________

Lesson 22

COMMON CORE STANDARD CC.2.NBT.1

Lesson Objective: Use place value to describe the values of digits in numbers to 1,000.

Place Value to 1,000

The value of each digit in 426 is shown by its place in the number.

Hundreds	Tens	Ones
4 hundreds	2 tens	6 ones
400	20	6

426

Circle the value or the meaning of the underlined digit.

1. 7<u>8</u>2	800	80	8
2. <u>3</u>52	3 hundreds	3 tens	3 ones
3. 7<u>4</u>2	4	40	400
4. 41<u>9</u>	9 hundreds	9 tens	9 ones
5. <u>5</u>84	500	50	5

Name ______________________________

Lesson **22**
CC.2.NBT.1

Place Value to 1,000

Circle the value or the meaning of the underlined digit.

1. 337	3	30	300
2. 462	200	20	2
3. 572	5	50	500
4. 567	7 ones	7 tens	7 hundreds
5. 462	4 hundreds	4 ones	4 tens
6. 1,000	1 ten	1 hundred	1 thousand

PROBLEM SOLVING

7. Write the 3-digit number that answers the riddle.
   - I have the same hundreds digit as ones digit.
   - The value of my tens digit is 50.
   - The value of my ones digit is 4. The number is ________.

Name ______________________

Lesson 23

COMMON CORE STANDARDS CC.2.NBT.1a, CC.2.NBT.1b

Lesson Objective: Understand that each group of 10 tens is equivalent to 1 hundred.

Group Tens as Hundreds

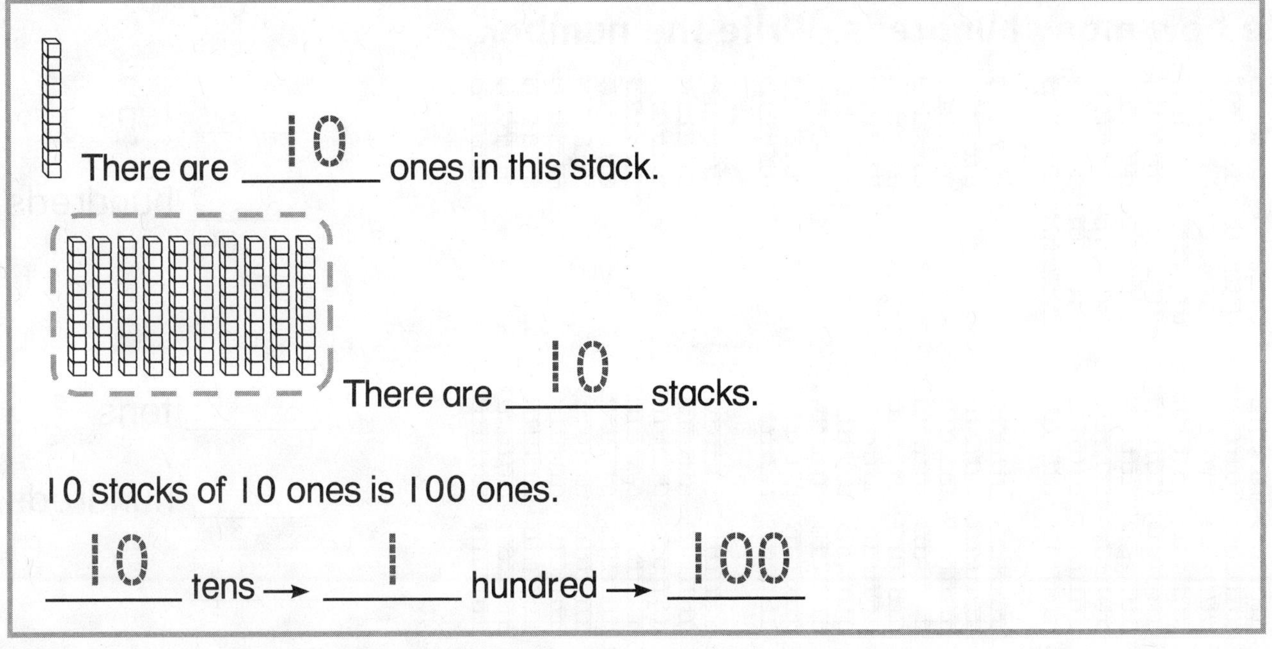

10 stacks of 10 ones is 100 ones.

10 tens → 1 hundred → 100

Write how many tens. Circle groups of 10 tens. Write how many hundreds. Write the number.

1. 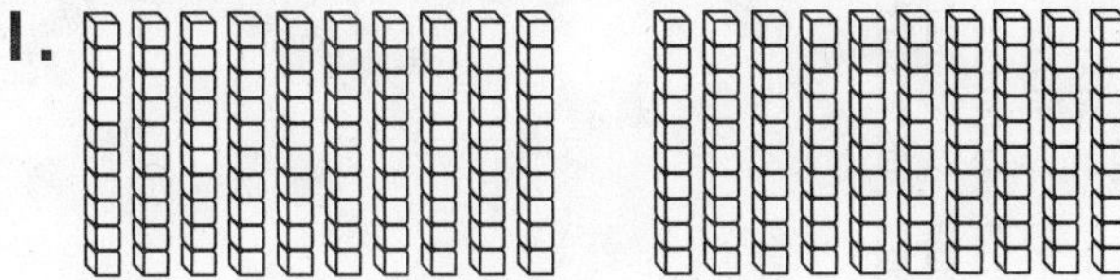

_____ tens

_____ hundreds

_____ blocks

2. 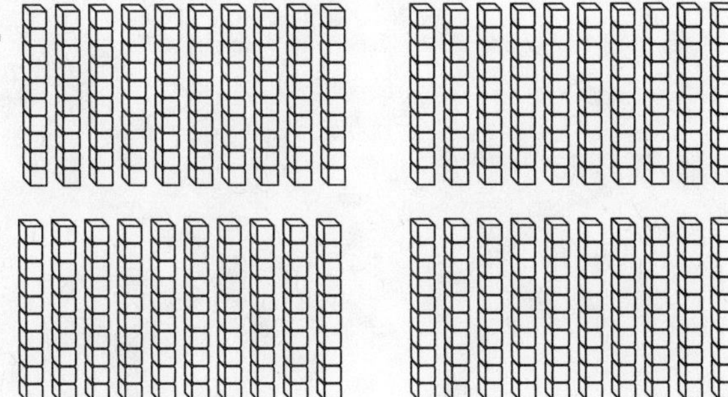

_____ tens

_____ hundreds

_____ blocks

Name ______________________

Group Tens as Hundreds

Write how many tens. Circle groups of 10 tens. Write how many hundreds. Write the number.

1. ______ tens

______ hundreds

______

2. ______ tens

______ hundreds

______

3. ______ tens

______ hundreds

______

PROBLEM SOLVING

Solve. Write or draw to explain.

4. Farmer Gray has 30 flowerpots. He planted 10 seeds in each pot. How many seeds did he plant?

______ seeds

Name ___________________________

Lesson 24

COMMON CORE STANDARD CC.2.NBT.2

Lesson Objective: Extend counting sequences within 100, counting by 1s, 5s, and 10s.

Counting Patterns Within 100

You can count different ways.

Count by fives.

5, 10, 15, 20, 25, 30, 35

Count by tens.

10, 20, 30, 40, 50, 60

Count by fives.

1. 5, 10, 15, 20, ____, ____, ____

2. 20, 25, 30, 35, ____, ____, ____

3. 55, 60, 65, 70, ____, ____, ____

Count by tens.

4. 10, 20, 30, ____, ____, ____

5. 30, 40, 50, 60, ____, ____, ____

Name ___________________________

Counting Patterns Within 100

Count by ones.

1. 58, 59, ____, ____, ____, ____, ____

Count by fives.

2. 45, 50, ____, ____, ____, ____, ____

3. 20, 25, ____, ____, ____, ____, ____

Count by tens.

4. 20, ____, ____, ____, ____, ____, ____

Count back by ones.

5. 87, 86, 85, ____, ____, ____

PROBLEM SOLVING

6. Tim counts his friends' fingers by fives.
He counts six hands. What numbers does he say?

5, ____, ____, ____, ____, ____

Name ______________________________

COMMON CORE STANDARD CC.2.NBT.2

Lesson Objective: Extend counting sequences within 1,000, counting by 1s, 5s, 10s, and 100s.

Counting Patterns Within 1,000

You can count in different ways.
Look for a pattern to use.

Count by tens.

500, 510, 520, 530, 540, 550

Count by hundreds.

300, 400, 500, 600, 700, 800

Count by tens.

1. 410, 420, 430, ____, ____

2. 730, 740, ____, ____, ____

3. 250, 260, ____, ____, ____

Count by hundreds.

4. 100, 200, 300, ____, ____

5. 500, 600, ____, ____, ____

Name ________________________

Counting Patterns Within 1,000

Count by fives.

1. 415, 420, ______, ______, ______, ______

2. 675, 680, ______, ______, ______, ______, ______

Count by tens.

3. 210, 220, ______, ______, ______, ______, ______

4. 840, 850, ______, ______, ______, ______, ______

Count by hundreds.

5. 300, 400, ______, ______, ______, ______, ______

Count back by ones.

6. 953, 952, ______, ______, ______, ______, ______

PROBLEM SOLVING

7. Lee has a jar of 100 pennies.
   She adds groups of 10 pennies to the jar.
   She adds 5 groups. What numbers does she say?

   ______, ______, ______, ______, ______

Name ________________________________

Lesson 26

COMMON CORE STANDARD CC.2.NBT.3

Lesson Objective: Use place value to describe the values of digits in 2-digit numbers.

Understand Place Value

0, 1, 2, 3, 4, 5, 6, 7, 8, and 9 are digits.
A digit's place in a number shows the value of the digit.

52 has two digits.

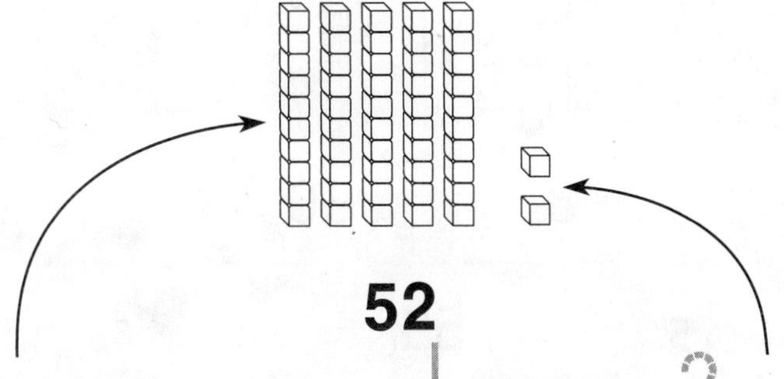

52

The digit __5__ is in the tens place.

The digit 5 shows __5__ tens.

Its value is __50__.

The digit __2__ is in the ones place.

The digit 2 shows __2__ ones.

Its value is __2__.

Circle the value of the underlined digit.

1. 27

20   2

2. 18

1   10

3. 56

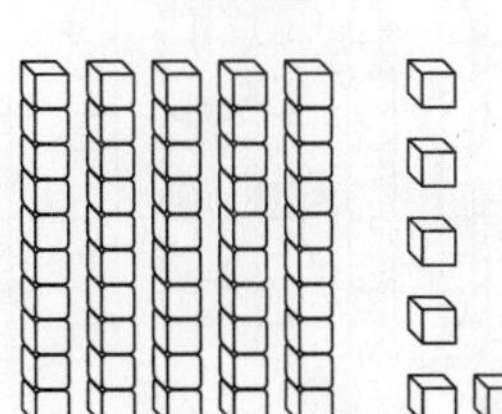

60   6

4. 30

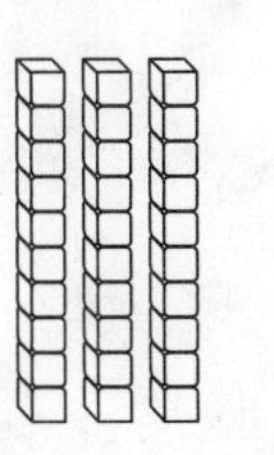

30   3

5. 75

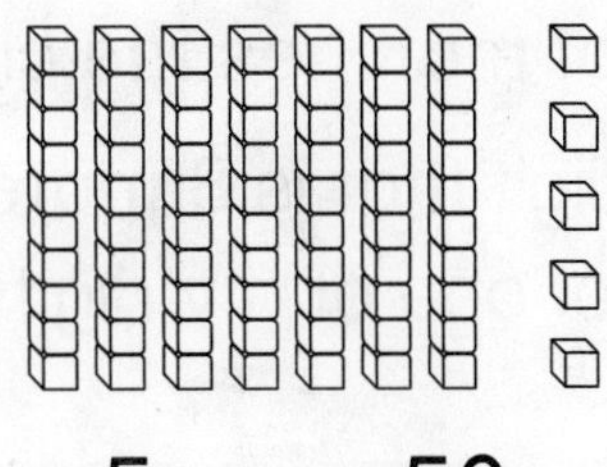

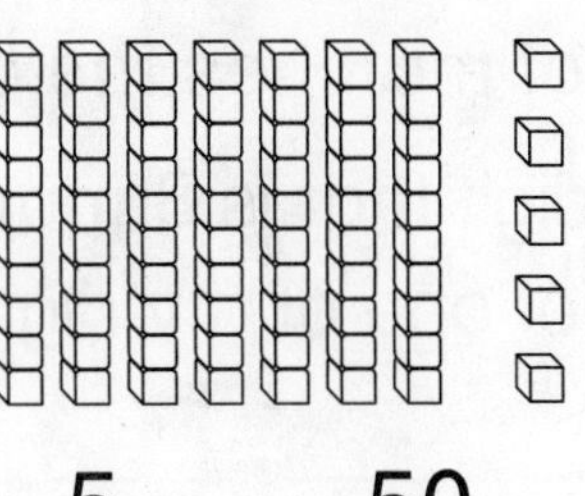

5   50

6. 41

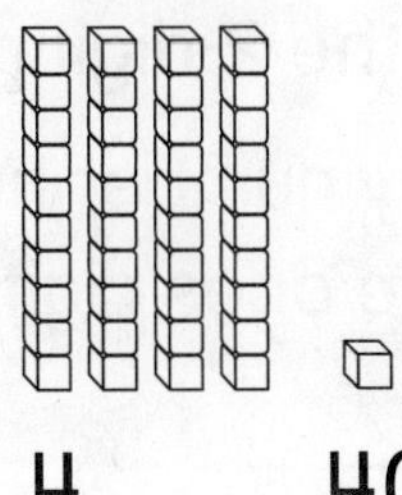

4   40

Name ______________________________

Lesson 26
CC.2.NBT.3

Understand Place Value

Circle the value of the underlined digit.

1. 23

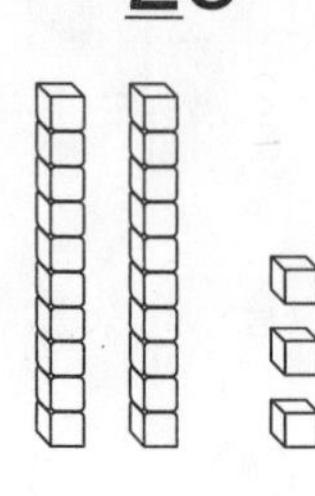

20   2

2. 48

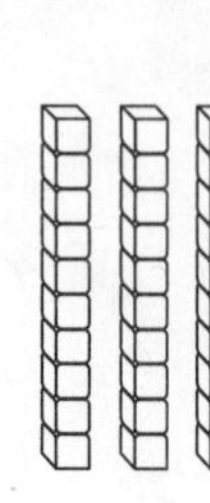
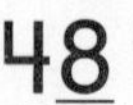
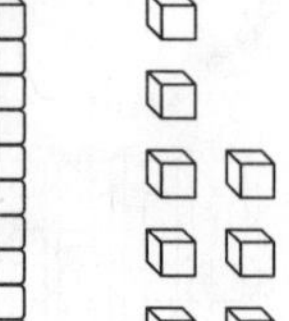

8   80

3. 18

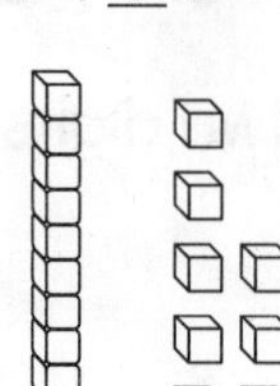

10   1

4. 43

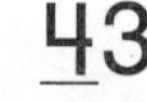
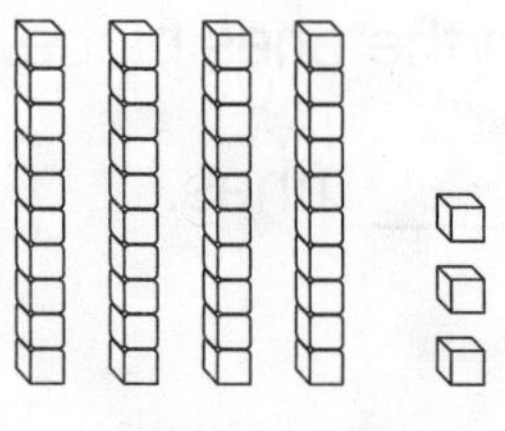

40   4

5. 54

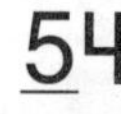
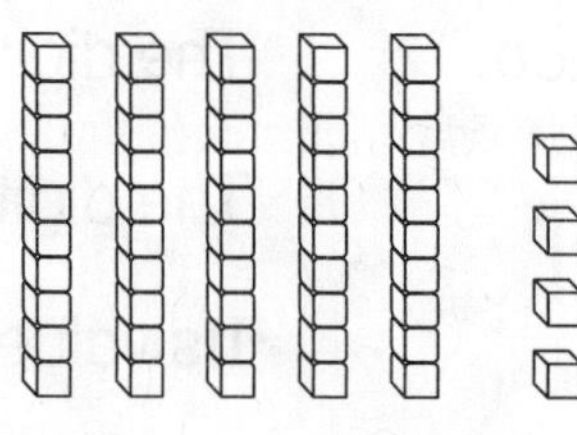

5   50

6. 65

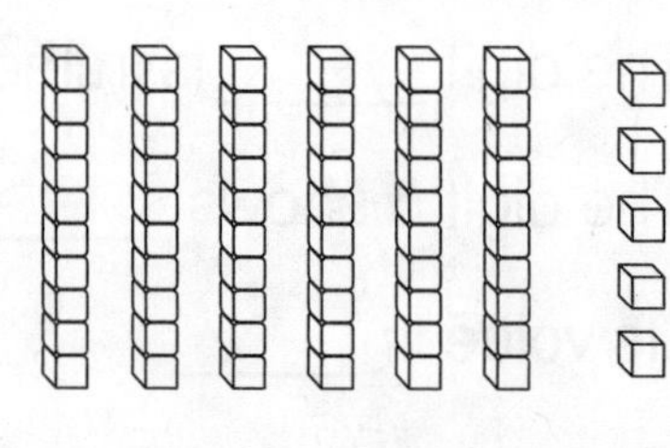

50   5

7. 70

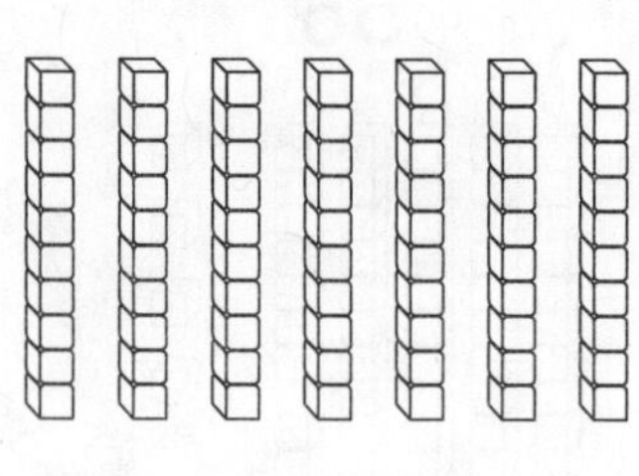

7   70

8. 37

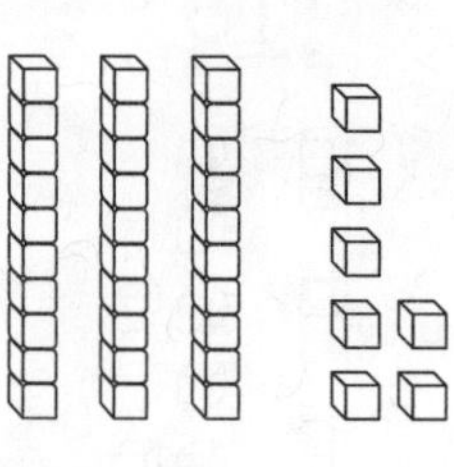

70   7

9. 22

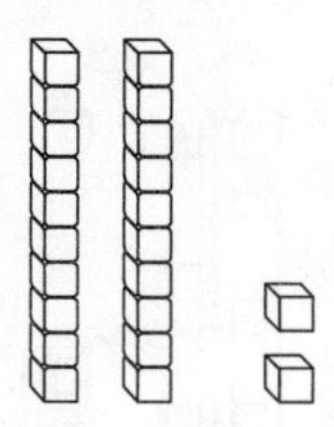

20   2

PROBLEM SOLVING

Write the 2-digit number that matches the clues.

10. My number has a tens digit that is 8 more than the ones digit. Zero is not one of my digits.

My number is _____.

Name ____________________

COMMON CORE STANDARD CC.2.NBT.3

Lesson Objective: Write 2-digit numbers in expanded form.

Expanded Form

Show tens and ones in 43.

Tens	Ones
4 tens	3 ones

How many tens? __4__ tens   How many ones? __3__ ones

__43__ is __4__ tens __3__ ones

__43__ is __40__ + __3__

Describe the number in two ways.

1. 35

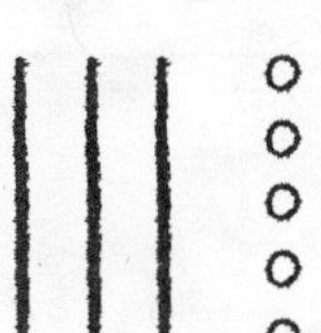

_____ tens _____ ones

_____ + _____

2. 63

_____ tens _____ ones

_____ + _____

3. 57

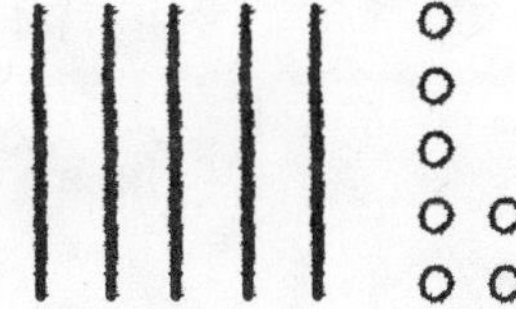

_____ tens _____ ones

_____ + _____

4. 19

_____ ten _____ ones

_____ + _____

Name ______________________

Lesson **27**
CC.2.NBT.3

Expanded Form

Draw a quick picture to show the number.
Describe the number in two ways.

1. 68

____ tens ____ ones

____ + ____

2. 21

____ tens ____ one

____ + ____

3. 70

____ tens ____ ones

____ + ____

4. 53

____ tens ____ ones

____ + ____

5. 35

____ tens ____ ones

____ + ____

6. 47

____ tens ____ ones

____ + ____

PROBLEM SOLVING

7. Circle the ways to write the number shown by the model.

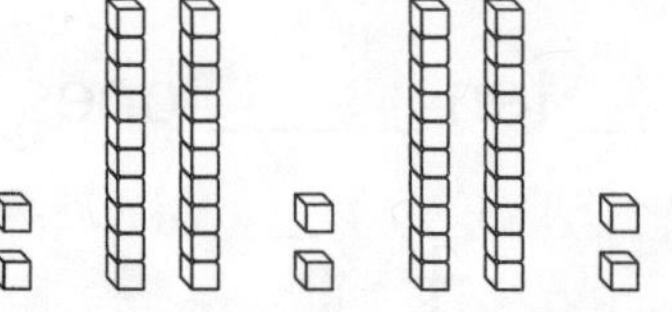

4 tens 6 ones	40 + 6	64
6 tens 4 ones	60 + 4	46

Name ___________________________

Lesson 28

COMMON CORE STANDARD CC.2.NBT.3

Lesson Objective: Write 2-digit numbers in word form, expanded form, and standard form.

Different Ways to Write Numbers

You can write numbers in different ways.

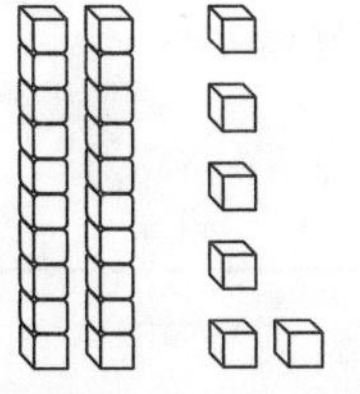

20 + 6

2 tens 6 ones

twenty-six

26

ones	teen words		tens	
1 one	11 eleven	1 ten 1 one	10 ten	1 ten
2 two	12 twelve	1 ten 2 ones	20 twenty	2 tens
3 three	13 thirteen	1 ten 3 ones	30 thirty	3 tens
4 four	14 fourteen	1 ten 4 ones	40 forty	4 tens
5 five	15 fifteen	1 ten 5 ones	50 fifty	5 tens
6 six	16 sixteen	1 ten 6 ones	60 sixty	6 tens
7 seven	17 seventeen	1 ten 7 ones	70 seventy	7 tens
8 eight	18 eighteen	1 ten 8 ones	80 eighty	8 tens
9 nine	19 nineteen	1 ten 9 ones	90 ninety	9 tens

Write the number another way.

1. twenty

   ____

2. 37

   _____ tens _____ ones

3. 40 + 5

   ____

4. eighty-one

   ____

5. 56

   ____

6. 9 tens 2 ones

   ____

7. 1 ten 8 ones

   ____

8. seventy-three

   _____ tens _____ ones

Name ______________________________

Different Ways to Write Numbers

Write the number another way.

1. 32

_____ tens _____ ones

2. forty-one

____

3. 9 tens 5 ones

____

4. 80 + 3

____

5. 57

_____ tens _____ ones

6. seventy-two

_____ + _____

7. 60 + 4

____

8. 4 tens 8 ones

____

9. twenty-eight

_____ + _____

10. 80

_____ tens _____ ones

PROBLEM SOLVING

11. A number has the digit 3 in the ones place and the digit 4 in the tens place. Which of these is another way to write this number? Circle it.

3 + 4   40 + 3   30 + 4

Name ____________________

COMMON CORE STANDARD CC.2.NBT.3

Lesson Objective: Apply place value concepts to find equivalent representations of numbers.

Algebra • Different Names for Numbers

Here are some ways to show 28.

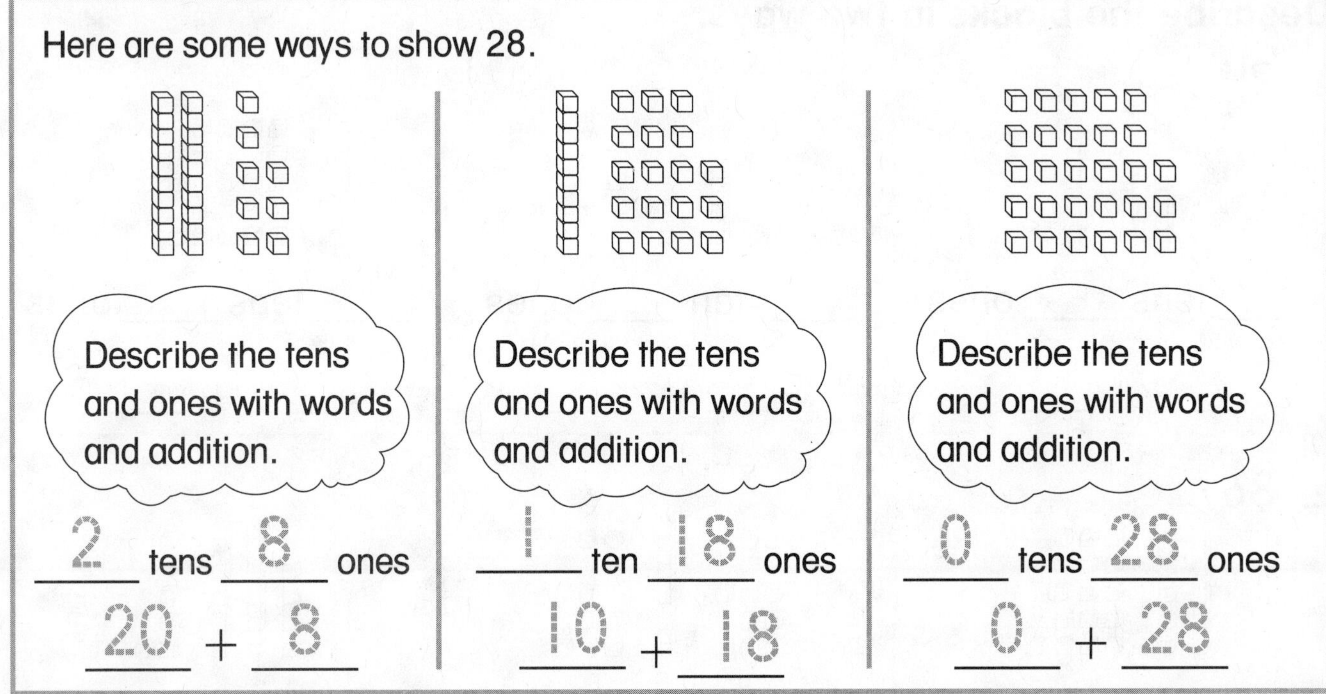

Describe the blocks in two ways.

1. 32

2. 47

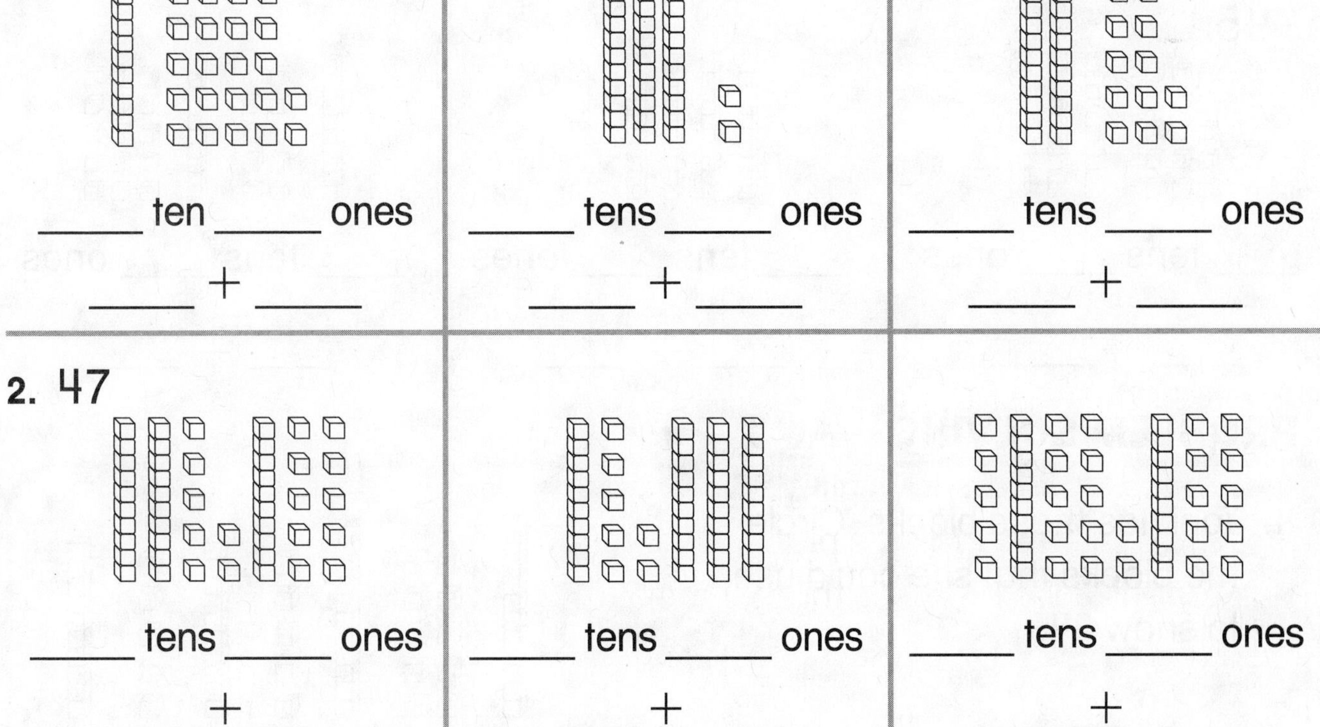

Name ___________________________

Algebra • Different Names for Numbers

The blocks show the number in different ways. Describe the blocks in two ways.

1. 24

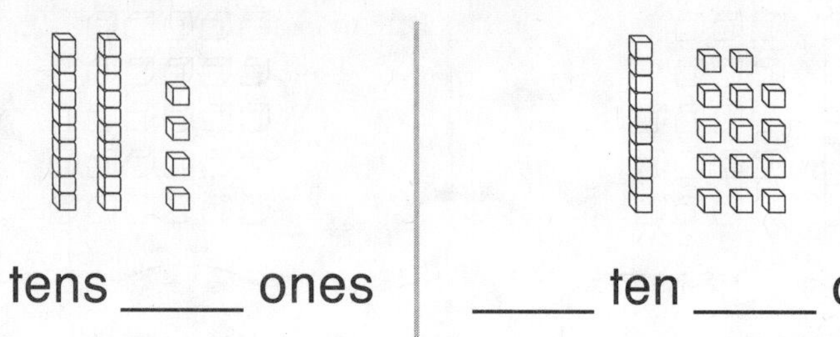

_____ tens _____ ones | _____ ten _____ ones | _____ tens _____ ones

_____ + _____ | _____ + _____ | _____ + _____

2. 36

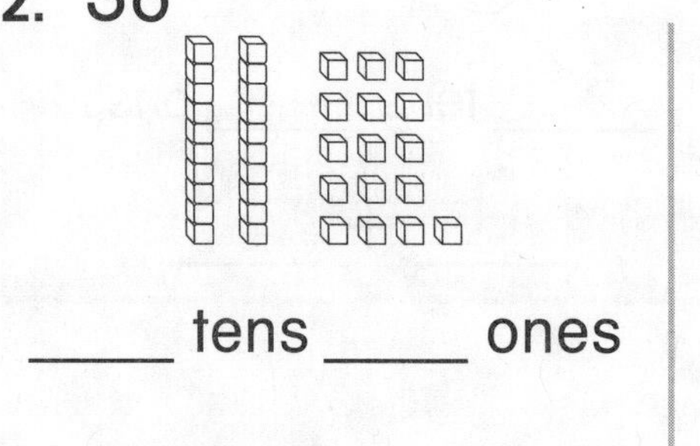

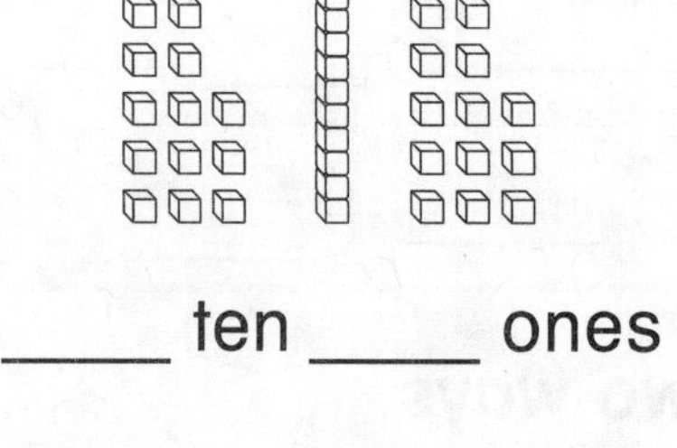

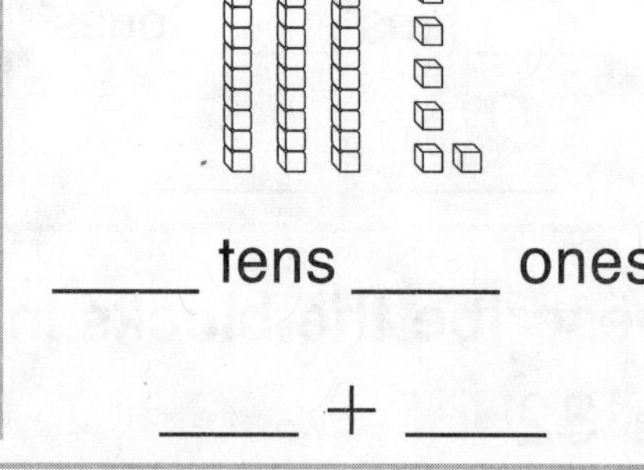

_____ tens _____ ones | _____ ten _____ ones | _____ tens _____ ones

_____ + _____ | _____ + _____ | _____ + _____

3. 45

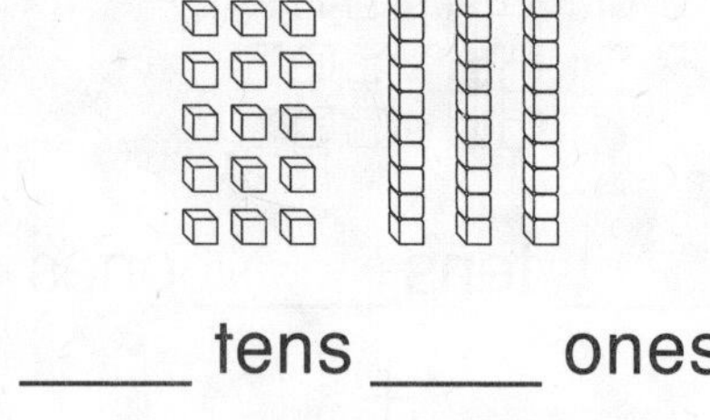

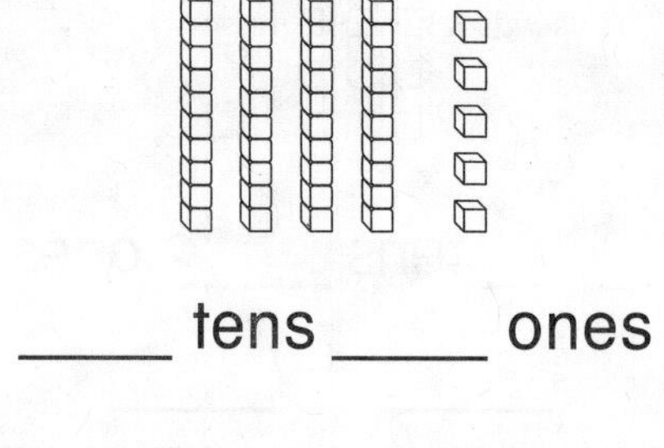

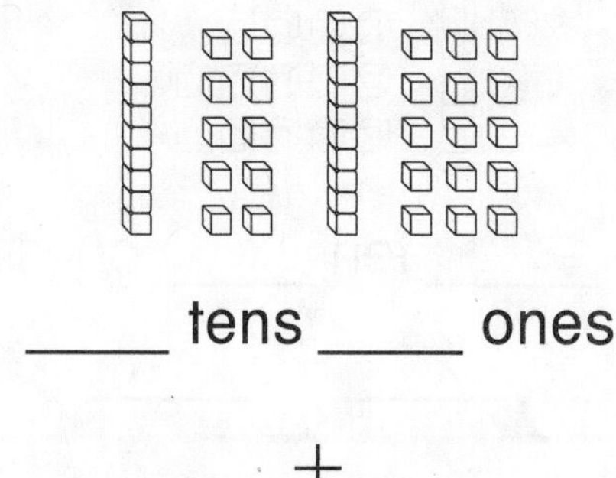

_____ tens _____ ones | _____ tens _____ ones | _____ tens _____ ones

_____ + _____ | _____ + _____ | _____ + _____

PROBLEM SOLVING REAL WORLD

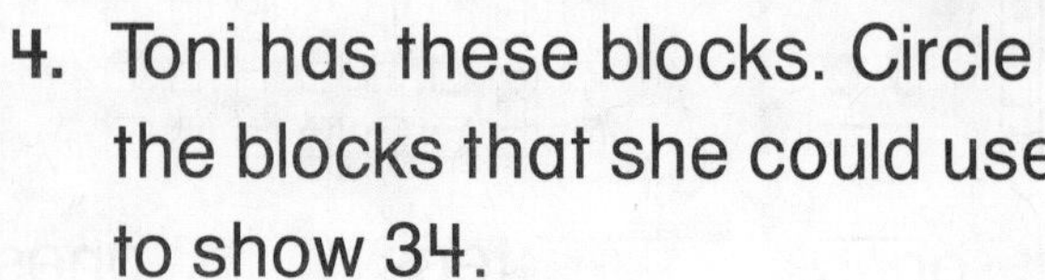

4. Toni has these blocks. Circle the blocks that she could use to show 34.

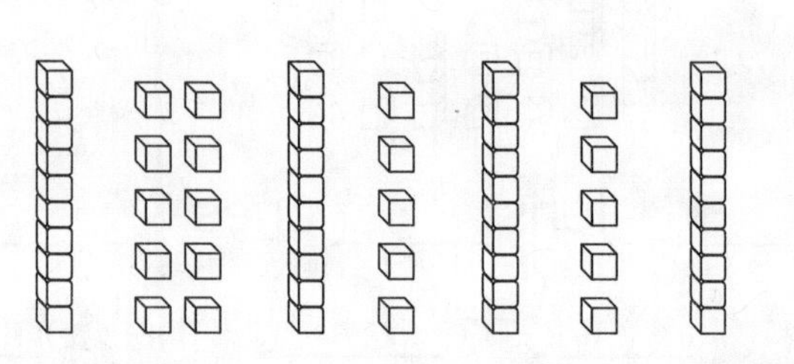

Name ______________________________

Lesson 30

COMMON CORE STANDARD CC.2.NBT.3

Lesson Objective: Solve problems by finding different combinations of tens and ones to represent 2-digit numbers using the strategy *find a pattern.*

Problem Solving • Tens and Ones

Anya has 25 toys. She can put them away in boxes of 10 toys or as single toys. What are the different ways Anya can put away the toys?

Unlock the Problem

What do I need to find?	What information do I need to use?
the different ways ______ Anya can put away the toys	She can put them away in boxes of 10 ______ toys or as single ______ toys.

Look for a pattern.

2 tens + 5 ones

1 ten + 15 ones

0 tens + 25 ones

Boxes of 10 toys	Single toys
2	5
1	15

Find a pattern to solve.

1. Mr. Moore is buying 29 apples. He can buy them in packs of 10 apples or as single apples. What are the different ways Mr. Moore can buy the apples?

Packs of 10 apples	Single apples
2	
1	
0	

Name ______________________________

Problem Solving • Tens and Ones

Find a pattern to solve.

1. Ann is grouping 38 rocks. She can put them into groups of 10 rocks or as single rocks. What are the different ways Ann can group the rocks?

Groups of 10 rocks	Single rocks

2. Mr. Grant needs 30 pieces of felt. He can buy them in packs of 10 or as single pieces. What are the different ways Mr. Grant can buy the felt?

Packs of 10 pieces	Single pieces

3. Ms. Sims is putting away 22 books. She can put them on the table in stacks of 10 or as single books. What are the different ways Ms. Sims can put away the books?

Stacks of 10 books	Single books

Name ______________________________

COMMON CORE STANDARD CC.2.NBT.3

Lesson Objective: Read and write 3-digit numbers in word form.

Number Names

You can write a number using words.

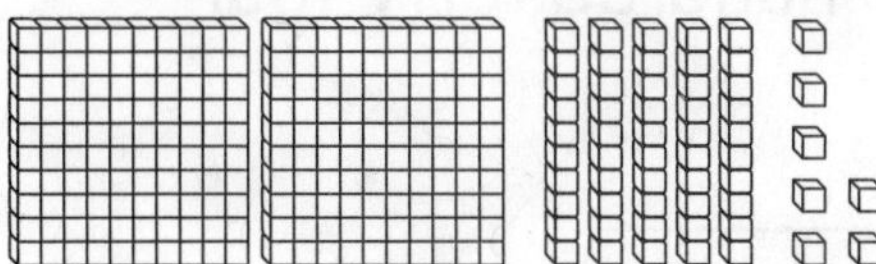

257

What is shown with the hundreds blocks?

two hundred

What is shown with the tens and ones blocks?

fifty-seven

So you write 257 as two hundred fifty-seven.

Write the number using words.

1. 163

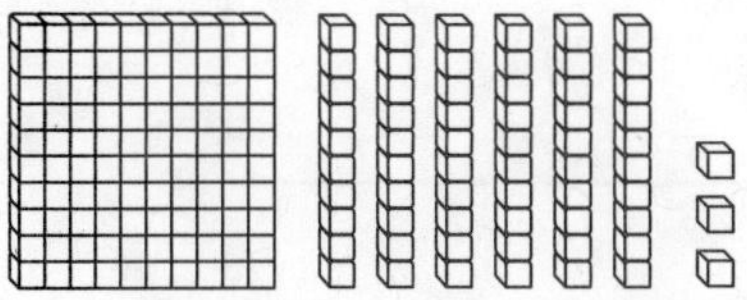

____

2. 427

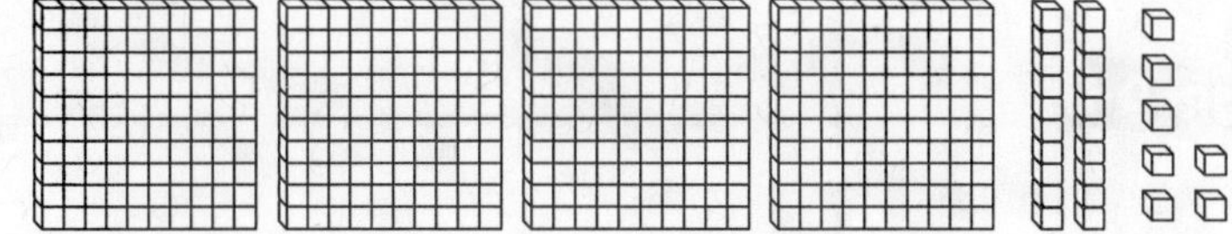

____

Write the number.

3. two hundred nine

____

4. five hundred seventy-nine

____

Name ___________________________

Number Names

Write the number.

1. two hundred thirty-two

____

2. five hundred forty-four

____

3. one hundred fifty-eight

____

4. nine hundred fifty

____

5. four hundred twenty

____

6. six hundred seventy-eight

____

Write the number using words.

7. 317

____

8. 457

____

PROBLEM SOLVING

Circle the answer.

9. Six hundred twenty-six children attend Elm Street School. Which is another way to write this number?

266 626 662

Name ____________________

Lesson 32

COMMON CORE STANDARD CC.2.NBT.3

Lesson Objective: Write 3-digit numbers in expanded form and in standard form.

Different Forms of Numbers

There is more than one way to show and write a number.

three hundred sixty-two

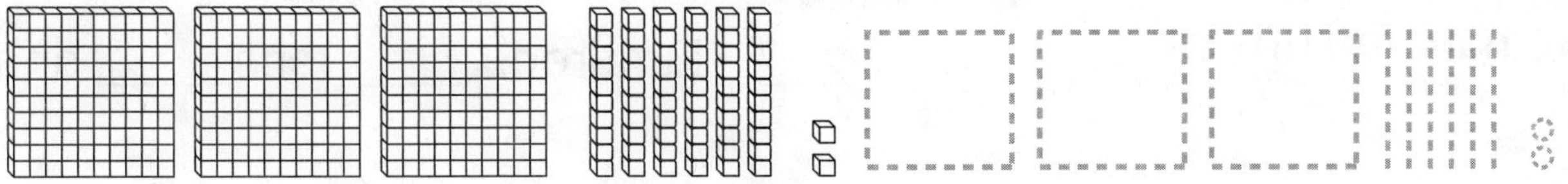

3 hundreds 6 tens 2 ones

300 + 60 + 2

362

Read the number and draw a quick picture.
Then write the number in different ways.

1. four hundred thirty-two

_____ hundreds _____ tens _____ ones

_____ + _____ + _____

_____

2. two hundred seventy-five

_____ hundreds _____ tens _____ ones

_____ + _____ + _____

_____

Name ______________________________

Different Forms of Numbers

Read the number and draw a quick picture. Then write the number in different ways.

1. two hundred fifty-one

____ hundreds ____ tens ____ one

________ + ________ + ________

____

2. three hundred twelve

____ hundreds ____ ten ____ ones

________ + ________ + ________

____

3. two hundred seven

____ hundreds ____ tens ____ ones

________ + ________ + ________

____

PROBLEM SOLVING

Write the number another way.

4. 200 + 30 + 7

____

5. 895

____

Name ______________________

Lesson 33

COMMON CORE STANDARD CC.2.NBT.3

Lesson Objective: Apply place value concepts to find equivalent representations of numbers.

Algebra • Different Ways to Show Numbers

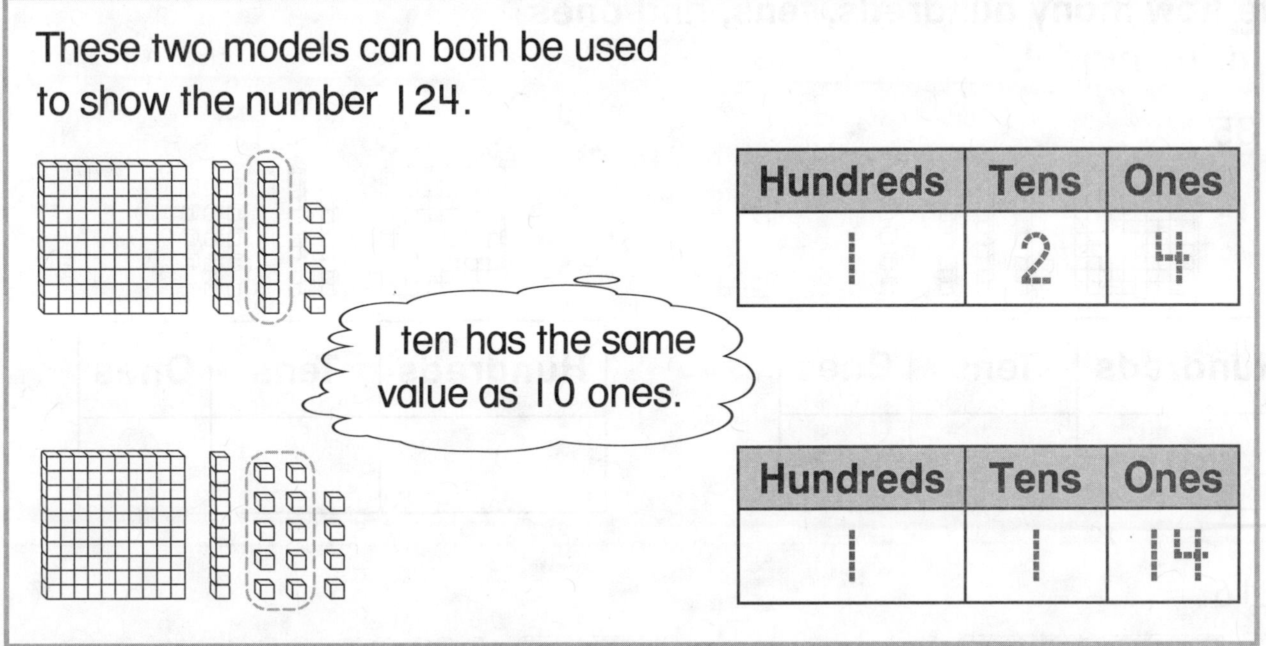

Hundreds	Tens	Ones
1	2	4

Hundreds	Tens	Ones
1	1	14

Write how many hundreds, tens, and ones are in the model.

1. 132

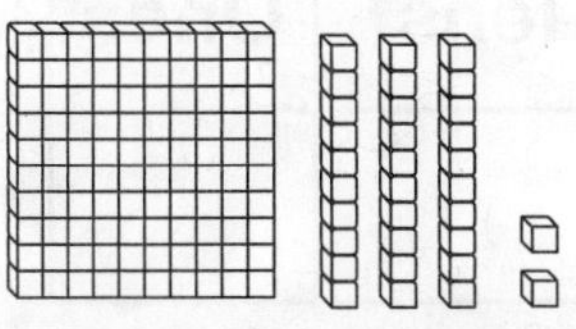

Hundreds	Tens	Ones

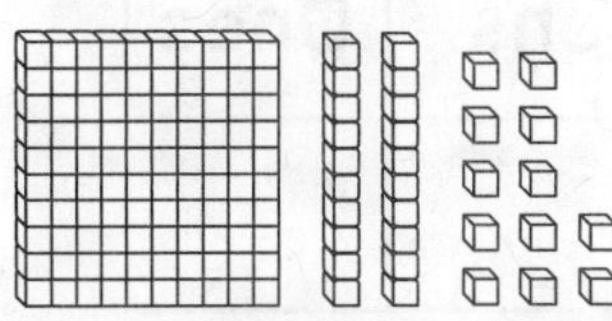

Hundreds	Tens	Ones

2. 246

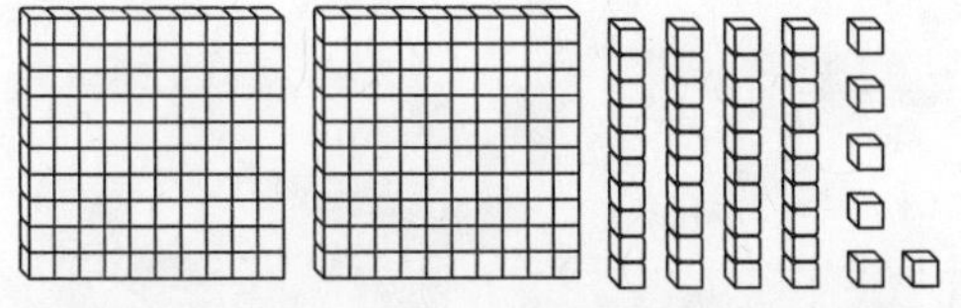

Hundreds	Tens	Ones

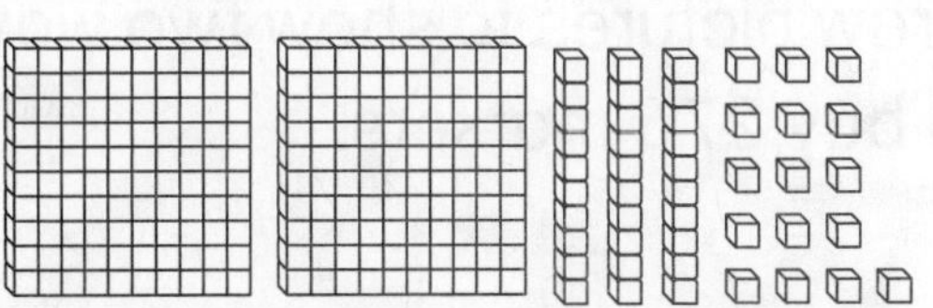

Hundreds	Tens	Ones

Name ______________________________

Lesson 33
CC.2.NBT.3

Algebra • Different Ways to Show Numbers

Write how many hundreds, tens, and ones are in the model.

1. 135

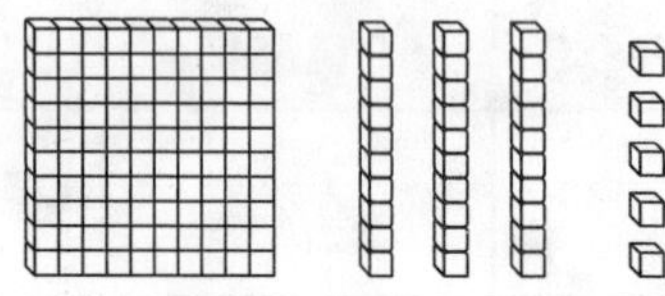

Hundreds	Tens	Ones

Hundreds	Tens	Ones

2. 216

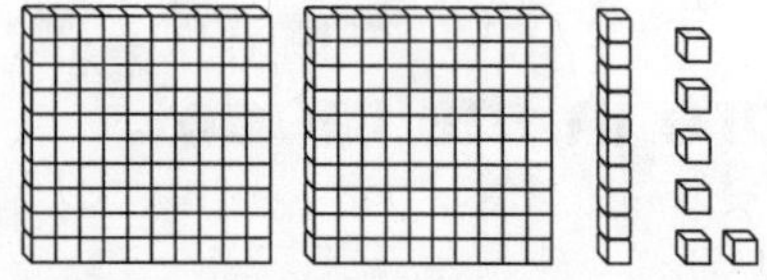

Hundreds	Tens	Ones

Hundreds	Tens	Ones

PROBLEM SOLVING

Markers are sold in boxes, packs, or as single markers. Each box has 10 packs. Each pack has 10 markers.

3. Draw pictures to show two ways to buy 276 markers.

Name ______________________________

Lesson 34

COMMON CORE STANDARD CC.2.NBT.4

Lesson Objective: Solve problems involving number comparisons by using the strategy *make a model.*

Problem Solving • Compare Numbers

At the zoo, there are 137 birds and 142 reptiles.
Are there more birds or more reptiles at the zoo?

Unlock the Problem

What do I need to find?	What information do I need to use?
I need to find if there are more birds or reptiles.	There are 137 birds. There are 142 reptiles.

Show how to solve the problem.

Birds

Reptiles

The number of hundreds is the same.
There are more tens in the number of reptiles.

There are more reptiles at the zoo.

Draw quick pictures to model the numbers.

1. There are 153 birds and 149 fish at the nature center.
Are there more birds or more fish?

There are more ______________________ .

Name ______________________

Lesson 34
CC.2.NBT.4

Problem Solving • Compare Numbers

Model the numbers. Draw quick pictures to show how you solved the problem.

1. Lauryn has 128 marbles. Kristin has 118 marbles. Who has more marbles?

____

2. Nick has 189 trading cards. Kyle has 198 trading cards. Who has fewer cards?

____

3. A piano has 36 black keys and 52 white keys. Are there more black keys or white keys on a piano?

____

4. There are 253 cookies in a bag. There are 266 cookies in a box. Are there fewer cookies in the bag or in the box?

____

Name ______________________

COMMON CORE STANDARD CC.2.NBT.4

Lesson Objective: Compare 3-digit numbers using the >, =, and < symbols.

Algebra • Compare Numbers

To compare 3-digit numbers, first compare hundreds.

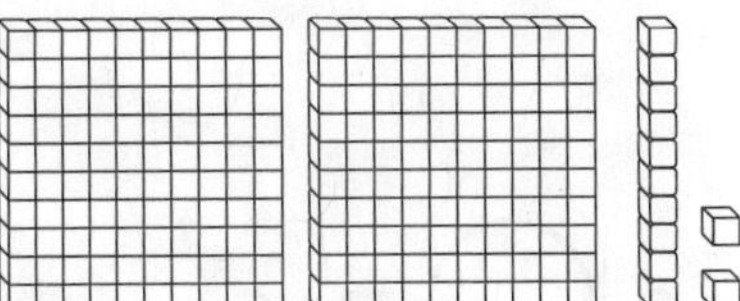

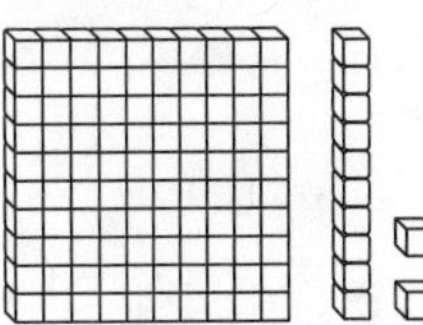

212 has more hundreds than 112.

212 (>) 112

If hundreds are equal, then compare tens.

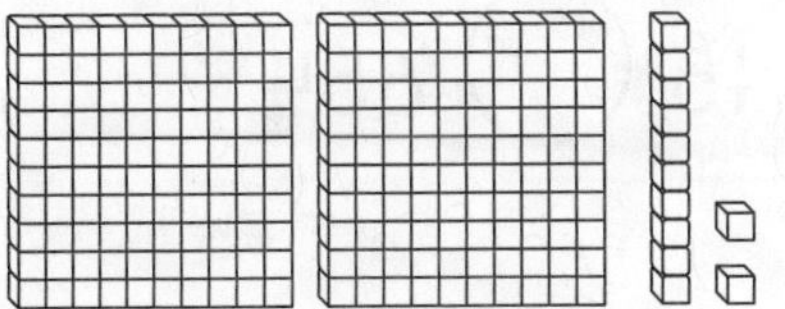

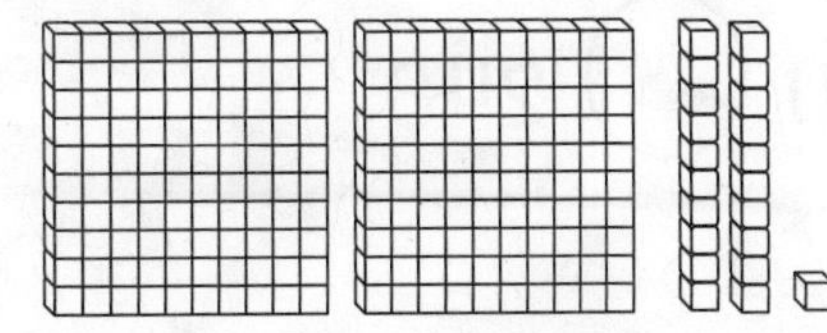

212 has fewer tens than 221.

212 (<) 221

If hundreds and tens are equal, then compare ones.

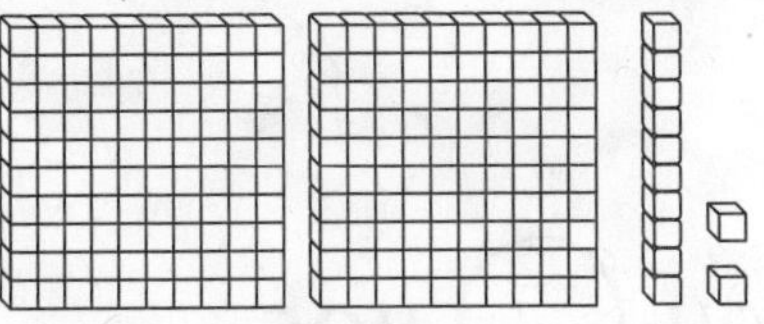

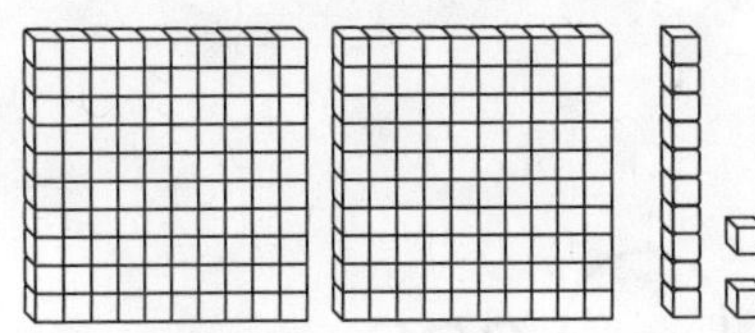

212 (=) 212

Compare the numbers. Write >, <, or =.

1. 317 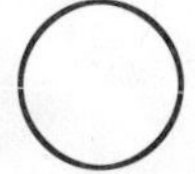 326

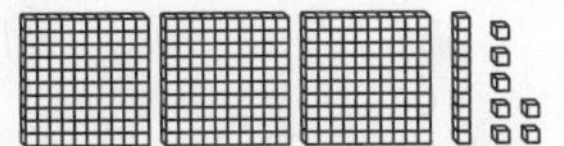

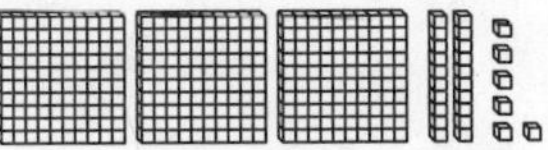

2. 582  634

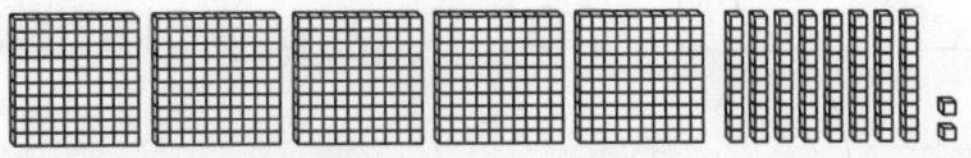

Name ____________________

Algebra • Compare Numbers

Compare the numbers. Write >, <, or =.

1. 489
   605

   489 ◯ 605

2. 719
   719

   719 ◯ 719

3. 370
   248

   370 ◯ 248

4. 645
   654

   645 ◯ 654

5. 205
   250

   205 ◯ 250

6. 813
   781

   813 ◯ 781

7. 397
   393

   397 ◯ 393

8. 504
   405

   504 ◯ 405

PROBLEM SOLVING

Solve. Write or draw to explain.

9. Toby has 178 pennies.
   Bella has 190 pennies.
   Who has more pennies?

   ________ has more pennies.

Name ______________________________

Lesson 36

COMMON CORE STANDARD CC.2.NBT.5

Lesson Objective: Record 2-digit addition using the standard algorithm.

2-Digit Addition

Add 27 and 36.

STEP 1

Model 27 and 36.
Add the ones.

$7 + 6 = 13$

Tens	Ones
☐	
2	7
+ 3	6

STEP 2

If you can make a 10, regroup 10 ones for 1 ten.

13 ones = 1 ten 3 ones

Tens	Ones
1	
2	7
+ 3	6
	3

STEP 3

Add the tens.
Remember to add the regrouped ten.

$1 + 2 + 3 = 6$

Tens	Ones
1	
2	7
+ 3	6
6	3

Regroup if you need to. Write the sum.

1.

Tens	Ones
☐	
5	4
+ 2	9

2.

Tens	Ones
☐	
1	7
+ 6	1

3.

Tens	Ones
☐	
4	1
+ 2	9

4.

Tens	Ones
☐	
3	5
+ 3	2

Name ____________________

2-Digit Addition

Regroup if you need to. Write the sum.

1.
$$\begin{array}{r} 47 \\ +25 \\ \hline \end{array}$$

2.
$$\begin{array}{r} 33 \\ +18 \\ \hline \end{array}$$

3.
$$\begin{array}{r} 28 \\ +64 \\ \hline \end{array}$$

4.
$$\begin{array}{r} 13 \\ +65 \\ \hline \end{array}$$

5.
$$\begin{array}{r} 17 \\ +26 \\ \hline \end{array}$$

6.
$$\begin{array}{r} 36 \\ +53 \\ \hline \end{array}$$

7.
$$\begin{array}{r} 58 \\ +25 \\ \hline \end{array}$$

8.
$$\begin{array}{r} 37 \\ +49 \\ \hline \end{array}$$

9.
$$\begin{array}{r} 52 \\ +29 \\ \hline \end{array}$$

10.
$$\begin{array}{r} 66 \\ +24 \\ \hline \end{array}$$

11.
$$\begin{array}{r} 74 \\ +14 \\ \hline \end{array}$$

12.
$$\begin{array}{r} 37 \\ +37 \\ \hline \end{array}$$

PROBLEM SOLVING

Solve. Write or draw to explain.

13. Angela drew 16 flowers on her paper in the morning. She drew 25 more flowers in the afternoon. How many flowers did she draw in all?

_____ flowers

Name ____________________

COMMON CORE STANDARD CC.2.NBT.5

Lesson Objective: Practice 2-digit addition with and without regrouping.

Practice 2-Digit Addition

Eliza sold 47 pencils in one week.
She sold 65 pencils the next week.
How many pencils did she sell in both weeks?

Add 47 and 65. Add the ones. $7 + 5 = 12$	Regroup. 12 ones = 1 ten and 2 ones	Add the tens. $1 + 4 + 6 = 11$
$\begin{array}{r} \square \\ 47 \\ +\ 65 \\ \hline \end{array}$	$\begin{array}{r} 1 \\ 47 \\ +\ 65 \\ \hline 2 \end{array}$	$\begin{array}{r} 1 \\ 47 \\ +\ 65 \\ \hline 112 \end{array}$

Write the sum.

1. $\begin{array}{r} \square \\ 43 \\ +\ 69 \\ \hline \end{array}$

2. $\begin{array}{r} \square \\ 76 \\ +\ 58 \\ \hline \end{array}$

3. $\begin{array}{r} \square \\ 38 \\ +\ 42 \\ \hline \end{array}$

4. $\begin{array}{r} \square \\ 85 \\ +\ 68 \\ \hline \end{array}$

5. $\begin{array}{r} \square \\ 82 \\ +\ 47 \\ \hline \end{array}$

6. $\begin{array}{r} \square \\ 81 \\ +\ 17 \\ \hline \end{array}$

7. $\begin{array}{r} \square \\ 27 \\ +\ 86 \\ \hline \end{array}$

8. $\begin{array}{r} \square \\ 51 \\ +\ 38 \\ \hline \end{array}$

Name ___________________________

Practice 2-Digit Addition

Write the sum.

1. 58 + 17	**2.** 44 + 86	**3.** 36 + 13
4. 49 + 72	**5.** 58 + 87	**6.** 32 + 59
7. 77 + 58	**8.** 45 + 45	**9.** 54 + 28

PROBLEM SOLVING

Solve. Write or draw to explain.

10. There are 45 books on the shelf. There are 37 books on the table. How many books in all are on the shelf and the table?

_____ books

Name ____________________

COMMON CORE STANDARD CC.2.NBT.5

Lesson Objective: Rewrite horizontal addition problems vertically in the standard algorithm format.

Rewrite 2-Digit Addition

Add. 43 + 19 = ?

STEP 1

What is the tens digit in 43? 4

Write 4 in the tens column.
Write the ones digit, 3, in the ones column.

Tens	Ones
□	
4	3
+	

STEP 2

What is the tens digit in 19? 1

Write 1 in the tens column.
Write the ones digit, 9, in the ones column.

Tens	Ones
□	
4	3
+ 1	9

STEP 3

Add the ones. Regroup if you need to.

Add the tens.

Tens	Ones
1	
4	3
+ 1	9
6	2

Rewrite the numbers. Then add.

1. 26 + 9

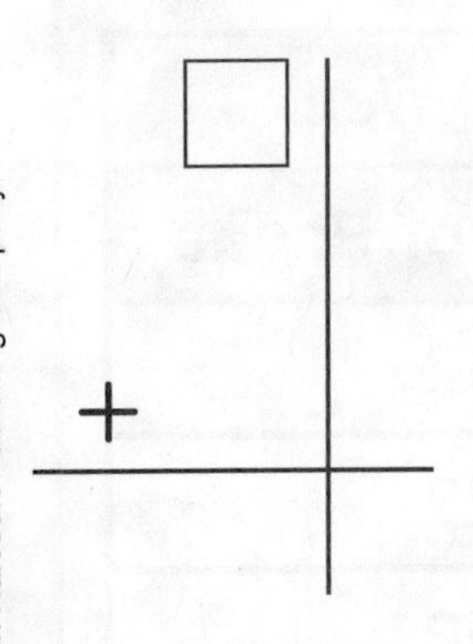

2. 16 + 43

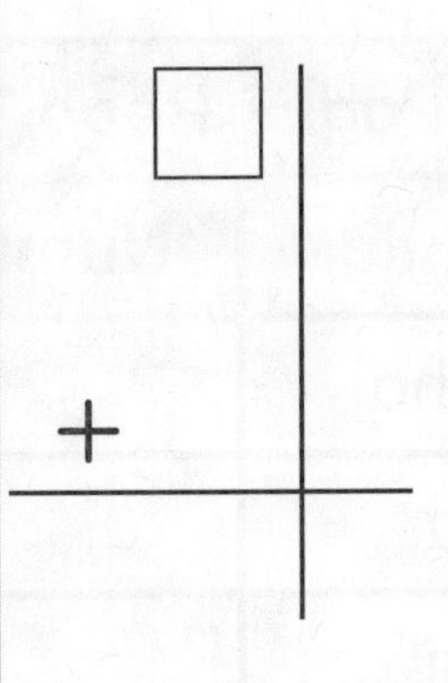

3. 32 + 38

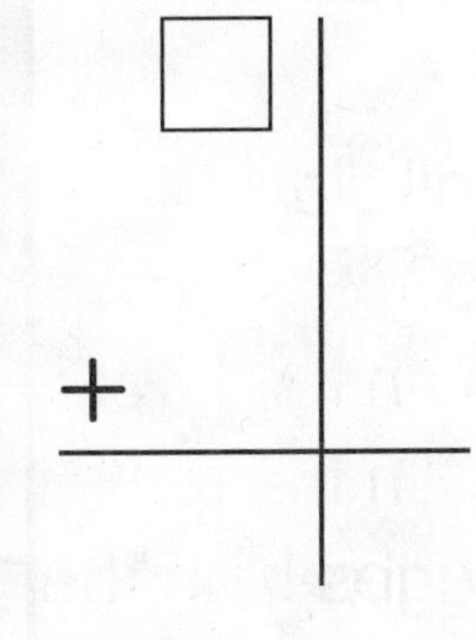

4. 23 + 26

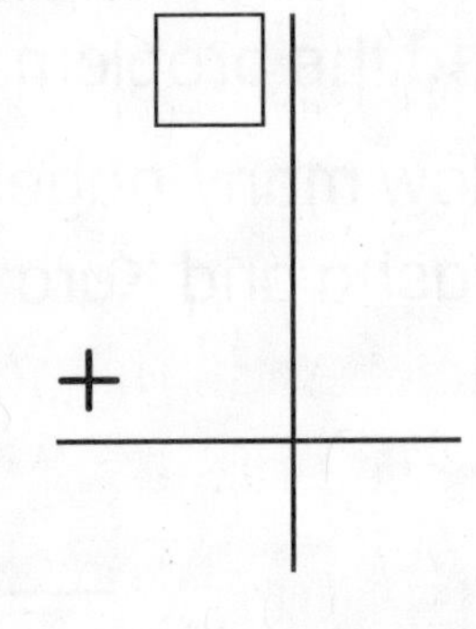

Name ________________________

Rewrite 2-Digit Addition

Lesson 38
CC.2.NBT.5

Rewrite the numbers. Then add.

1. 27 + 19

   +

2. 36 + 23

   +

3. 31 + 29

   +

4. 48 + 23

   +

5. 53 + 12

   +

6. 69 + 13

   +

7. 24 + 38

   +

8. 46 + 37

   +

PROBLEM SOLVING

Use the table. Show how you solved the problem.

9. How many pages in all did Sasha and Kara read?

   _____ pages

Pages Read This Week	
Child	**Number of Pages**
Sasha	62
Kara	29
Juan	50

Name ______________________

COMMON CORE STANDARD CC.2.NBT.5

Lesson Objective: Break apart a 1-digit subtrahend to subtract it from a 2-digit number.

Algebra • Break Apart Ones to Subtract

To subtract a one-digit number, break it apart.

Break apart ones in 7.

- Use 4 because 44 has a 4 in the ones place.
- The other part is 3.

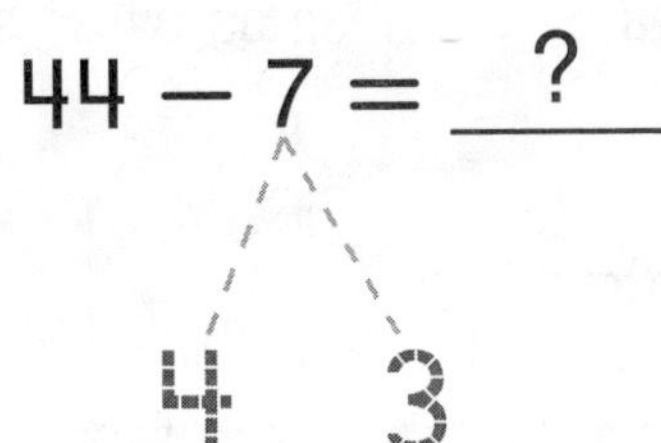

Start at 44.
Subtract 4, and then subtract 3.

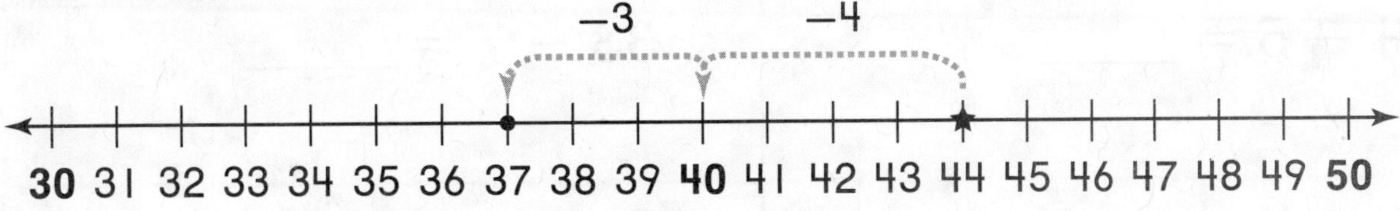

So, 44 − 7 = 37.

Break apart ones to subtract. Write the difference.

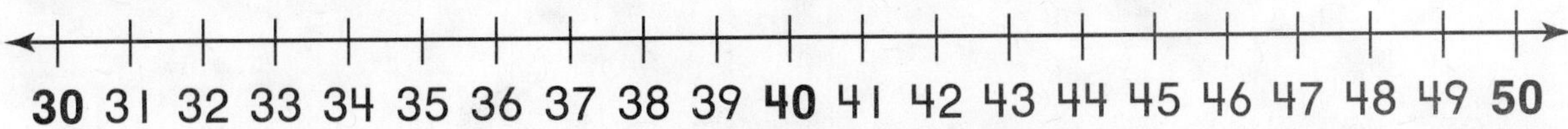

1. 42 − 8 = ______

2. 47 − 8 = ______

3. 43 − 5 = ______

4. 41 − 8 = ______

Name ______________________________

Algebra • Break Apart Ones to Subtract

Break apart ones to subtract.
Write the difference.

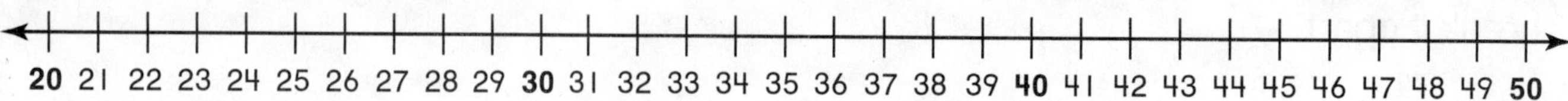

1. 36 − 7 = _____
2. 35 − 8 = _____
3. 37 − 9 = _____
4. 41 − 6 = _____
5. 44 − 5 = _____
6. 33 − 7 = _____
7. 32 − 4 = _____
8. 31 − 6 = _____
9. 46 − 9 = _____
10. 43 − 5 = _____

PROBLEM SOLVING

Choose a way to solve. Write or draw to explain.

11. Beth had 44 marbles. She gave 9 marbles to her brother. How many marbles does Beth have now?

_____ marbles

Name ____________________

Lesson 40

COMMON CORE STANDARD CC.2.NBT.5

Lesson Objective: Break apart a 2-digit subtrahend to subtract it from a 2-digit number.

Algebra • Break Apart Numbers to Subtract

To subtract a two-digit number, break it apart.

First break apart 16 into tens and ones.

Now break apart ones in 6.

- Use 4 because 54 has a 4 in the ones place.
- The other part is 2.

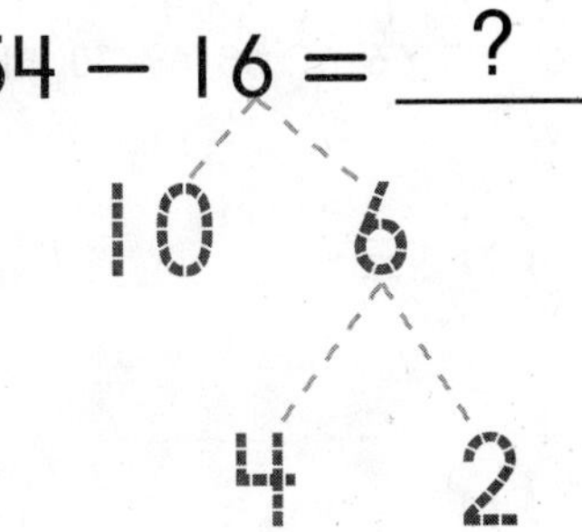

Use the number line to subtract the three parts.

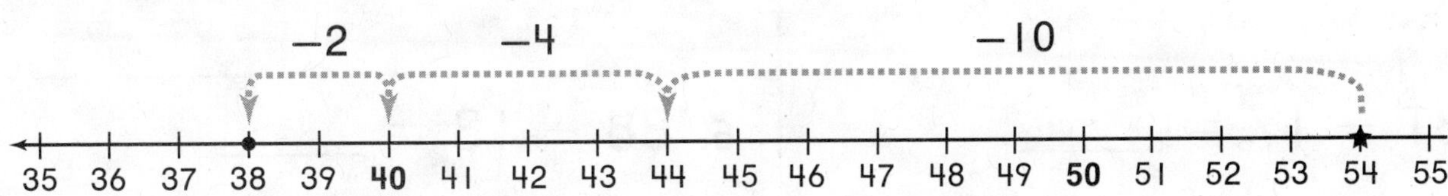

So, 54 − 16 = 38.

Break apart the number you are subtracting. Write the difference.

30 31 32 33 34 35 36 37 38 39 40 41 42 43 44 45 46 47 48 49 50 51 52 53 54 55 56 57 58 59 60

1. 51 − 16 = ______

2. 57 − 18 = ______

3. 54 − 17 = ______

4. 52 − 18 = ______

Name ______________________

Lesson 40

CC.2.NBT.5

Algebra • Break Apart Numbers to Subtract

Break apart the number you are subtracting. Write the difference.

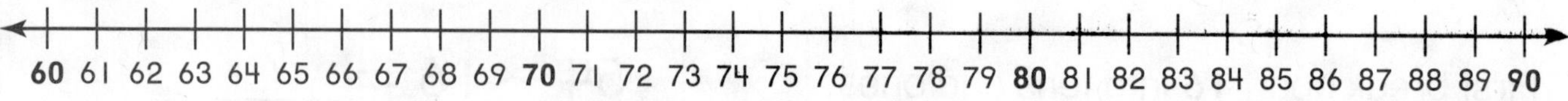

1. 81 − 14 = ______
2. 84 − 16 = ______
3. 77 − 14 = ______
4. 83 − 19 = ______
5. 81 − 17 = ______
6. 88 − 13 = ______
7. 84 − 19 = ______
8. 86 − 18 = ______
9. 84 − 17 = ______
10. 76 − 15 = ______
11. 86 − 12 = ______
12. 82 − 19 = ______

PROBLEM SOLVING

Solve. Write or draw to explain.

13. Mr. Pearce bought 43 plants. He gave 14 plants to his sister. How many plants does Mr. Pearce have now?

______ plants

Name ______________________________

Lesson 41

COMMON CORE STANDARD CC.2.NBT.5

Lesson Objective: Draw quick pictures and record 2-digit subtraction using the standard algorithm.

Model and Record 2-Digit Subtraction

Subtract.

$$\begin{array}{r} 54 \\ -\ 15 \\ \hline \end{array}$$

Are there enough ones to subtract 5? no

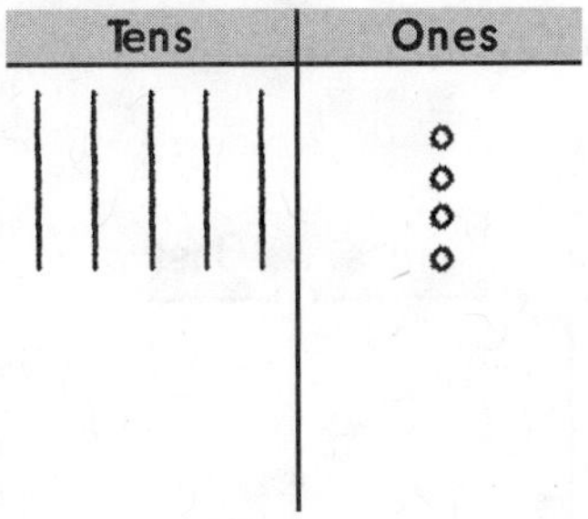

Tens	Ones
☐	☐
5	4
− 1	5

Regroup 1 ten as 10 ones.

Write the new number of tens and ones.

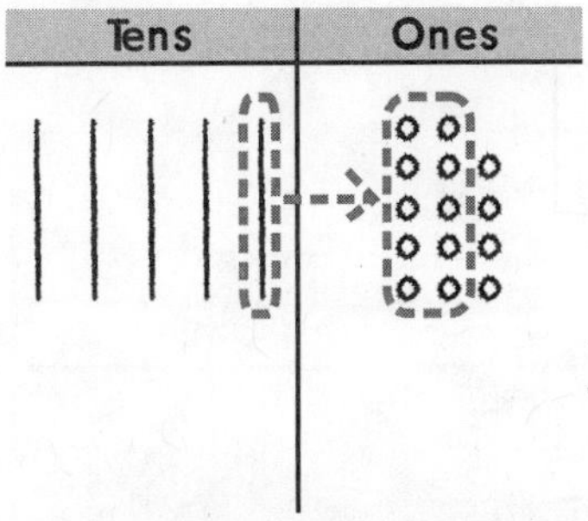

Tens	Ones
4	14
~~5~~	~~4~~
− 1	5

Subtract the ones.

14 ones − 5 ones = 9 ones

Write that number in the ones place.

Subtract the tens.

4 tens − 1 ten = 3 tens

Write that number in the tens place.

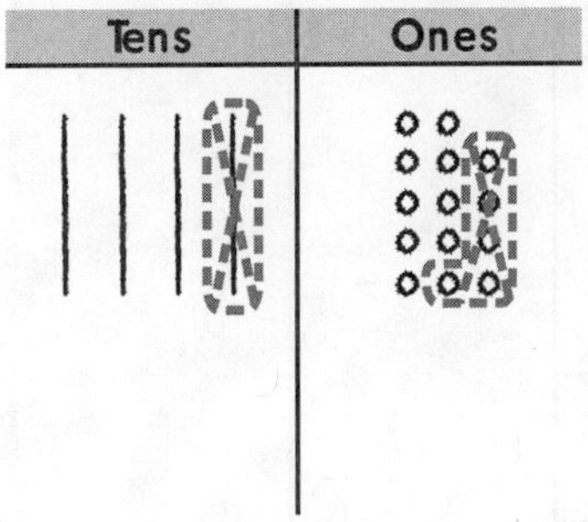

Tens	Ones
4	14
~~5~~	~~4~~
− 1	5
3	9

Draw a quick picture to solve. Write the difference.

1.

Tens	Ones
☐	☐
4	3
− 1	6

Tens	Ones

2.

Tens	Ones
☐	☐
3	1
− 1	7

Tens	Ones

Name ____________________

Model and Record 2-Digit Subtraction

Draw a quick picture to solve.
Write the difference.

1.

	Tens	Ones
	☐	☐
	4	3
−	1	7

Tens	Ones

2.

	Tens	Ones
	☐	☐
	3	8
−	2	9

Tens	Ones

3.

	Tens	Ones
	☐	☐
	5	2
−	3	7

Tens	Ones

4.

	Tens	Ones
	☐	☐
	3	5
−	1	9

Tens	Ones

PROBLEM SOLVING

Solve. Write or draw to explain.

5. Kendall has 63 stickers.
Her sister has 57 stickers.
How many more stickers does Kendall have than her sister?

_______ more stickers

Name ______________________

Lesson 42

COMMON CORE STANDARD CC.2.NBT.5

Lesson Objective: Record 2-digit subtraction using the standard algorithm.

2-Digit Subtraction

Subtract. 54 − 28

Are there enough ones to subtract 8? no

Tens	Ones
☐	☐
5	4
− 2	8

Regroup 1 ten as 10 ones.

Write the new number of tens and ones.

Tens	Ones
4	14
~~5~~	~~4~~
− 2	8

Subtract the ones.

14 ones − 8 ones = 6 ones

Write that number in the ones place.

Tens	Ones
4	14
~~5~~	~~4~~
− 2	8
	6

Subtract the tens.

4 tens − 2 tens = 2 tens

Write that number in the tens place.

Tens	Ones
4	14
~~5~~	~~4~~
− 2	8
2	6

Regroup if you need to. Write the difference.

1.

Tens	Ones
☐	☐
7	2
− 4	5

2.

Tens	Ones
☐	☐
5	1
− 1	3

3.

Tens	Ones
☐	☐
3	8
− 1	6

Name ____________________

2-Digit Subtraction

Regroup if you need to. Write the difference.

1.

Tens	Ones
☐	☐
4	7
− 2	8

2.

Tens	Ones
☐	☐
3	3
− 1	8

3.

Tens	Ones
☐	☐
2	8
− 1	4

4.

Tens	Ones
☐	☐
6	6
− 1	9

5.

7	7
− 2	6

6.

5	8
− 3	4

7.

5	2
− 2	5

8.

8	7
− 4	9

PROBLEM SOLVING

Solve. Write or draw to explain.

9. Mrs. Paul bought 32 erasers. She gave 19 erasers to students. How many erasers does she still have?

_____ erasers

Name ____________________

Lesson 43

COMMON CORE STANDARD CC.2.NBT.5

Lesson Objective: Practice 2-digit subtraction with and without regrouping.

Practice 2-Digit Subtraction

Clay scored 80 points. Meg scored 61 points.
How many more points did Clay score than Meg?

STEP 1

More ones are needed. Regroup 8 tens 0 ones as 7 tens 10 ones.

7	10
8	0
− 6	1

STEP 2

Subtract in the ones column.

7	10
8	0
− 6	1
	9

STEP 3

Subtract in the tens column.

7	10
8	0
− 6	1
1	9

Write the difference.

1. $60 - 27$

2. $37 - 22$

3. $61 - 48$

4. $70 - 26$

5. $37 - 19$

6. $55 - 14$

Name ______________________________

Practice 2-Digit Subtraction

Write the difference.

1. $\begin{array}{r} 50 \\ -18 \\ \hline \end{array}$	**2.** $\begin{array}{r} 43 \\ -17 \\ \hline \end{array}$	**3.** $\begin{array}{r} 75 \\ -18 \\ \hline \end{array}$
4. $\begin{array}{r} 22 \\ -\ \ 6 \\ \hline \end{array}$	**5.** $\begin{array}{r} 60 \\ -35 \\ \hline \end{array}$	**6.** $\begin{array}{r} 42 \\ -34 \\ \hline \end{array}$
7. $\begin{array}{r} 21 \\ -\ \ 8 \\ \hline \end{array}$	**8.** $\begin{array}{r} 39 \\ -27 \\ \hline \end{array}$	**9.** $\begin{array}{r} 61 \\ -37 \\ \hline \end{array}$

PROBLEM SOLVING

Solve. Write or draw to explain.

10. Julie has 42 sheets of paper. She gives 17 sheets to Kari. How many sheets of paper does Julie have now?

_____ sheets of paper

Name ______________________________

Lesson 44

COMMON CORE STANDARD CC.2.NBT.5

Lesson Objective: Rewrite horizontal subtraction problems vertically in the standard algorithm format.

Rewrite 2-Digit Subtraction

62 − 38 = ?

Rewrite 62 first.

62

The 6 is in the tens place. Write it in the tens column.

The 2 is in the ones place. Write it in the ones column.

	Tens	Ones
	☐	☐
	6	2
−		

Then rewrite 38.

38

The 3 is in the tens place. Write it in the tens column.

The 8 is in the ones place. Write it in the ones column.

	Tens	Ones
	☐	☐
	6	2
−	3	8

Now the ones digits are in a column and the tens digits are in a column.

Subtract. Write the difference.

	Tens	Ones
	5	12
	~~6~~	~~2~~
−	3	8
	2	4

Rewrite the subtraction problem. Find the difference.

1. 56 − 24

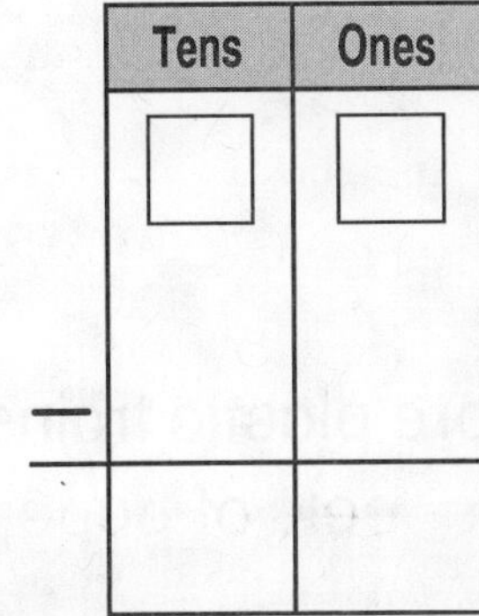

2. 74 − 37

	Tens	Ones
	☐	☐
−		

3. 43 − 15

	Tens	Ones
	☐	☐
−		

Name ___________________________

Rewrite 2-Digit Subtraction

Rewrite the subtraction problem.
Then find the difference.

1. 35 − 19

−
______

2. 47 − 23

−
______

3. 55 − 28

−
______

4. 22 − 15

−
______

5. 61 − 32

−
______

6. 70 − 37

−
______

PROBLEM SOLVING

Solve. Write or draw to explain.

7. Jimmy went to the toy store. He saw 23 wooden trains and 41 plastic trains. How many more plastic trains than wooden trains did he see?

_____ more plastic trains

Name ______________________

Lesson 45

COMMON CORE STANDARD CC.2.NBT.5

Lesson Objective: Use addition to find differences.

Add to Find Differences

Count up to solve. 34 − 27 = ?
Start at 27. Count up 3 to 30.

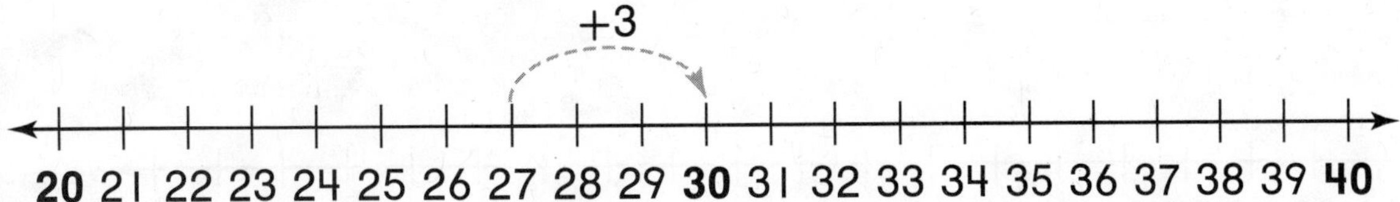

To get to 34 from 30, count up 4 more.

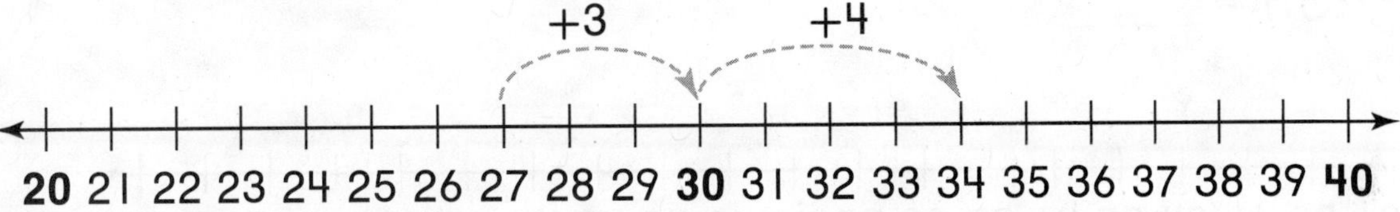

7 was added to get to 34.

So, 34 − 27 = 7.

Count up to find the difference.

1. 41 − 37 = ____

2. 43 − 38 = ____

Name ____________________

Add to Find Differences

Use the number line. Count up to find the difference.

1. 36 − 29 = ____

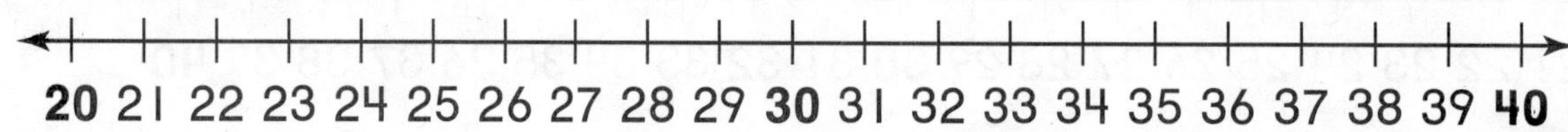

2. 43 − 38 = ____

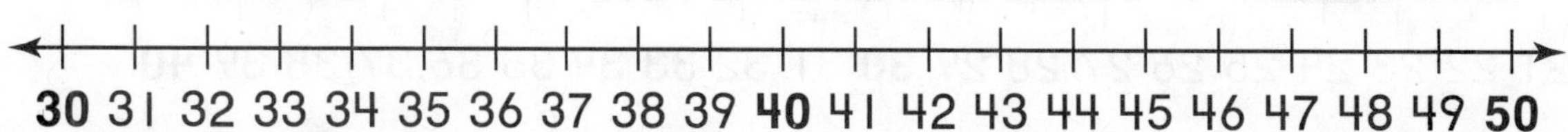

3. 76 − 68 = ____

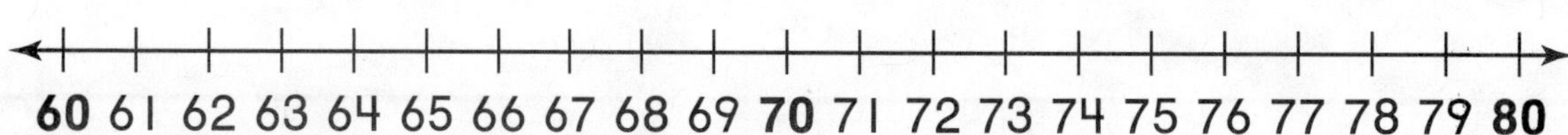

PROBLEM SOLVING REAL WORLD

Solve. You may wish to use the number line.

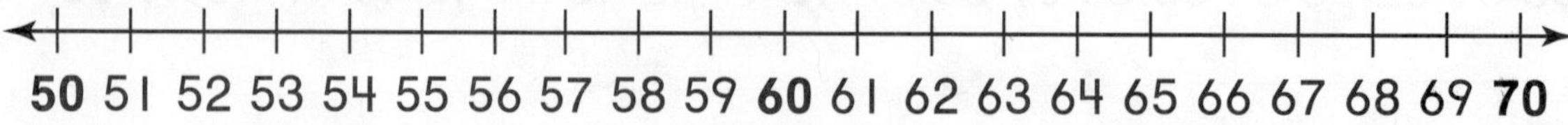

4. Jill has 63 index cards. She uses 57 of them for a project. How many index cards does Jill have now?

____ index cards

Name ________________

COMMON CORE STANDARD CC.2.NBT.6

Lesson Objective: Find a sum by breaking apart a 1-digit addend to make a 2-digit addend a multiple of 10.

Break Apart Ones to Add

Sometimes when you are adding, you can break apart ones to make a ten.

$37 + 8 = \underline{?}$

Look at the two-digit addend, 37. What digit is in the ones place? 7

Decide how many you need to add to the ones digit to make 10.

$7 + \underline{3} = 10$, and $37 + \underline{3} = 40$

Break apart that number from the one-digit addend, 8.

$8 - 3 = 5$

Finally, write the new number sentence. $40 + 5 = \underline{45}$

Break apart ones to make a ten. Then add and write the sum.

1. $28 + 6 =$ ____

2. $34 + 7 =$ ____

Name ______________________

Lesson 46
CC.2.NBT.6

Break Apart Ones to Add

Break apart ones to make a ten. Then add and write the sum.

1. 62 + 9 = ____
2. 27 + 7 = ____
3. 28 + 5 = ____
4. 17 + 8 = ____
5. 57 + 6 = ____
6. 23 + 9 = ____
7. 39 + 7 = ____
8. 26 + 5 = ____
9. 13 + 8 = ____
10. 18 + 7 = ____
11. 49 + 8 = ____
12. 27 + 5 = ____
13. 39 + 4 = ____
14. 18 + 8 = ____

PROBLEM SOLVING

Solve. Write or draw to explain.

15. Jimmy had 18 toy airplanes. His mother bought him 7 more toy airplanes. How many toy airplanes does he have now?

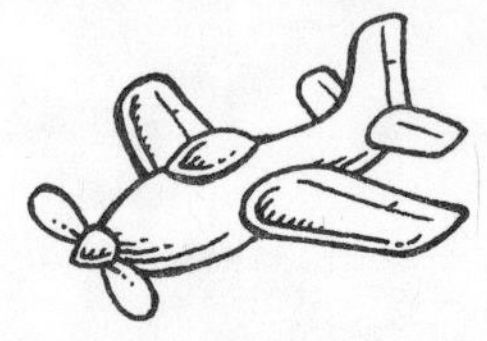

____ toy airplanes

Name ______________________________

Lesson 47

COMMON CORE STANDARD CC.2.NBT.6

Lesson Objective: Use compensation to develop flexible thinking for 2-digit addition.

Use Compensation

This is a way to add 2-digit numbers.
Take ones from one addend to make the other addend a tens number.

$27 + 38 = \underline{\ ?\ }$

First, find the addend with the greater ones digit. <u>38</u>
How many ones would you need to add to make it a tens number?

$38 + \_\_\_ = 40$ Add <u>2</u> to make <u>40</u>.

Next, take that many ones away from the other addend.

$27 - 2 = 25$ The two new addends are <u>25</u> and <u>40</u>.

Write the new addition sentence to find the sum.

<u>25</u> + <u>40</u> = <u>65</u>

Show how to make one addend the next tens number. Complete the new addition sentence.

1. $28 + 16 = ?$

___ + ___ = ___

2. $37 + 24 = ?$

___ + ___ = ___

Name ______________________________

Use Compensation

Show how to make one addend the next tens number. Complete the new addition sentence.

1. 15 + 37 = ?

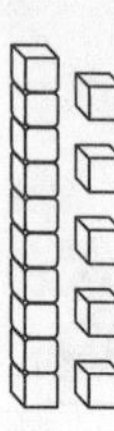
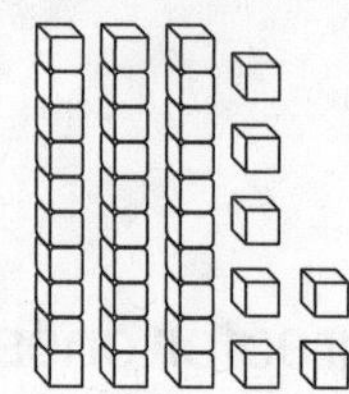

____ + ____ = ____

2. 22 + 49 = ?

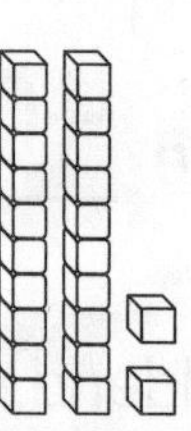
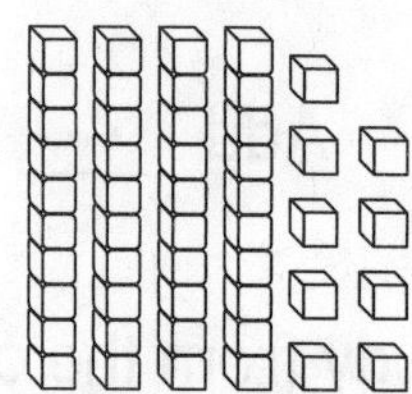

____ + ____ = ____

3. 38 + 26 = ?

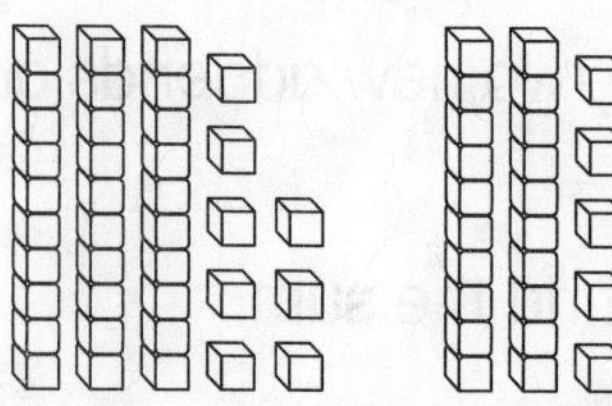

____ + ____ = ____

4. 27 + 47 = ?

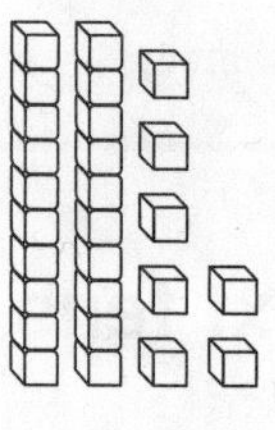
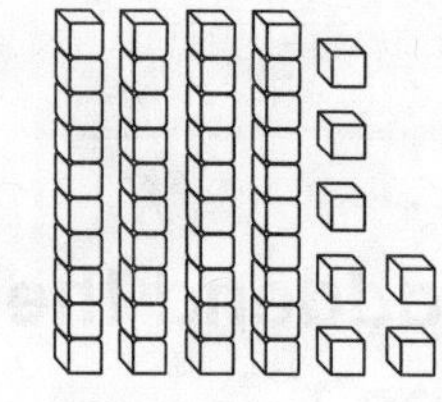

____ + ____ = ____

PROBLEM SOLVING

Solve. Write or draw to explain.

5. The oak tree at the school was 34 feet tall. Then it grew 18 feet taller. How tall is the oak tree now?

____ feet tall

Name ______________________________

Lesson 48

COMMON CORE STANDARD CC.2.NBT.6

Lesson Objective: Apply place-value concepts when using a break-apart strategy for 2-digit addition.

Break Apart Addends as Tens and Ones

25 + 46 = ?

Break apart 25 into tens and ones. Break apart 46 into tens and ones.

Then, add the tens from the two addends. 20 + 40 = 60

Add the ones from the two addends. 5 + 6 = 11

Add the two sums. 60 + 11 = 71

So, 25 + 46 = 71.

Break apart the addends to find the sum.

1. 12 + 48 = ?

___ + ___ + ___ + ___

Add the tens. ___ + ___ = ___

Add the ones. ___ + ___ = ___

How many in all? ___ + ___ = ___

So, 12 + 48 = ___.

Name ______________________________

Break Apart Addends as Tens and Ones

Break apart the addends to find the sum.

1.

18	→	____ + ____
+ 21	→	____ + ____
		____ + ____ = ____

2.

33	→	____ + ____
+ 49	→	____ + ____
		____ + ____ = ____

3.

72	→	____ + ____
+ 18	→	____ + ____
		____ + ____ = ____

PROBLEM SOLVING

Choose a way to solve.
Write or draw to explain.

4. Christopher has 28 baseball cards. Justin has 18 baseball cards. How many baseball cards do they have in all?

____ baseball cards

Name ______________________________

COMMON CORE STANDARD CC.2.NBT.6

Lesson Objective: Draw quick pictures and record 2-digit addition using the standard algorithm.

Model and Record 2-Digit Addition

Model 33 + 19.

How many ones are there in all? 12 ones

Can you make a ten? yes

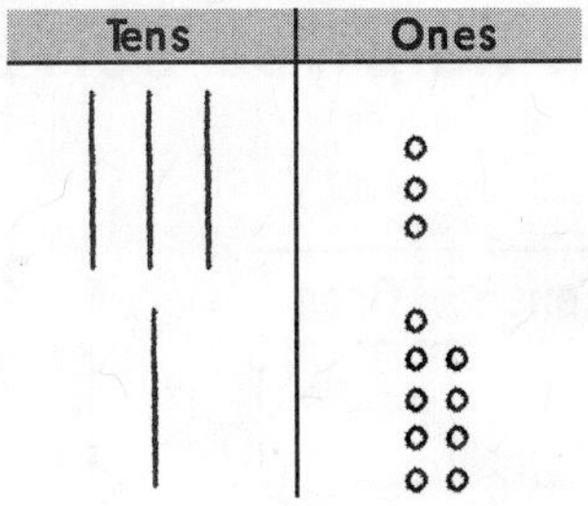

Tens	Ones
☐	
3	3
+ 1	9

Regroup 10 ones as 1 ten. Write a 1 in the tens column to show the regrouped ten.

How many ones are left after regrouping? 2 ones

Write that number in the ones place.

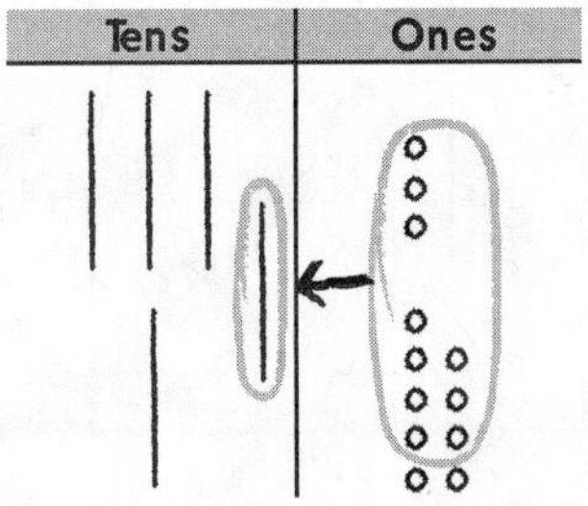

Tens	Ones
1	
3	3
+ 1	9
	2

How many tens are there in all? 5 tens

Write that number in the tens place.

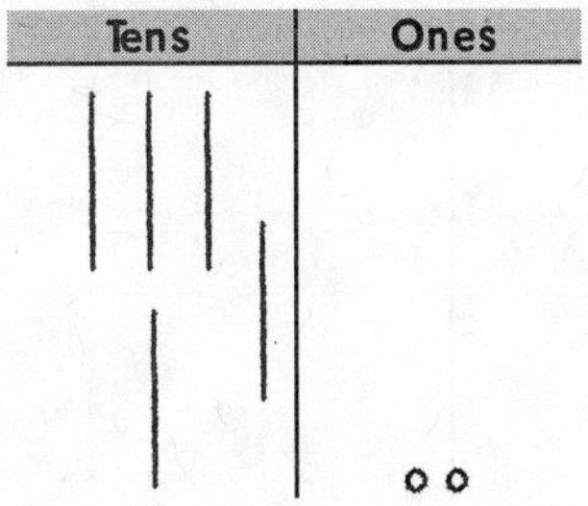

Tens	Ones
1	
3	3
+ 1	9
5	2

Draw quick pictures to help you solve. Write the sum.

1.

Tens	Ones
☐	
4	7
+ 2	5

Tens	Ones

2.

Tens	Ones
☐	
3	6
+ 4	6

Tens	Ones

Name ____________________

Model and Record 2-Digit Addition

Draw quick pictures to help you solve.
Write the sum.

1.

	Tens	Ones
	☐	
	3	8
+	1	7

Tens	Ones

2.

	Tens	Ones
	☐	
	5	8
+	2	6

Tens	Ones

3.

	Tens	Ones
	☐	
	4	2
+	3	7

Tens	Ones

4.

	Tens	Ones
	☐	
	5	3
+	3	8

Tens	Ones

PROBLEM SOLVING

Choose a way to solve.
Write or draw to explain.

5. There were 37 children at the park on Saturday and 25 children at the park on Sunday. How many children were at the park on those two days?

_____ children

Name ____________________

Lesson 50

COMMON CORE STANDARD CC.2.NBT.6

Lesson Objective: Find sums of three 2-digit numbers.

Algebra • Find Sums for 3 Addends

You can add three numbers in different ways.
Start by adding the ones first.

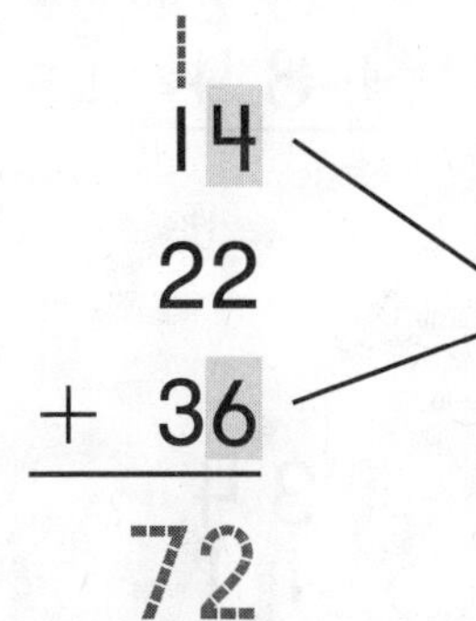

Look at the column of ones digits. Choose two of the digits to add first. Then add the other digit.

$4 + 6 = 10$

$10 + 2 = 12$

Then add the tens.

$1 + 1 + 2 + 3 = 7$

$$\begin{array}{r} 1 \\ 14 \\ 22 \\ +\ 36 \\ \hline 72 \end{array}$$

Start at the top of the ones column. Add the first two digits, and then add the third digit.

$4 + 2 = 6$

$6 + 6 = 12$

Then add the tens.

$1 + 1 + 2 + 3 = 7$

Add.

1.
$$\begin{array}{r} 18 \\ 25 \\ +\ 32 \\ \hline \end{array}$$

2.
$$\begin{array}{r} 40 \\ 37 \\ +\ 16 \\ \hline \end{array}$$

3.
$$\begin{array}{r} 13 \\ 21 \\ +\ 34 \\ \hline \end{array}$$

4.
$$\begin{array}{r} 26 \\ 22 \\ +\ 23 \\ \hline \end{array}$$

Name ______________________________

Lesson 50
CC.2.NBT.6

Algebra • Find Sums for 3 Addends

Add.

1.
```
  23
  20
+ 25
----
```

2.
```
  15
  22
+ 38
----
```

3.
```
  13
  52
+ 34
----
```

4.
```
  27
  40
+ 19
----
```

5.
```
  31
  45
+ 24
----
```

6.
```
  34
  11
+ 28
----
```

7.
```
  42
  36
+ 11
----
```

8.
```
  18
  22
+ 34
----
```

9.
```
  53
  19
+ 25
----
```

PROBLEM SOLVING

Solve. Write or draw to explain.

10. Liam has 24 yellow pencils, 15 red pencils, and 9 blue pencils. How many pencils does he have altogether?

_____ pencils

Name ____________________

COMMON CORE STANDARD CC.2.NBT.6

Lesson Objective: Find sums of four 2-digit numbers.

Algebra • Find Sums for 4 Addends

You can add 4 numbers in different ways.
One way is to add pairs of digits in the ones column.

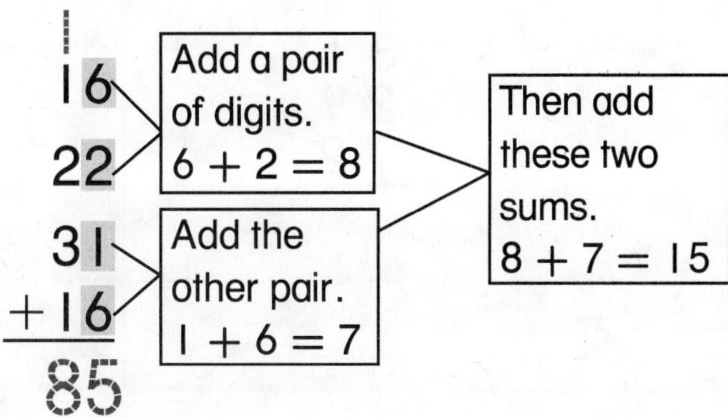

Then add the digits in the tens column.

Add.

1.
```
  43
  57
  32
+  2
```

2.
```
  24
  21
  19
+ 32
```

3.
```
  21
  14
  20
+ 42
```

Name ____________________

Algebra • Find Sums for 4 Addends

Add.

1.
$$\begin{array}{r} 18 \\ 32 \\ 23 \\ +\ 3 \\ \hline \end{array}$$

2.
$$\begin{array}{r} 45 \\ 31 \\ 29 \\ +72 \\ \hline \end{array}$$

3.
$$\begin{array}{r} 24 \\ 62 \\ 70 \\ +33 \\ \hline \end{array}$$

4.
$$\begin{array}{r} 83 \\ 32 \\ 61 \\ +22 \\ \hline \end{array}$$

5.
$$\begin{array}{r} 37 \\ 15 \\ 31 \\ +12 \\ \hline \end{array}$$

6.
$$\begin{array}{r} 21 \\ 13 \\ 96 \\ +18 \\ \hline \end{array}$$

PROBLEM SOLVING

Solve. Show how you solved the problem.

7. Kinza jogs 16 minutes on Monday, 13 minutes on Tuesday, 9 minutes on Wednesday, and 20 minutes on Thursday. What is the total number of minutes she jogged?

_____ minutes

Name ______________________________

Lesson 52

COMMON CORE STANDARD CC.2.NBT.7

Lesson Objective: Draw quick pictures to represent 3-digit addition.

Draw to Represent 3-Digit Addition

Add 213 and 124.
Draw quick pictures of 213 and 124.

Count the hundreds, tens, and ones.

3 hundreds 3 tens 7 ones

Write the number. 337

Hundreds	Tens	Ones

Draw quick pictures. Write how many hundreds, tens, and ones in all. Write the number.

1. Add 135 and 214.

Hundreds	Tens	Ones

_____ hundreds _____ tens _____ ones

_____

2. Add 121 and 143.

Hundreds	Tens	Ones

_____ hundreds _____ tens _____ ones

_____

Name ______________________

Lesson 52
CC.2.NBT.7

Draw to Represent 3-Digit Addition

Draw quick pictures. Write how many hundreds, tens, and ones in all. Write the number.

1. Add 142 and 215.

Hundreds	Tens	Ones

____ hundreds ____ tens ____ ones

____

2. Add 263 and 206.

Hundreds	Tens	Ones

____ hundreds ____ tens ____ ones

____

PROBLEM SOLVING

Solve. Write or draw to explain.

3. A farmer sold 324 lemons and 255 limes. How many pieces of fruit did the farmer sell altogether?

________ pieces of fruit

Name ______________________

Lesson 53

COMMON CORE STANDARD CC.2.NBT.7

Lesson Objective: Apply place value concepts when using a break apart strategy for 3-digit addition.

Break Apart 3-Digit Addends

743
+ 124

Break apart each addend.
Write the value of each digit.

743 = 700 + 40 + 3

124 = 100 + 20 + 4

Add the hundreds, tens, and ones.
Then add these sums together.

	Hundreds		Tens		Ones		
743 →	700	+	40	+	3		
+ 124 →	100	+	20	+	4		
	800	+	60	+	7	=	867

Break apart the addends to find the sum.

	Hundreds		Tens		Ones		
1. 253 →	____	+	____	+	____		
+ 536 →	____	+	____	+	____		
	____	+	____	+	____	=	____

Name ______________________

Break Apart 3-Digit Addends

Break apart the addends to find the sum.

1. 518 → ______ + ______ + ______

   \+ 221 → ______ + ______ + ______

   ______ + ______ + ______ = ______

2. 438 → ______ + ______ + ______

   \+ 142 → ______ + ______ + ______

   ______ + ______ + ______ = ______

3. 324 → ______ + ______ + ______

   \+ 239 → ______ + ______ + ______

   ______ + ______ + ______ = ______

PROBLEM SOLVING

Solve. Write or draw to explain.

4. There are 126 crayons in a bucket. A teacher puts 144 more crayons in the bucket. How many crayons are in the bucket now?

______ crayons

Name ______________________

Lesson 54

COMMON CORE STANDARD CC.2.NBT.7

Lesson Objective: Record 3-digit addition using the standard algorithm with possible regrouping of ones.

3-Digit Addition: Regroup Ones

Add. 318
+ 256

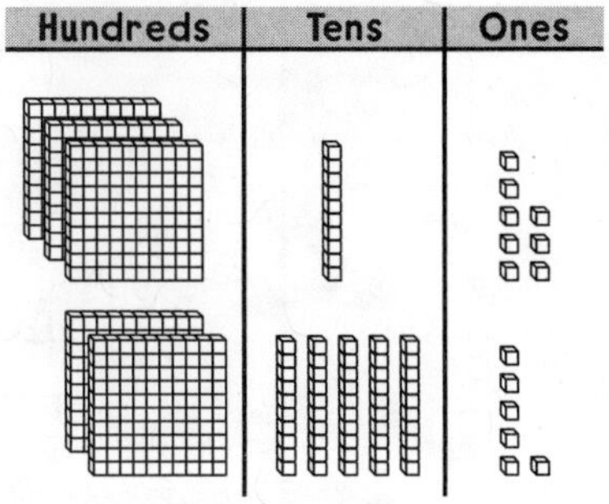

Hundreds	Tens	Ones
	☐	
3	1	8
+ 2	5	6

Add the ones.

8 + 6 = 14

Do you need to regroup? yes

Regroup 10 ones as 1 ten.

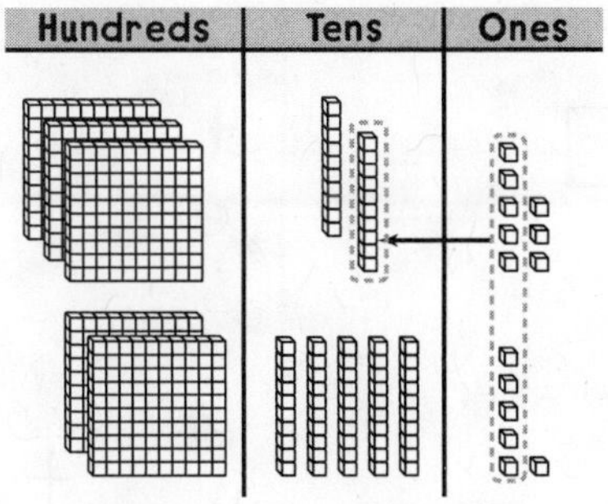

Hundreds	Tens	Ones
	1	
3	1	8
+ 2	5	6
		4

Add the tens.

1 + 1 + 5 = 7

Add the hundreds.

3 + 2 = 5

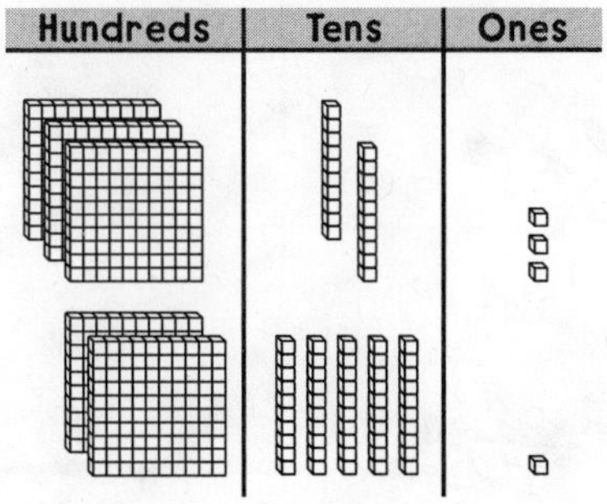

Hundreds	Tens	Ones
	1	
3	1	8
+ 2	5	6
5	7	4

Write the sum.

1.

Hundreds	Tens	Ones
	☐	
5	2	6
+ 1	4	2

2.

Hundreds	Tens	Ones
	☐	
4	5	7
+ 3	3	5

Name ____________________

3-Digit Addition: Regroup Ones

Write the sum.

1.

	Hundreds	Tens	Ones
		☐	
	1	4	8
+	2	3	4

2.

	Hundreds	Tens	Ones
		☐	
	3	2	1
+	3	1	8

3.

	Hundreds	Tens	Ones
		☐	
	4	1	4
+	1	7	9

4.

	Hundreds	Tens	Ones
		☐	
	6	0	2
+	2	5	8

PROBLEM SOLVING

Solve. Write or draw to explain.

5. In the garden, there are 258 yellow daisies and 135 white daisies. How many daisies are in the garden altogether?

__________ daisies

Name ______________________________

Lesson 55

COMMON CORE STANDARD CC.2.NBT.7

Lesson Objective: Record 3-digit addition using the standard algorithm with possible regrouping of tens.

3-Digit Addition: Regroup Tens

Add. 271
+ 158

Add the ones.

1 + 8 = 9

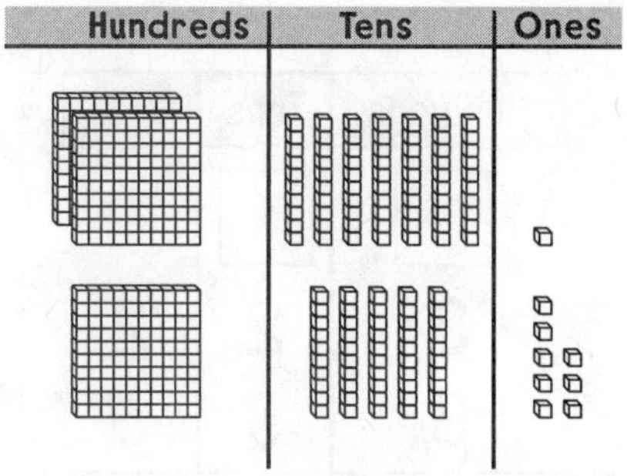

Hundreds	Tens	Ones
2	7	1
+ 1	5	8
		9

Add the tens.

7 + 5 = 12

Do you need to regroup? yes

Regroup 12 tens as 1 hundred 2 tens.

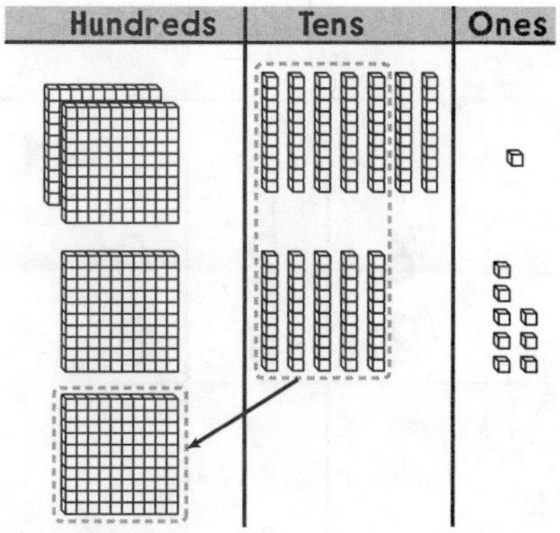

Hundreds	Tens	Ones
1		
2	7	1
+ 1	5	8
	2	9

Add the hundreds.

1 + 2 + 1 = 4

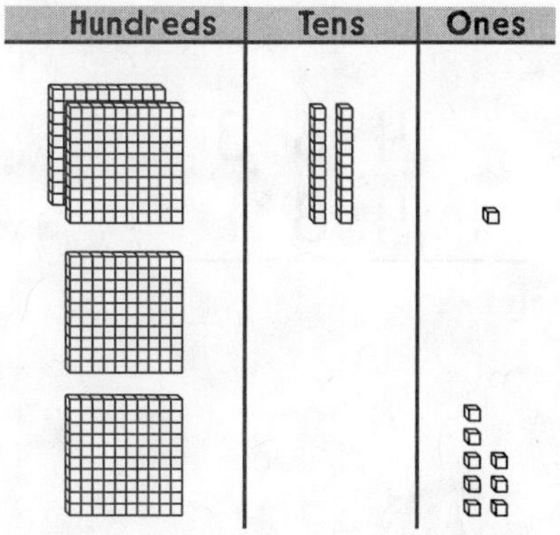

Hundreds	Tens	Ones
1		
2	7	1
+ 1	5	8
4	2	9

Write the sum.

1.

Hundreds	Tens	Ones
2	6	4
+ 1	4	5

2.

Hundreds	Tens	Ones
2	3	2
+ 6	0	6

Name ___________________________

Lesson 55
CC.2.NBT.7

3-Digit Addition: Regroup Tens

Write the sum.

1.

	Hundreds	Tens	Ones
	□	□	
	1	8	7
+	2	3	2

2.

	Hundreds	Tens	Ones
	□	□	
	3	2	2
+	3	5	6

3.

	Hundreds	Tens	Ones
	□	□	
	2	8	5
+	5	3	1

4.

	4	4	5
+		3	4

5.

	6	2	0
+	2	8	8

6.

	5	5	7
+	1	8	0

7.
$$\begin{array}{r} 671 \\ +\,154 \\ \hline \end{array}$$

8.
$$\begin{array}{r} 463 \\ +\,481 \\ \hline \end{array}$$

9.
$$\begin{array}{r} 746 \\ +\,133 \\ \hline \end{array}$$

PROBLEM SOLVING 

Solve. Write or draw to explain.

10. There are 142 blue toy cars and 293 red toy cars at the toy store. How many toy cars are there in all?

________ toy cars

Name ______________________

Lesson 56

COMMON CORE STANDARD CC.2.NBT.7

Lesson Objective: Record 3-digit addition using the standard algorithm with possible regrouping of both ones and tens.

Addition: Regroup Ones and Tens

Sometimes, you may need to regroup more than once.

$$\begin{array}{r} 189 \\ +\,623 \\ \hline \end{array}$$

Step 1 Add the ones.
There are 12 ones in all.
Regroup 12 ones as 1 ten 2 ones.

	1	
1	8	9
+ 6	2	3
		2

Step 2 Add the tens.
There are 11 tens in all.
Regroup 11 tens as 1 hundred 1 ten.

1	1	
1	8	9
+ 6	2	3
	1	2

Step 3 Add the hundreds.
There are 8 hundreds in all.

1	1	
1	8	9
+ 6	2	3
8	1	2

Write the sum.

1.

2	7	8
+ 4	6	5

2.

1	5	7
+ 7	7	1

3.

3	6	4
+ 4	1	9

Name ______________________

Addition: Regroup Ones and Tens

Write the sum.

1. $\begin{array}{r} 547 \\ +\ 435 \\ \hline \end{array}$	**2.** $\begin{array}{r} 367 \\ +\ 284 \\ \hline \end{array}$	**3.** $\begin{array}{r} 485 \\ +\ 456 \\ \hline \end{array}$
4. $\begin{array}{r} 187 \\ +\ 306 \\ \hline \end{array}$	**5.** $\begin{array}{r} 647 \\ +\ 128 \\ \hline \end{array}$	**6.** $\begin{array}{r} 523 \\ +\ 174 \\ \hline \end{array}$
7. $\begin{array}{r} 255 \\ +\ 231 \\ \hline \end{array}$	**8.** $\begin{array}{r} 294 \\ +\ 176 \\ \hline \end{array}$	**9.** $\begin{array}{r} 375 \\ +\ 364 \\ \hline \end{array}$

PROBLEM SOLVING

Solve. Write or draw to explain.

10. Saul and Luisa each scored 167 points on a computer game. How many points did they score in all?

__________ points

Name ______________________

Lesson 57

COMMON CORE STANDARD CC.2.NBT.7

Lesson Objective: Solve problems involving 3-digit subtraction by using the strategy *make a model.*

Problem Solving • 3-Digit Subtraction

There were 237 books on the shelves.
Mr. Davies took 126 books off the shelves.
How many books were still on the shelves?

Unlock the Problem

What do I need to find?	What information do I need to use?
how many books were still on the shelves	There were 237 books on the shelves. Mr. Davies took 126 books off the shelves.

Show how to solve the problem.

There were 111 books still on the shelves.

Make a model to solve. Then draw a quick picture of your model.

1. Mr. Cho has 256 pencils. Then he sells 132 pencils. How many pencils does he have now?

_______ pencils

Name ______________________________

Problem Solving • 3-Digit Subtraction

Make a model to solve. Then draw a quick picture of your model.

1. On Saturday, 770 people went to the snack shop. On Sunday, 628 people went. How many more people went to the snack shop on Saturday than on Sunday?

_________ more people

2. There were 395 lemon ice cups at the snack shop. People bought 177 lemon ice cups. How many lemon ice cups are still at the snack shop?

_________ cups

3. There were 576 bottles of water at the snack shop. People bought 469 bottles of water. How many bottles of water are at the snack shop now?

_________ bottles

4. There were 279 bags of apple chips at the snack shop. Then 134 bags of apple chips were bought. How many bags of apple chips are at the snack shop now?

_________ bags

Name ______________________

Lesson 58

COMMON CORE STANDARD CC.2.NBT.7

Lesson Objective: Record 3-digit subtraction using the standard algorithm with possible regrouping of tens.

3-Digit Subtraction: Regroup Tens

Subtract. 463
−317

Are there enough ones to subtract 7? no
Regroup 1 ten as 10 ones.

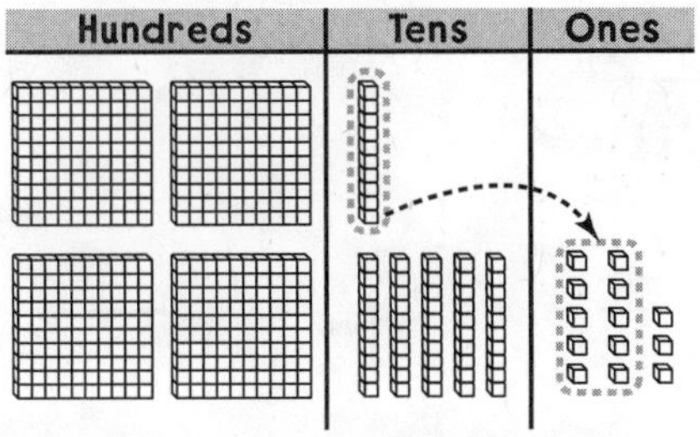

Hundreds	Tens	Ones
	☐	☐
4	6	3
− 3	1	7

There are 13 ones and 5 tens.

Subtract the ones.
$13 - 7 =$ 6

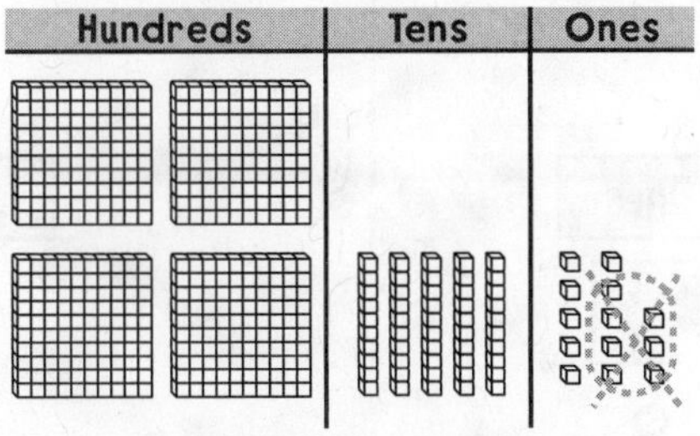

Hundreds	Tens	Ones
	5	13
4	~~6~~	~~3~~
− 3	1	7
		6

Subtract the tens.
$5 - 1 =$ 4

Subtract the hundreds.
$4 - 3 =$ 1

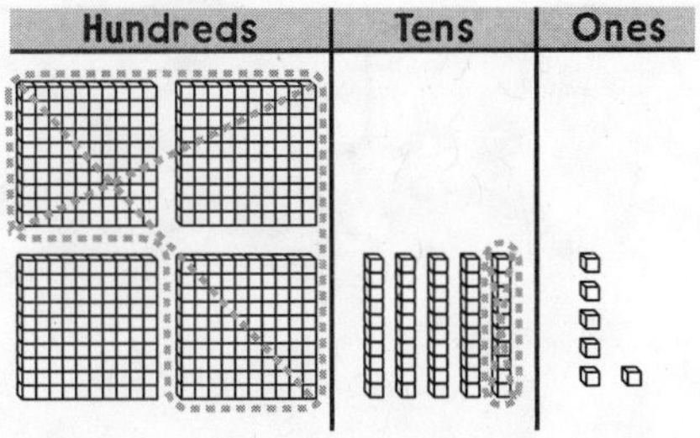

Hundreds	Tens	Ones
	5	13
4	~~6~~	~~3~~
− 3	1	7
1	4	6

Solve. Write the difference.

1.

Hundreds	Tens	Ones
	☐	☐
8	6	2
− 3	2	8

2.

Hundreds	Tens	Ones
	☐	☐
6	7	8
− 2	4	5

Name ______________________________

3-Digit Subtraction: Regroup Tens

Solve. Write the difference.

1.

	Hundreds	Tens	Ones
		☐	☐
	7	7	4
−	2	3	6

2.

	Hundreds	Tens	Ones
		☐	☐
	5	5	1
−	1	1	3

3.

	Hundreds	Tens	Ones
		☐	☐
	4	8	9
−	2	7	3

4.

	Hundreds	Tens	Ones
		☐	☐
	7	7	2
−	2	5	4

PROBLEM SOLVING

Solve. Write or draw to explain.

5. There were 985 pencils. Some pencils were sold. Then there were 559 pencils left. How many pencils were sold?

__________ pencils

Name ____________________

Lesson 5.9

COMMON CORE STANDARD CC.2.NBT.7

Lesson Objective: Record 3-digit subtraction using the standard algorithm with possible regrouping of hundreds.

3-Digit Subtraction: Regroup Hundreds

Subtract. 326
− 174

Subtract the ones.

6 − 4 = 2

Are there enough tens to subtract 7 tens? no

Regroup 1 hundred as 10 tens.

Hundreds	Tens	Ones
2	12	
3	2	6
− 1	7	4
		2

Now there are 12 tens and 2 hundreds.

Subtract the tens.

12 − 7 = 5

Subtract the hundreds.

2 − 1 = 1

Hundreds	Tens	Ones
2	12	
~~3~~	~~2~~	6
− 1	7	4
1	5	2

Solve. Write the difference.

1.

Hundreds	Tens	Ones
6	7	9
− 2	6	1

2.

Hundreds	Tens	Ones
5	2	5
− 2	9	3

Name ______________________________

3-Digit Subtraction: Regroup Hundreds

Solve. Write the difference.

1.

	Hundreds	Tens	Ones
	☐	☐	☐
	7	2	7
−	2	5	6

2.

	Hundreds	Tens	Ones
	☐	☐	☐
	9	6	7
−	1	5	3

3.

	6	3	9
−	4	7	2

4.

	4	4	8
−	3	6	3

PROBLEM SOLVING

Solve. Write or draw to explain.

5. There were 537 people in the parade. 254 of these people were playing an instrument. How many people were not playing an instrument?

_________ people

Name ______________________________

Lesson 60

COMMON CORE STANDARD CC.2.NBT.7

Lesson Objective: Record 3-digit subtraction using the standard algorithm with possible regrouping of both hundreds and tens.

Subtraction: Regroup Hundreds and Tens

You may need to regroup more than once.

$$\begin{array}{r} 282 \\ -\ 198 \\ \hline \end{array}$$

Regroup 1 ten as 10 ones. Subtract the ones.

$$\begin{array}{r} 7\,12 \\ 2\,\not{8}\,\not{2} \\ -1\,9\,8 \\ \hline 4 \end{array}$$

Regroup 1 hundred as 10 tens. Subtract the tens.

$$\begin{array}{r} 17 \\ 1\,\not{7}\,12 \\ \not{2}\,\not{8}\,\not{2} \\ -1\,9\,8 \\ \hline 8\,4 \end{array}$$

Subtract the hundreds.

$$\begin{array}{r} 17 \\ 1\,\not{7}\,12 \\ \not{2}\,\not{8}\,\not{2} \\ -1\,9\,8 \\ \hline 8\,4 \end{array}$$

Solve. Write the difference.

1. $\begin{array}{r} 481 \\ -176 \\ \hline \end{array}$

2. $\begin{array}{r} 746 \\ -\ 28 \\ \hline \end{array}$

3. $\begin{array}{r} 331 \\ -148 \\ \hline \end{array}$

4. $\begin{array}{r} 395 \\ -131 \\ \hline \end{array}$

5. $\begin{array}{r} 524 \\ -265 \\ \hline \end{array}$

6. $\begin{array}{r} 748 \\ -603 \\ \hline \end{array}$

Name ____________________

Subtraction: Regroup Hundreds and Tens

Solve. Write the difference.

1.

$$\begin{array}{r} 816 \\ -\ 345 \\ \hline \end{array}$$

2.

$$\begin{array}{r} 942 \\ -\ 163 \\ \hline \end{array}$$

3.

$$\begin{array}{r} 796 \\ -\ 468 \\ \hline \end{array}$$

4.

$$\begin{array}{r} 723 \\ -\ 543 \\ \hline \end{array}$$

5.

$$\begin{array}{r} 986 \\ -\ 712 \\ \hline \end{array}$$

6.

$$\begin{array}{r} 547 \\ -\ 289 \\ \hline \end{array}$$

PROBLEM SOLVING

Solve.

7. Mia's coloring book has 432 pages. She has already colored 178 pages. How many pages in the book are left to color?

________ pages

Name ____________________

Lesson 61

COMMON CORE STANDARD CC.2.NBT.7

Lesson Objective: Record subtraction using the standard algorithm when there are zeros in the minuend.

Regrouping with Zeros

Subtract 138 from 305.

There are not enough ones to subtract 8.

Since there are 0 tens, regroup 3 hundreds as 2 hundreds 10 tens.

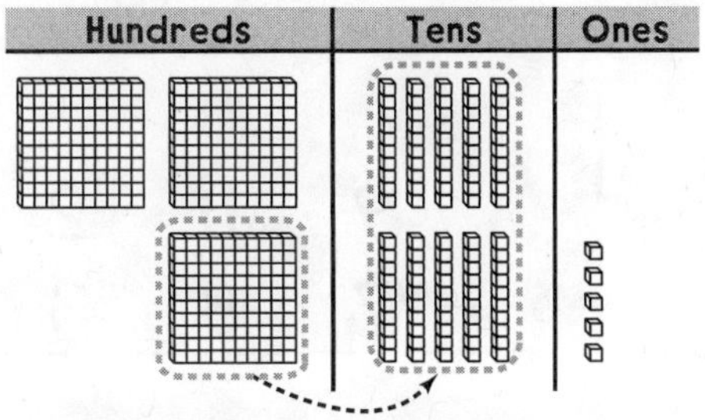

Hundreds	Tens	Ones

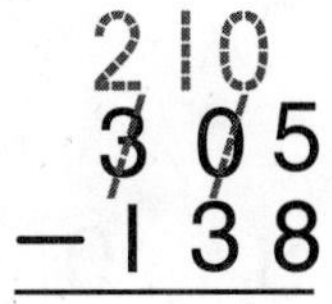

$$\begin{array}{r} \overset{2}{\cancel{3}}\,\overset{10}{\cancel{0}}\,5 \\ -\,1\,3\,8 \\ \hline \end{array}$$

Then regroup 10 tens 5 ones as 9 tens 15 ones.

Subtract the ones.

$15 - 8 = 7$

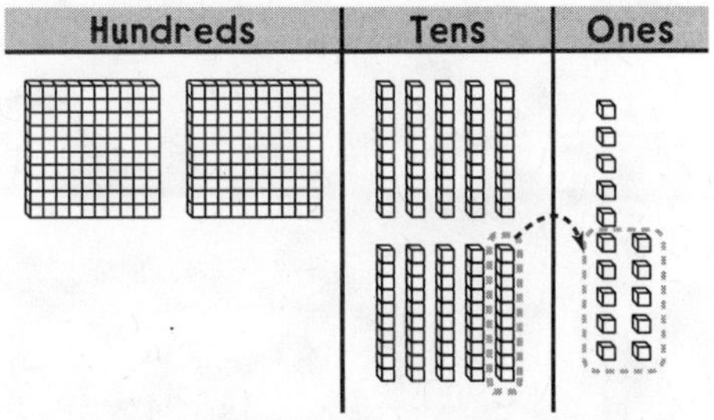

Hundreds	Tens	Ones

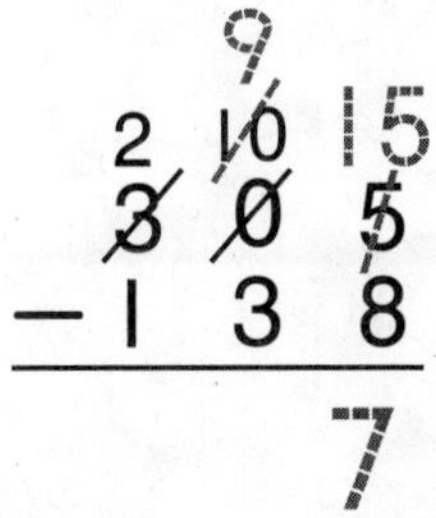

$$\begin{array}{r} \overset{2}{\cancel{3}}\,\overset{\overset{9}{\cancel{10}}}{\cancel{0}}\,\overset{15}{\cancel{5}} \\ -\,1\,3\,8 \\ \hline 7 \end{array}$$

Subtract the tens.

$9 - 3 = 6$

Subtract the hundreds.

$2 - 1 = 1$

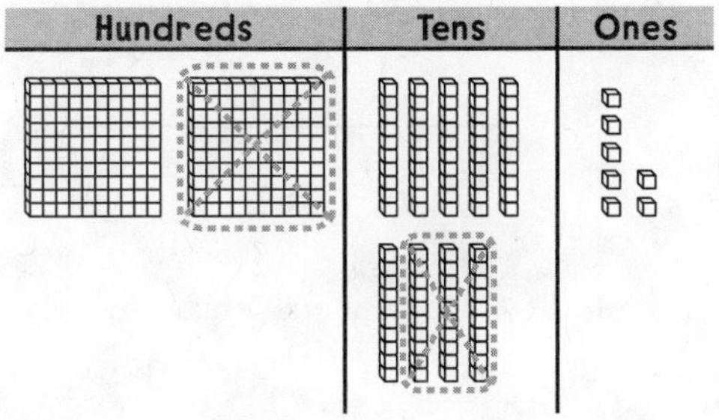

Hundreds	Tens	Ones

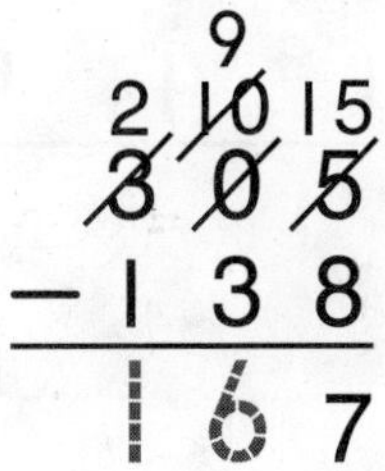

$$\begin{array}{r} \overset{2}{\cancel{3}}\,\overset{\overset{9}{\cancel{10}}}{\cancel{0}}\,\overset{15}{\cancel{5}} \\ -\,1\,3\,8 \\ \hline 1\,6\,7 \end{array}$$

So, $305 - 138 =$ 167.

Solve. Write the difference.

1. $\begin{array}{r} 801 \\ -\,375 \\ \hline \end{array}$

2. $\begin{array}{r} 693 \\ -\,241 \\ \hline \end{array}$

3. $\begin{array}{r} 907 \\ -\,624 \\ \hline \end{array}$

Name ______________________________

Regrouping with Zeros

Solve. Write the difference.

1.	2.	3.
$\begin{array}{r} 806 \\ -345 \\ \hline \end{array}$	$\begin{array}{r} 902 \\ -783 \\ \hline \end{array}$	$\begin{array}{r} 794 \\ -268 \\ \hline \end{array}$

4.	5.	6.
$\begin{array}{r} 687 \\ -144 \\ \hline \end{array}$	$\begin{array}{r} 505 \\ -167 \\ \hline \end{array}$	$\begin{array}{r} 307 \\ -154 \\ \hline \end{array}$

PROBLEM SOLVING

Solve.

7. There are 303 students.
There are 147 girls.
How many boys are there?

________ boys

Name ________________________

Lesson 62

COMMON CORE STANDARD CC.2.NBT.8

Lesson Objective: Identify 10 more, 10 less, 100 more, or 100 less than a given number.

Count On and Count Back by 10 and 100

10 less than 234

2 hundreds 2 tens 4 ones.

224

100 less than 234

1 hundred 3 tens 4 ones.

134

Notice what digit changes.

10 more than 234

2 hundreds 4 tens 4 ones.

244

100 more than 234

3 hundreds 3 tens 4 ones.

334

Write the number.

1. 10 more than 719 ______

2. 10 less than 246 ______

3. 100 more than 291 ______

4. 100 less than 687 ______

5. 10 less than 568 ______

6. 100 more than 649 ______

Name ______________________

Count On and Count Back by 10 and 100

Write the number.

1. 10 more than 451 ______	**2.** 10 less than 770 ______
3. 100 more than 367 ______	**4.** 100 less than 895 ______
5. 10 less than 812 ______	**6.** 100 more than 543 ______
7. 10 more than 218 ______	**8.** 100 more than 379 ______
9. 100 less than 324 ______	**10.** 10 less than 829 ______

PROBLEM SOLVING

Solve. Write or draw to explain.

11. Sarah has 128 stickers. Alex has 10 fewer stickers than Sarah. How many stickers does Alex have?

______ stickers

Name ______________________________

Lesson 63

COMMON CORE STANDARD CC.2.NBT.8

Lesson Objective: Extend number patterns by counting on by tens or hundreds.

Algebra • Number Patterns

Find a counting pattern.

421, 431, 441, 451, ■, ■

Which digit changes from number to number?

The __tens__ digit changes.

How does it change?

by __one__ each time

Look at the chart. Find the next two numbers in the pattern.

401	402	403	404	405	406	407	408	409	410
411	412	413	414	415	416	417	418	419	420
421	422	423	424	425	426	427	428	429	430
431	432	433	434	435	436	437	438	439	440
441	442	443	444	445	446	447	448	449	450
451	452	453	454	455	456	457	458	459	460
461	462	463	464	465	466	467	468	469	470
471	472	473	474	475	476	477	478	479	480
481	482	483	484	485	486	487	488	489	490
491	492	493	494	495	496	497	498	499	500

The next two numbers are __461__ and __471__.

Look at the digits to find the next two numbers.

1. 937, 947, 957, 967, ■, ■

The next two numbers are ______ and ______.

2. 135, 235, 335, 435, ■, ■

The next two numbers are ______ and ______.

Name ________________________

Lesson 63
CC.2.NBT.8

Algebra • Number Patterns

Look at the digits to find the next two numbers.

1. 232, 242, 252, 262, ▢, ▢

The next two numbers are ________ and ________.

2. 185, 285, 385, 485, ▢, ▢

The next two numbers are ________ and ________.

3. 428, 528, 628, 728, ▢, ▢

The next two numbers are ________ and ________.

4. 654, 664, 674, 684, ▢, ▢

The next two numbers are ________ and ________.

5. 333, 433, 533, 633, ▢, ▢

The next two numbers are ________ and ________.

PROBLEM SOLVING

6. What are the missing numbers in the pattern?

431, 441, 451, 461, ▢, 481, 491, ▢

The missing numbers are ________ and ________.

Name ___________________________

Lesson 64

COMMON CORE STANDARD CC.2.NBT.9

Lesson Objective: Model 2-digit addition with regrouping.

Model Regrouping for Addition

Add 18 and 25.
Show 18 and 25 with tens and ones blocks.
Count the ones.
How many ones are there in all? 13 ones

Can you make a ten? yes

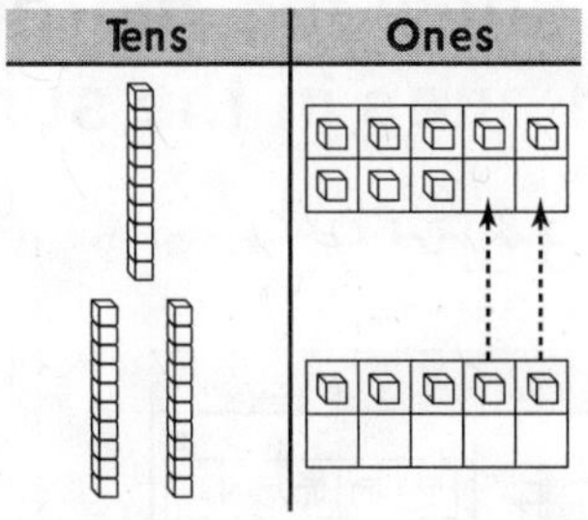

Tens	Ones

Trade 10 ones for 1 ten.
This is called regrouping.

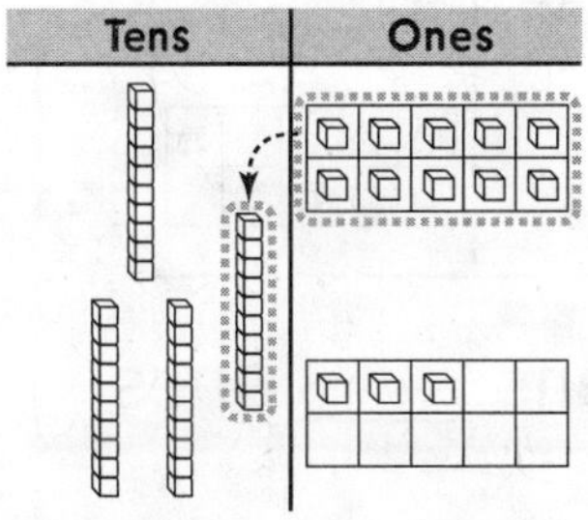

Tens	Ones

Count the tens. How many tens are there in all? 4 tens

Count the ones. How many ones are there in all? 3 ones

4 tens 3 ones is the same as 43.

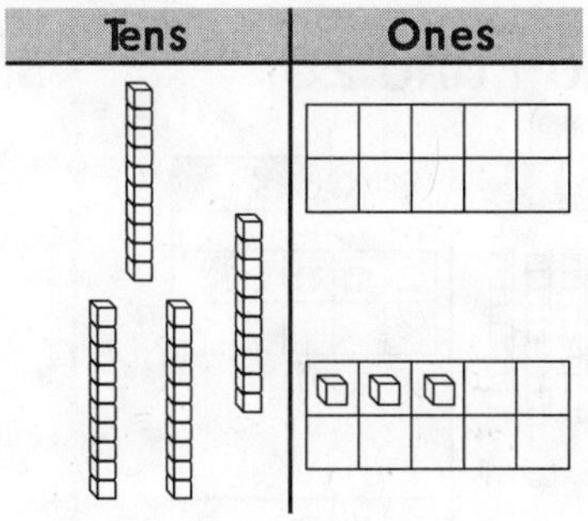

Tens	Ones

Write how many tens and ones in the sum.
Write the sum.

1. Add 46 and 19.

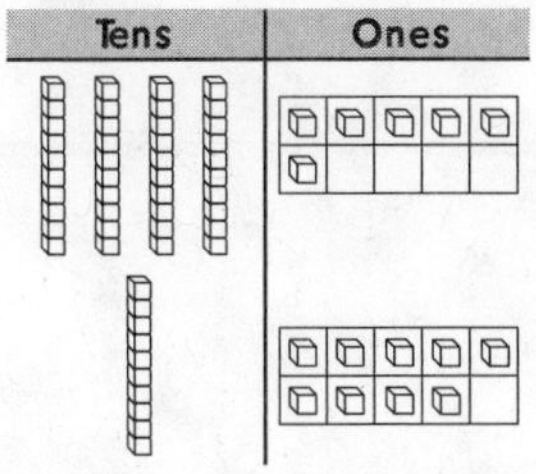

Tens	Ones

____ tens ____ ones

____

2. Add 45 and 27.

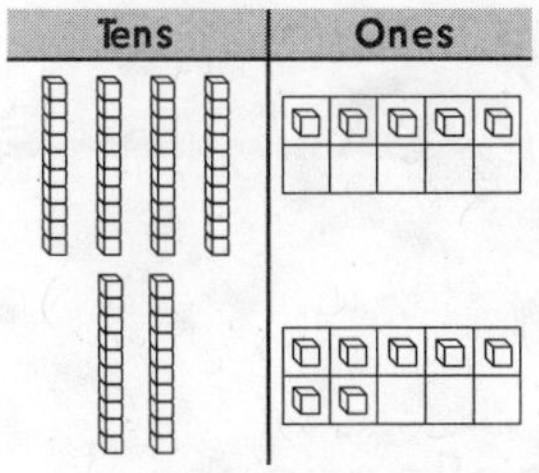

Tens	Ones

____ tens ____ ones

____

3. Add 58 and 38.

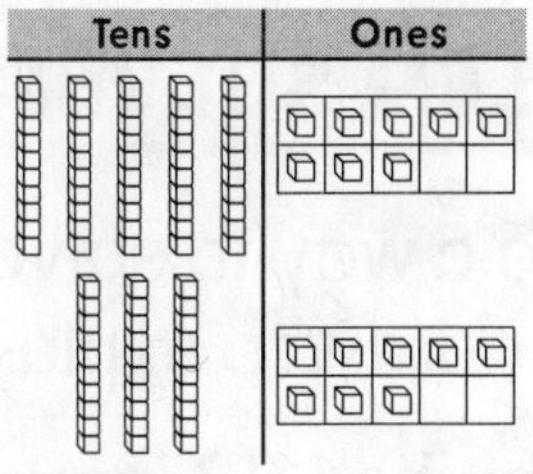

Tens	Ones

____ tens ____ ones

____

Name ______________________

Lesson 64
CC.2.NBT.9

Model Regrouping for Addition

Draw to show the regrouping. Write how many tens and ones in the sum. Write the sum.

1. Add 63 and 9.

Tens	Ones

_____ tens _____ ones

_____

2. Add 25 and 58.

Tens	Ones

_____ tens _____ ones

_____

3. Add 58 and 18.

Tens	Ones

_____ tens _____ ones

_____

4. Add 64 and 26.

Tens	Ones

_____ tens _____ ones

_____

5. Add 17 and 77.

Tens	Ones

_____ tens _____ ones

_____

6. Add 16 and 39.

Tens	Ones

_____ tens _____ ones

_____

PROBLEM SOLVING REAL WORLD

Choose a way to solve.
Write or draw to explain.

7. Cathy has 43 leaves in her collection. Jane has 38 leaves. How many leaves do the two children have?

_____ leaves

Name ______________________

COMMON CORE STANDARD CC.2.NBT.9

Lesson Objective: Model 2-digit subtraction with regrouping.

Model Regrouping for Subtraction

Subtract 37 from 65.

Are there enough ones to subtract 7? no

So, you will need to regroup.

Trade 1 ten for 10 ones.

Subtract the ones. Then subtract the tens.

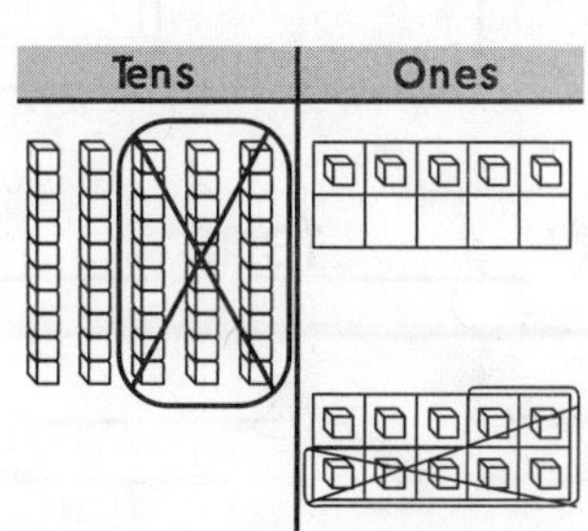

15 ones − 7 ones = 8 ones

5 tens − 3 tens = 2 tens

2 tens 8 ones is the same as 28.

The difference is 28.

Draw to show the regrouping. Write the tens and ones that are in the difference. Write the number.

1. Subtract 18 from 43.

_____ tens _____ ones

_____

2. Subtract 19 from 55.

_____ tens _____ ones

_____

Name ____________________

Lesson 65
CC.2.NBT.9

Model Regrouping for Subtraction

Draw to show the regrouping. Write the difference two ways. Write the tens and ones. Write the number.

1. Subtract 9 from 35.

Tens	Ones
3 tens	5 ones

_____ tens _____ ones

_____

2. Subtract 14 from 52.

Tens	Ones
5 tens	2 ones

_____ tens _____ ones

_____

3. Subtract 17 from 46.

Tens	Ones
4 tens	6 ones

_____ tens _____ ones

_____

4. Subtract 28 from 63.

Tens	Ones
6 tens	3 ones

_____ tens _____ ones

_____

PROBLEM SOLVING

Choose a way to solve. Write or draw to explain.

5. Mr. Ortega made 51 cookies. He gave 14 cookies away. How many cookies does he have now?

_____ cookies

Name ______________________

COMMON CORE STANDARD CC.2.MD.1

Lesson Objective: Use concrete models to measure the lengths of objects in inches.

Measure With Inch Models

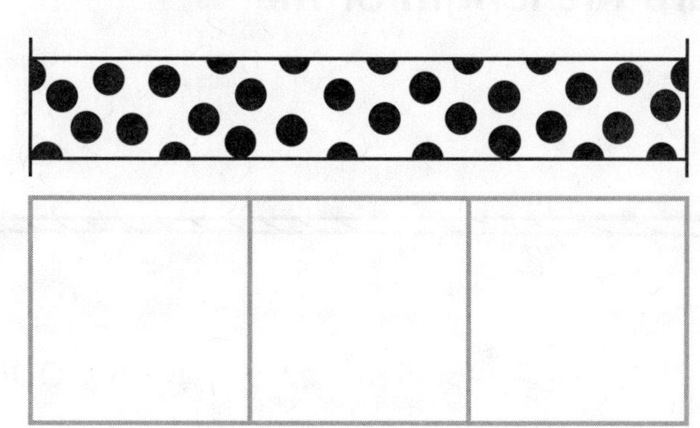

Place tiles on the squares. How many tiles? __3__ tiles
Each tile is about 1 inch long.

How long is the ribbon? about __3__ inches

Use color tiles. Measure the length of the object in inches.

1.

about _____ inches

2.

about _____ inches

3.

about _____ inches

Name ______________________________

Lesson 66
CC.2.MD.1

Measure with Inch Models

Use color tiles. Measure the length of the object in inches.

1.

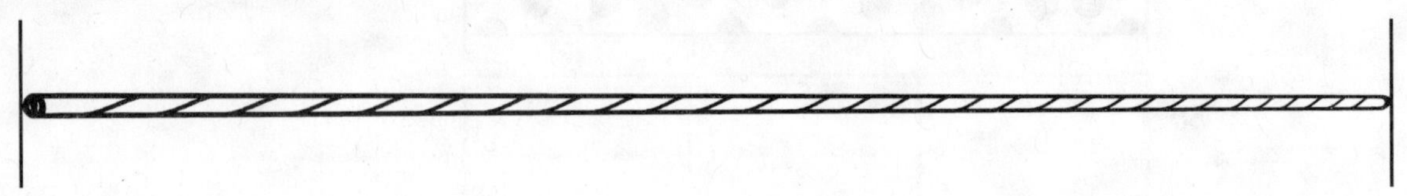

about _____ inches

2.

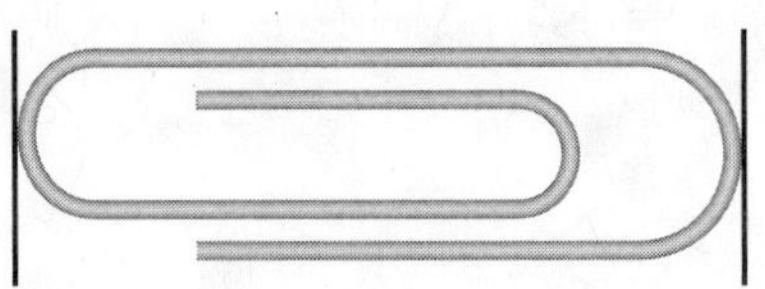

about _____ inches

3.

about _____ inches

4.

about _____ inches

PROBLEM SOLVING

5. Look around your classroom.
Find an object that is about 4 inches long.
Draw and label the object.

Name ______________________________

COMMON CORE STANDARD CC.2.MD.1

Lesson Objective: Make an inch ruler and use it to measure the lengths of objects.

Make and Use a Ruler

Use a paper strip. Mark the sides of a color tile.
Mark 6 tiles. Color each part.

Each part is about ___1 inch___ long.

Line up the left edge of the bracelet with the first mark. Count the inches.

The bracelet is about ___5___ inches long.

Measure the length with your ruler.
Count the inches.

1.

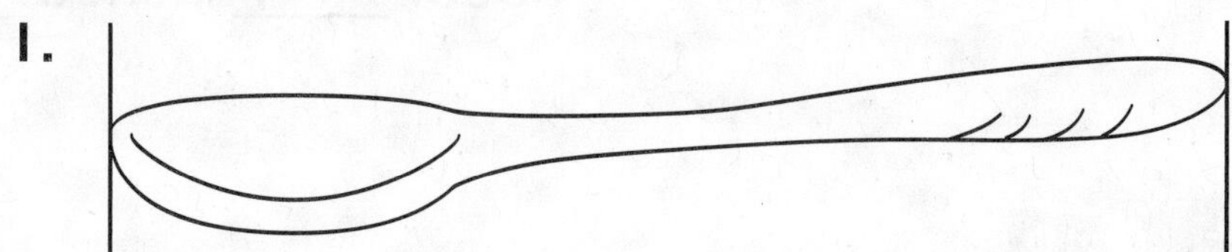

about _____ inches

2.

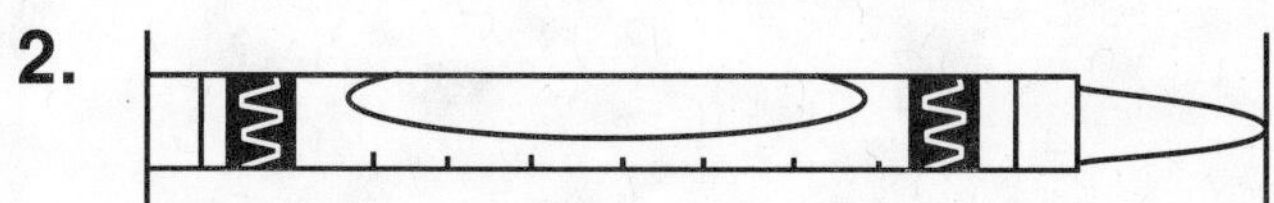

about _____ inches

Name ______________________________

Make and Use a Ruler

Measure the length with your ruler. Count the inches.

1.

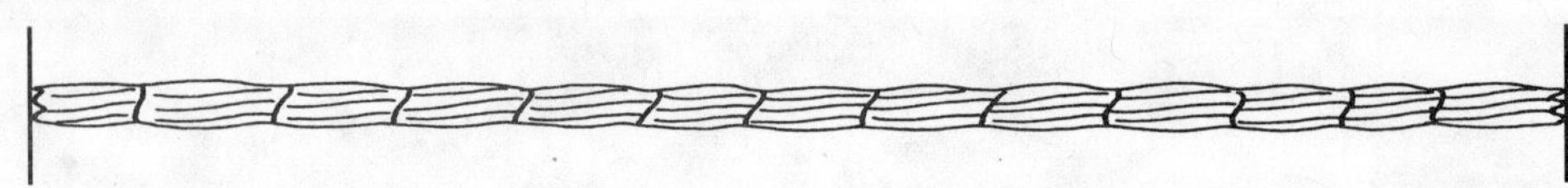

about _____ inches

2.

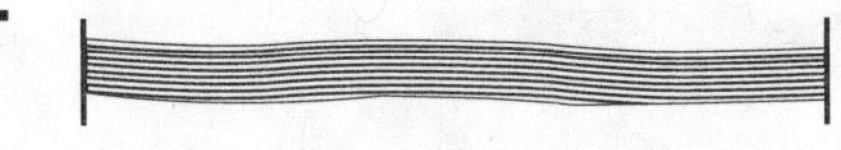

about _____ inches

3.

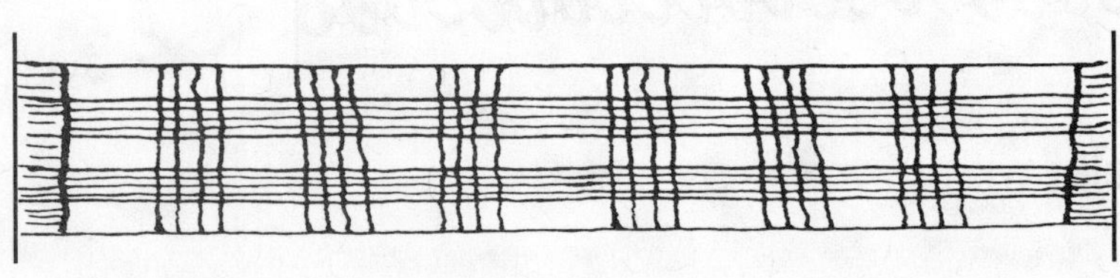

about _____ inches

4.

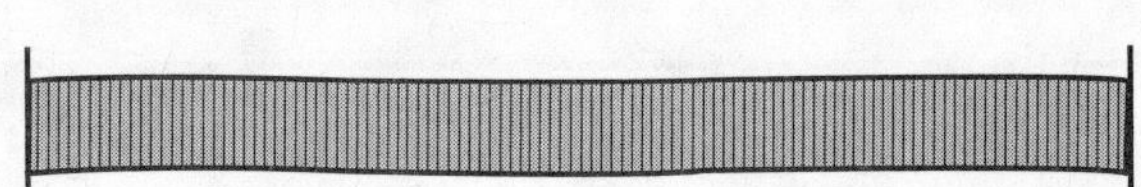

about _____ inches

PROBLEM SOLVING

5. Use your ruler. Measure the width of this page in inches.

about _____ inches

Name ____________________________________

Lesson 68

COMMON CORE STANDARD CC.2.MD.1

Lesson Objective: Measure the lengths of objects to the nearest inch using an inch ruler.

Measure with an Inch Ruler

1. Line up one end with 0.
2. Find the inch mark closest to the other end.
3. Read the number of inches at that mark.

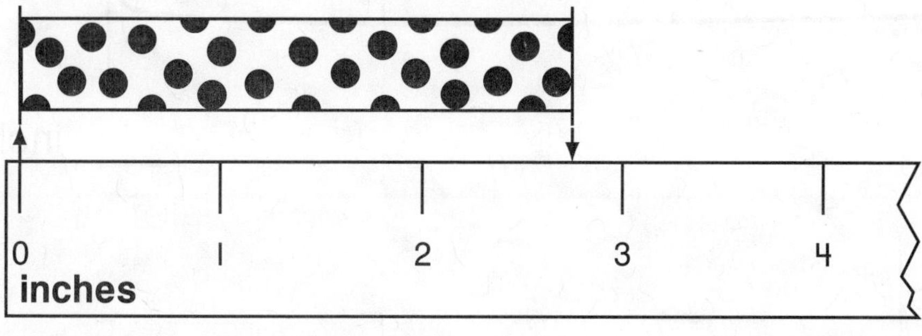

The ribbon is about __3__ inches long.

Measure the length to the nearest inch.

1. 

_____ inches

2. _____ inches

3. 

_____ inches

Name ______________________

Lesson 68

CC.2.MD.1

Measure with an Inch Ruler

Measure the length to the nearest inch.

1.

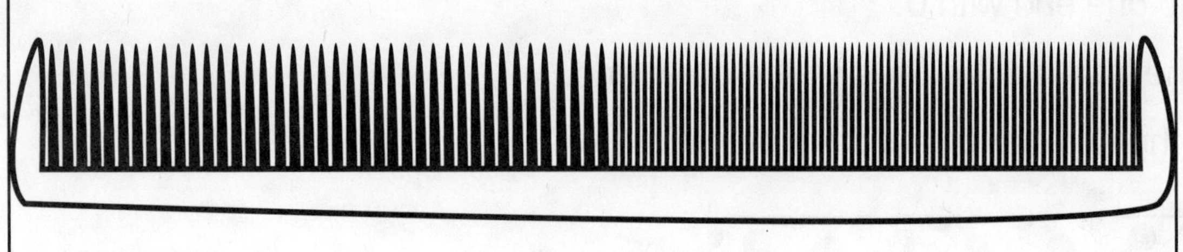

_____ inches

2.

_____ inches

3.

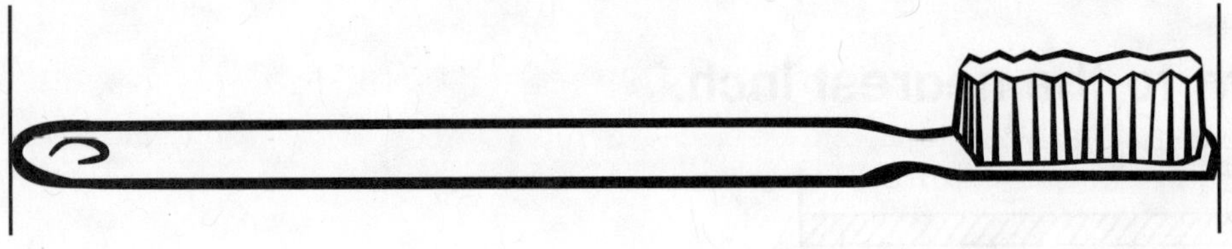

_____ inches

4.

_____ inches

PROBLEM SOLVING

5. Measure the string. What is its total length?

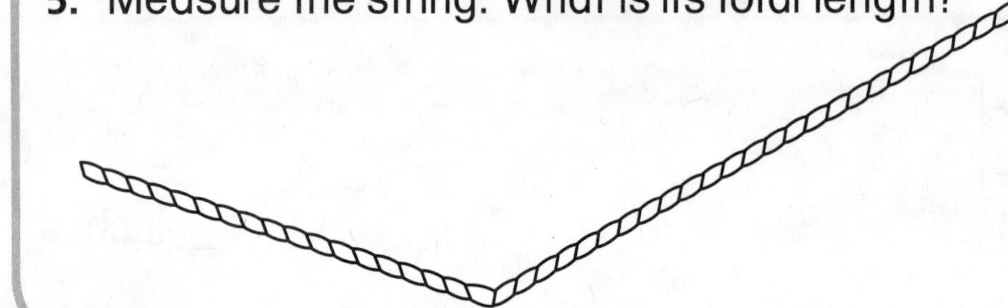

_____ inches

Name ______________________

Lesson 69

COMMON CORE STANDARD CC.2.MD.1

Lesson Objective: Select appropriate tools for measuring different lengths.

Choose a Tool

Use an inch ruler to measure short lengths.

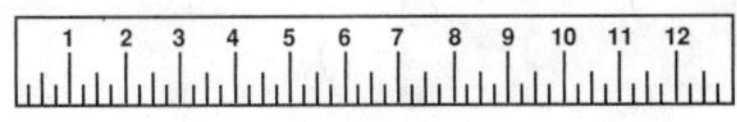

Use a yardstick to measure greater lengths.

Use a measuring tape to measure lengths that are not flat.

Choose the best tool for measuring the real object. Then measure and record the length.

1. a pencil

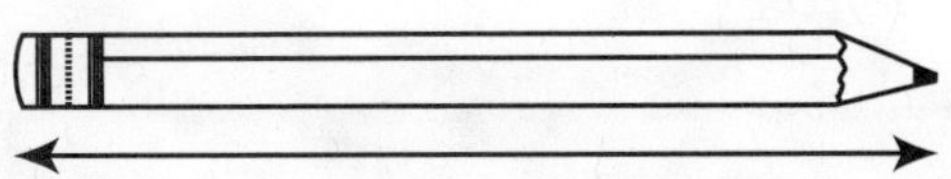

Tool: ______________________

Length: ______________________

2. a chalkboard

Tool: ______________________

Length: ______________________

Name ______________________

Lesson 69
CC.2.MD.1

Choose a Tool

Choose the best tool for measuring the real object. Then measure and record the length or distance.

inch ruler yardstick measuring tape

1. the length of your desk

Tool: ______________________

Length: ______________________

2. the distance around a basket

Tool: ______________________

Length: ______________________

PROBLEM SOLVING

Choose the better tool for measuring.
Explain your choice.

3. Mark wants to measure the length of his room. Should he use an inch ruler or a yardstick?

Mark should use ______________________ because

____

____

Name ______________________

COMMON CORE STANDARD CC.2.MD.1

Lesson Objective: Use a concrete model to measure the lengths of objects in centimeters.

Measure with a Centimeter Model

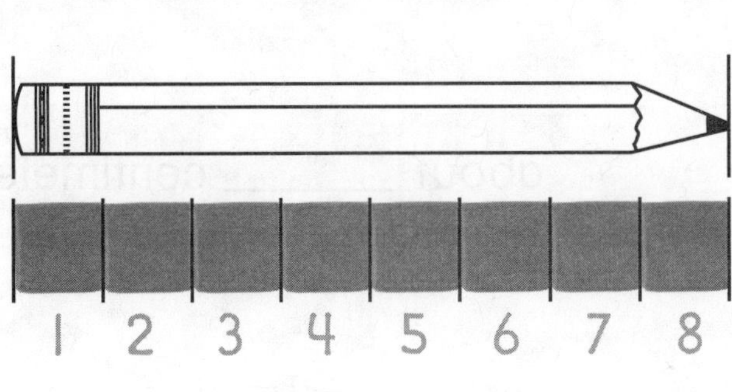

Place unit cubes on the squares.

How many cubes long is the pencil?

The pencil is __8__ cubes long.

Each unit cube is about 1 centimeter long.

So, the pencil is about __8__ centimeters long.

Use a unit cube. Measure the length in centimeters.

1.

about ______ centimeters

2.

about ______ centimeters

3.

about ______ centimeters

Name ______________________________

Lesson 70
CC.2.MD.1

Measure with a Centimeter Model

Use a unit cube. Measure the length in centimeters.

1.

about ______ centimeters

2.

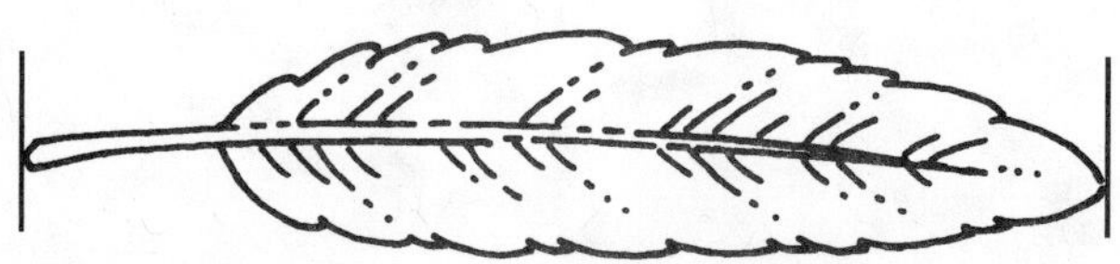

about ______ centimeters

3.

about ______ centimeters

4.

about ______ centimeters

PROBLEM SOLVING

Solve. Write or draw to explain.

5. Susan has a pencil that is 3 centimeters shorter than this string. How long is the pencil?

about ______ centimeters

Name ______________________________

Lesson 71

COMMON CORE STANDARD CC.2.MD.1

Lesson Objective: Measure lengths of objects to the nearest centimeter using a centimeter ruler.

Measure with a Centimeter Ruler

Line up the left end of the ribbon with the zero mark on the ruler.

Which centimeter mark is closest to the other end of the ribbon?

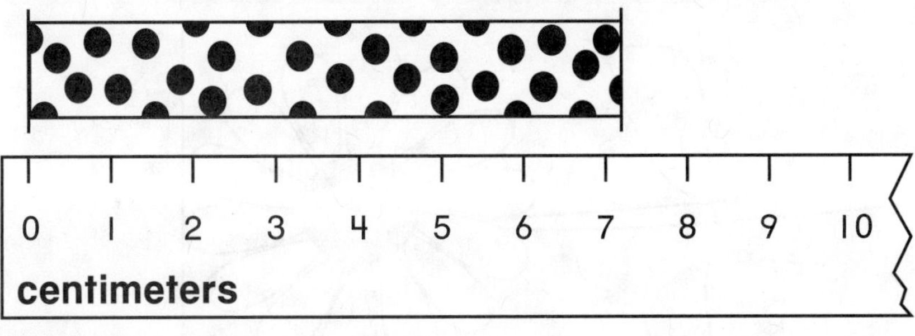

The ribbon is about __7__ centimeters long.

Measure the length to the nearest centimeter.

1.

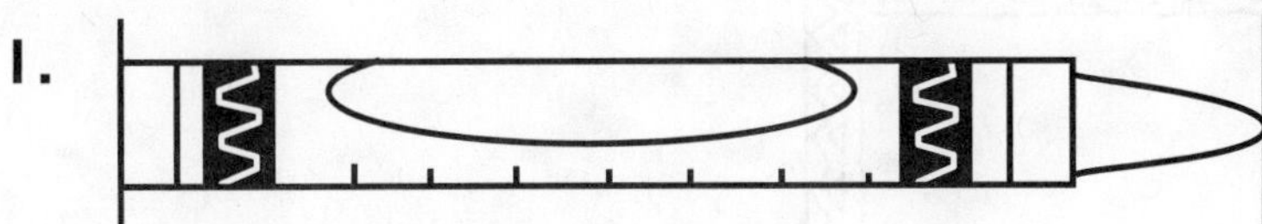

______ centimeters

2.

______ centimeters

3.

______ centimeters

Name ______________________

Lesson 71

CC.2.MD.1

Measure with a Centimeter Ruler

Measure the length to the nearest centimeter.

1\.

_____ centimeters

2\.

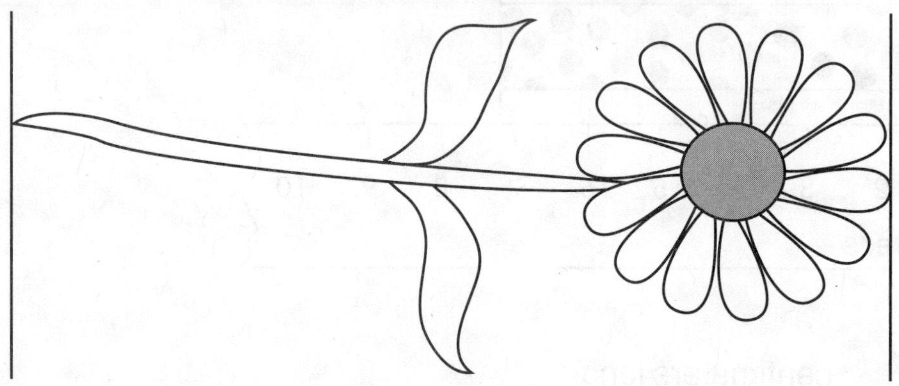

_____ centimeters

3\.

_____ centimeters

PROBLEM SOLVING

4\. Draw a string that is about 8 centimeters long.
Then use a centimeter ruler to check the length.

Name ________________________________

Lesson 72

COMMON CORE STANDARD CC.2.MD.2

Lesson Objective: Measure the lengths of objects in both inches and feet to explore the inverse relationship between size and number of units.

Measure in Inches and Feet

The real folder is about 12 inches wide.
The real folder is also about 1 foot wide.

12 inches is the same as 1 foot.

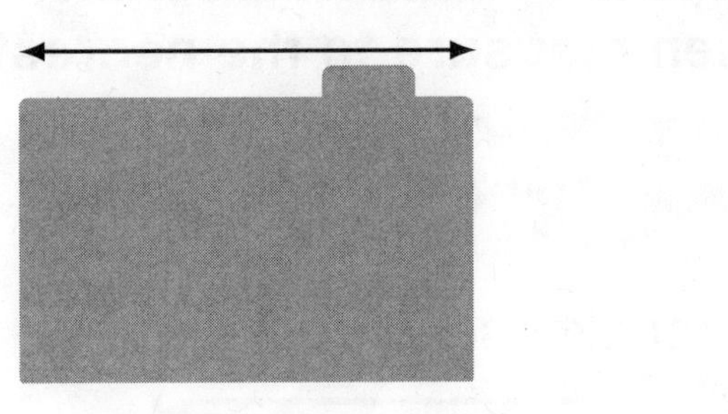

Measure to the nearest inch.
Then measure to the nearest foot.

	Find the real object.	Measure.
1.	desk	_____ inches _____ feet
2.	rug	_____ inches _____ feet
3.	map	_____ inches _____ feet

Name ______________________________

Measure in Inches and Feet

Measure to the nearest inch.
Then measure to the nearest foot.

Find the real object.	Measure.
1. bookcase	______ inches ______ feet
2. window	______ inches ______ feet
3. chair	______ inches ______ feet

PROBLEM SOLVING

4. Jake has a piece of yarn that is 4 feet long.
   Blair has a piece of yarn that is 4 inches long.
   Who has the longer piece of yarn? Explain.

____

____

Name ____________________

COMMON CORE STANDARD CC.2.MD.2

Lesson Objective: Measure the lengths of objects in both centimeters and meters to explore the inverse relationship between size and number of units.

Centimeters and Meters

You can measure longer lengths in meters.

1 meter is the same as 100 centimeters.

The real board is about 100 centimeters tall.
So, the real board is about 1 meter tall.

Measure to the nearest centimeter.
Then measure to the nearest meter.

	Find the real object.	Measure.
1.	desk	______ centimeters ______ meters
2.	door	______ centimeters ______ meters
3.	classroom floor	______ centimeters ______ meters

Name ______________________

Lesson 73
CC.2.MD.2

Centimeters and Meters

Measure to the nearest centimeter.
Then measure to the nearest meter.

Find the real object.	Measure.
1. bookcase	________ centimeters ________ meters
2. window	________ centimeters ________ meters
3. map	________ centimeters ________ meters

PROBLEM SOLVING

4. Sally will measure the length of a wall in both centimeters and meters. Will there be fewer centimeters or fewer meters? Explain.

____

____

____

Name ______________________________

Lesson 74

COMMON CORE STANDARD CC.2.MD.3

Lesson Objective: Estimate the lengths of objects by mentally partitioning the lengths into inches.

Estimate Lengths in Inches

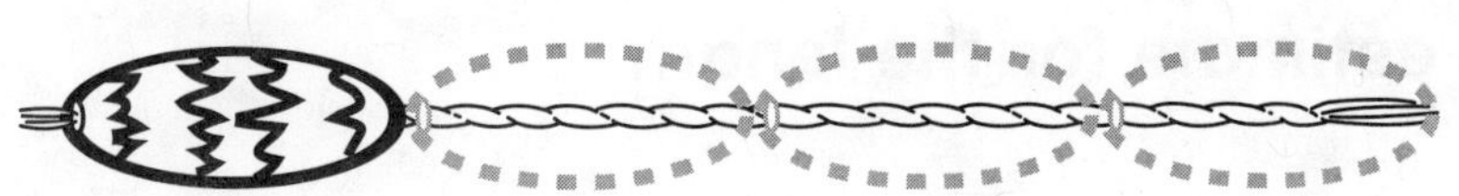

The bead is 1 inch long. How many beads will fit on the string?
Four beads will fit on the string.

About how long is the string? The string is about __4__ inches long.

Circle the best estimate for the length of the string.

1. 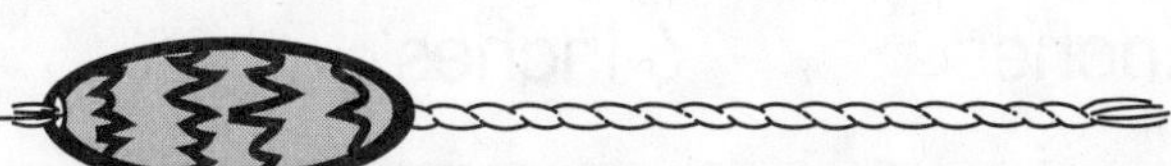

2 inches 4 inches 6 inches

2. 

1 inch 3 inches 5 inches

3.

1 inch 2 inches 4 inches

4. 

5 inches 8 inches 10 inches

Name ______________________________

Lesson 74
CC.2.MD.3

Estimate Lengths in Inches

**The bead is 1 inch long.
Circle the best estimate for the length of the string.**

1. 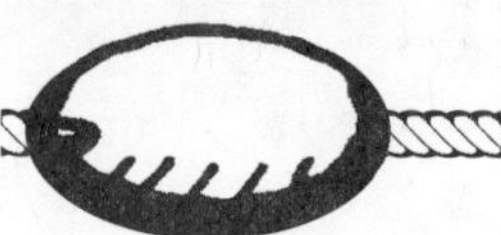

1 inch   4 inches   7 inches

2. 

3 inches   6 inches   9 inches

3. 

2 inches   3 inches   6 inches

4. 

2 inches   5 inches   8 inches

PROBLEM SOLVING

Solve. Write or draw to explain.

5. Ashley has some beads. Each bead is 2 inches long. How many beads will fit on a string that is 8 inches long?

_____ beads

Name ________________________

COMMON CORE STANDARD CC.2.MD.3

Lesson Objective: Estimate the lengths of objects in feet.

Estimate Lengths in Feet

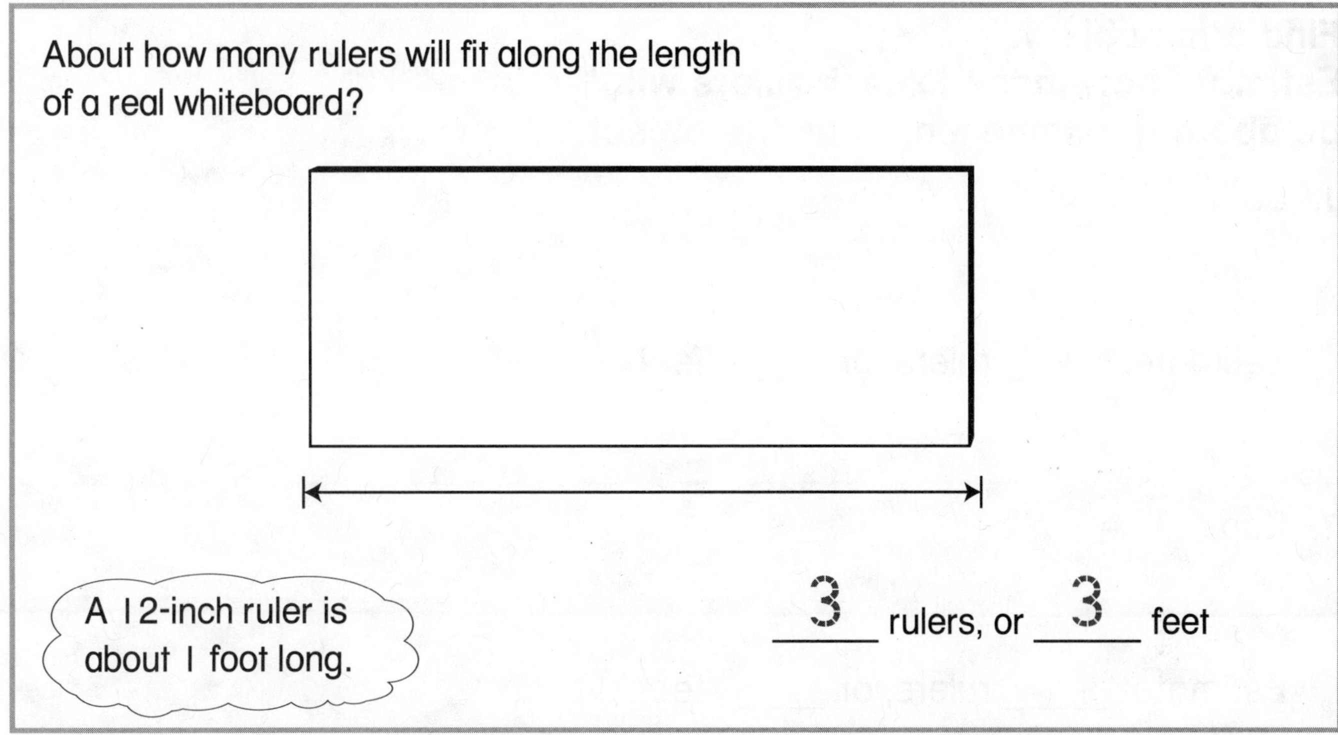

Find each object. Estimate how many 12-inch rulers will be about the same length as the object.

1. chalkboard

Estimate: ______ rulers, or ______ feet

2. poster

Estimate: ______ rulers, or ______ feet

Name ______________________________

Estimate Lengths in Feet

Find each object.
Estimate how many 12-inch rulers will be about the same length as the object.

1. door

Estimate: _____ rulers, or _____ feet

2. flag

Estimate: _____ rulers, or _____ feet

3. wall of a small room

Estimate: _____ rulers, or _____ feet

PROBLEM SOLVING

Solve. Write or draw to explain.

4. Mr. and Mrs. Baker place 12-inch rulers along the length of a rug. They each line up 3 rulers along the edge of the rug. What is the length of the rug?

about _____ feet

Name ______________________

Lesson 76

COMMON CORE STANDARD CC.2.MD.3

Lesson Objective: Estimate lengths of objects in centimeters by comparing them to known lengths.

Estimate Lengths in Centimeters

The ribbon is about 8 centimeters long. How can you find the most reasonable estimate for the length of the string?

ribbon

string

1 centimeter

6 centimeters

10 centimeters

Think: 1 centimeter is not reasonable because the string is much longer than 1 cube.

Think: 10 centimeters is not reasonable because the string is shorter than the ribbon.

1. The rope is about 7 centimeters long. Circle the best estimate for the length of the yarn.

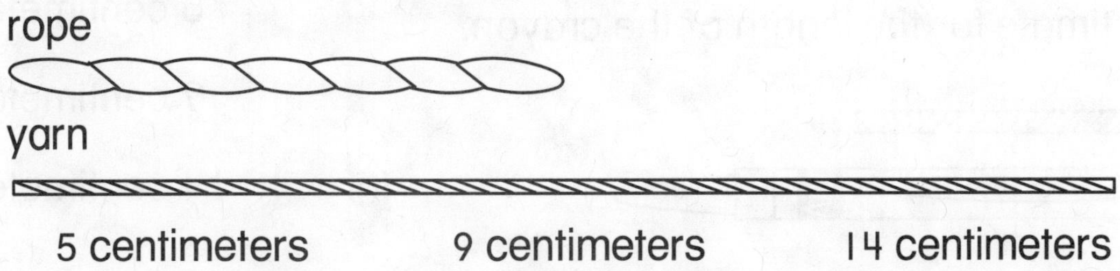

5 centimeters   9 centimeters   14 centimeters

2. The pencil is about 10 centimeters long. Circle the best estimate for the length of the ribbon.

5 centimeters   9 centimeters   12 centimeters

Name ______________________________

Estimate Lengths in Centimeters

1. The toothpick is about 6 centimeters long. Circle the best estimate for the length of the yarn.

6 centimeters

9 centimeters

12 centimeters

2. The pen is about 11 centimeters long. Circle the best estimate for the length of the eraser.

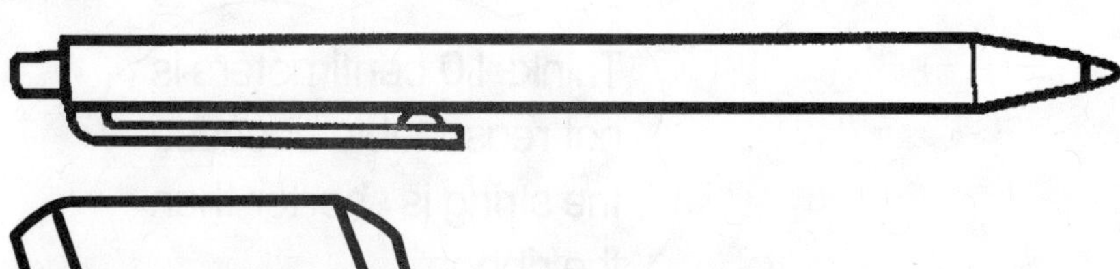

4 centimeters

10 centimeters

14 centimeters

3. The string is about 6 centimeters long. Circle the best estimate for the length of the crayon.

5 centimeters

9 centimeters

14 centimeters

PROBLEM SOLVING

4. The string is about 6 centimeters long. Draw a pencil that is about 12 centimeters long.

Name ______________________________

COMMON CORE STANDARD CC.2.MD.3

Lesson Objective: Estimate the lengths of objects in meters.

Estimate Lengths in Meters

Estimate the length of the chalk tray.

The chalk tray is about the same length as 2 meter sticks.

So, the chalk tray is about ___2___ meters long.

Find the real object.
Estimate its length in meters.

1. window

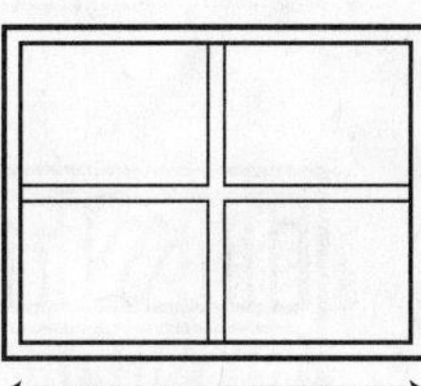

about ________ meters

2. bookshelf

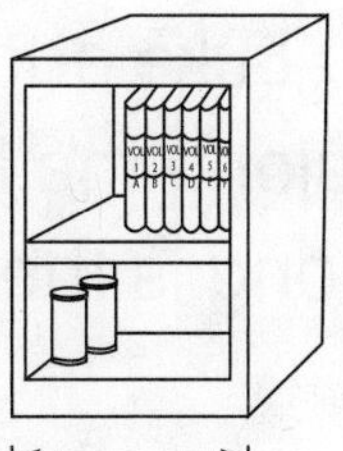

about ________ meters

Name ______________________________

Estimate Lengths in Meters

Find the real object.
Estimate its length in meters.

1. poster

about ________ meters

2. chalkboard

about ________ meters

3. bookshelf

about ________ meters

PROBLEM SOLVING

4. Barbara and Luke each placed 2 meter sticks end-to-end along the length of a large table. About how long is the table?

about ________ meters

Name ________________________

COMMON CORE STANDARD CC.2.MD.4

Lesson Objective: Measure and then find the difference in the lengths of two objects.

Measure and Compare Lengths

Which object is longer? How much longer?

1. Measure the leaf.

The leaf is __9__ centimeters.

2. Measure the stick.

The stick is __5__ centimeters.

3. Complete the number sentence to find the difference.

__9__ centimeters − __5__ centimeters = __4__ centimeters

The leaf is __4__ centimeters longer than the stick.

Measure the length of each object. Write a number sentence to find the difference between the lengths.

1.

______ centimeters

______ centimeters

______ centimeters − ______ centimeters = ______ centimeters

The string is ______ centimeters longer than the paper clip.

Name ______________________________

Lesson 78
CC.2.MD.4

Measure and Compare Lengths

Measure the length of each object. Write a number sentence to find the difference between the lengths.

1.

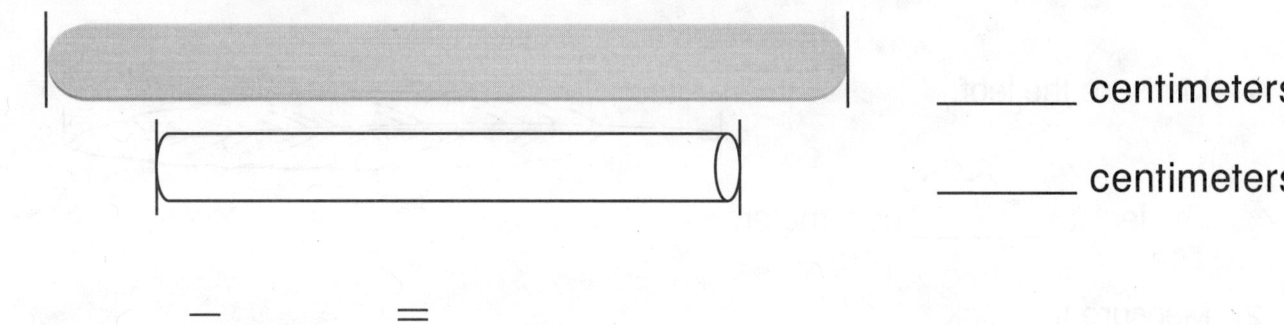

______ centimeters

______ centimeters

______ centimeters − ______ centimeters = ______ centimeters

The craft stick is ______ centimeters longer than the chalk.

2.

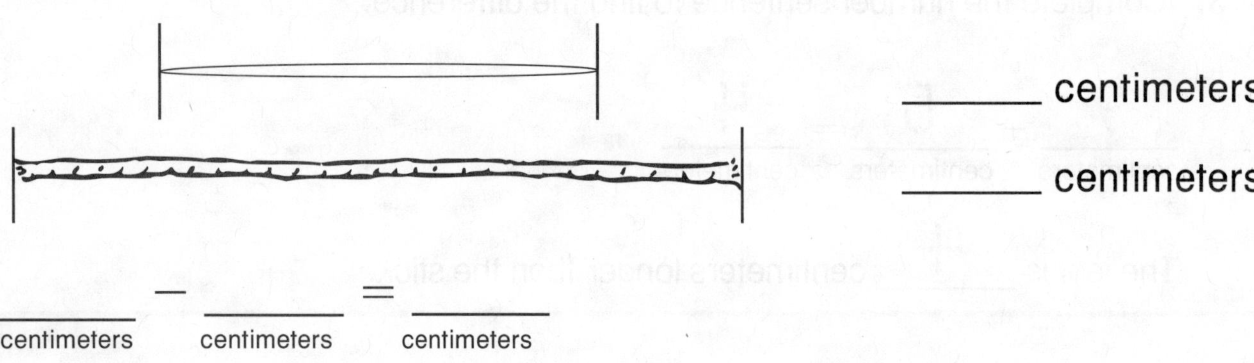

______ centimeters

______ centimeters

______ centimeters − ______ centimeters = ______ centimeters

The string is ______ centimeters longer than the toothpick.

PROBLEM SOLVING

Solve. Write or draw to explain.

3. A string is 11 centimeters long, a ribbon is 24 centimeters long, and a large paper clip is 5 centimeters long. How much longer is the ribbon than the string?

______ centimeters

Name ___________________________

Lesson 79

COMMON CORE STANDARD CC.2.MD.5

Lesson Objective: Solve addition and subtraction problems involving the lengths of objects by using the strategy *draw a diagram.*

Problem Solving • Add and Subtract in Inches

Zack has two strings. One string is 12 inches long and the other string is 5 inches long. How long are Zack's strings altogether?

Unlock the Problem

What do I need to find?	What information do I need to use?
how long Zack's strings are in all	One string is 12 inches long. The other string is 5 inches long.

Show how to solve the problem.

12 + 5 = ■ The strings are 17 inches long in all.

Write a number sentence using a ■ for the missing number. Solve.

1. Sara has two pieces of yarn. Each piece is 7 inches long. How many inches of yarn does she have in all?

_______________ Sara has _____ inches of yarn in all.

Name ______________________________

Problem Solving • Add and Subtract in Inches

Draw a diagram. Write a number sentence using a ■ for the missing number. Solve.

1. Molly had a ribbon that was 23 inches long. She cut 7 inches off the ribbon. How long is her ribbon now?

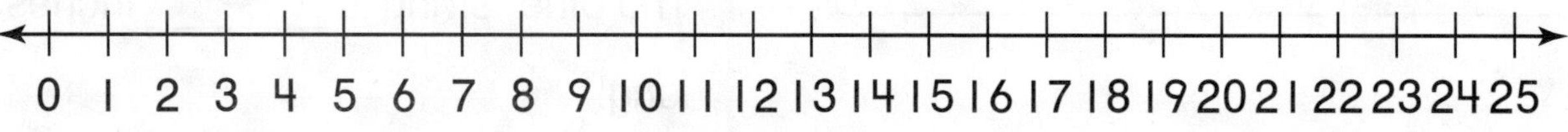

____

Molly's ribbon is ________ inches long now.

2. Jed has a paper clip chain that is 11 inches long. He adds 7 inches of paper clips to the chain. How long is the paper clip chain now?

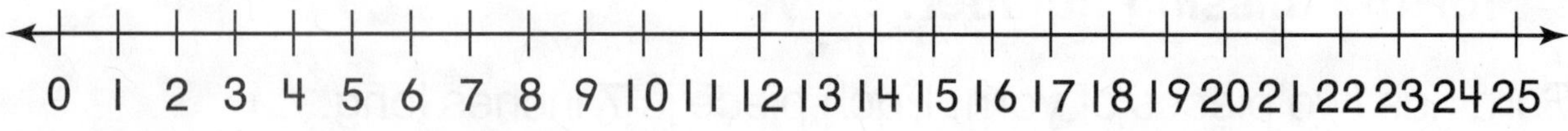

____

The paper clip chain is ________ inches long now.

Name ___________________________________

Lesson 80

COMMON CORE STANDARD CC.2.MD.6

Lesson Objective: Solve problems involving adding and subtracting lengths by using the strategy *draw a diagram.*

Problem Solving • Add and Subtract Lengths

Christy has a ribbon that is 12 centimeters long. Erin has a ribbon that is 9 centimeters long. How many centimeters of ribbon do they have altogether?

Unlock the Problem

What do I need to find?	What information do I need to use?
how much ribbon they have altogether	Christy has 12 centimeters of ribbon. Erin has 9 centimeters of ribbon.

Show how to solve the problem.

12 9

0 1 2 3 4 5 6 7 8 9 10 11 12 13 14 15 16 17 18 19 20 21 22 23 24 25

12 + 9 = ■

They have 21 centimeters of ribbon altogether.

Write a number sentence using a ■ for the missing number. Then solve.

1. Lucas has one string that is 9 centimeters long and another string that is 8 centimeters long. How many centimeters of string are there in all?

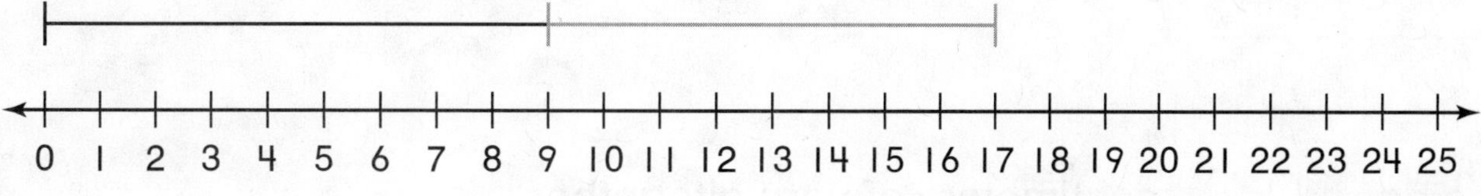

___________________________ _____ centimeters of string in all

Name ______________________

Problem Solving • Add and Subtract Lengths

Draw a diagram. Write a number sentence using a ▭ for the missing number. Then solve.

1. A straw is 20 centimeters long. Mr. Jones cuts off 8 centimeters of the straw. How long is the straw now?

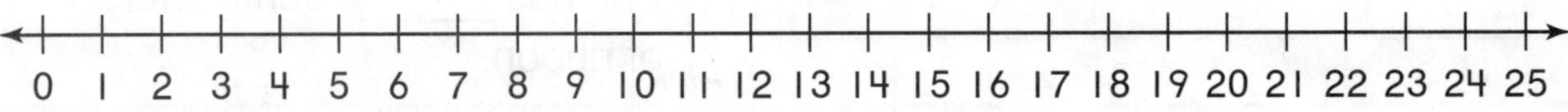

____

The straw is ______ centimeters long now.

2. Ella has a piece of blue yarn that is 14 centimeters long. She has a piece of red yarn that is 9 centimeters long. How many centimeters of yarn does she have altogether?

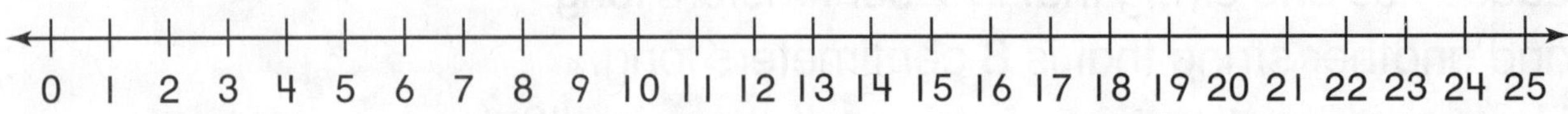

____

She has ______ centimeters of yarn altogether.

Name ______________________________

Lesson 81

COMMON CORE STANDARD CC.2.MD.7

Lesson Objective: Tell and write time to the hour and half hour.

Time to the Hour and Half Hour

It is zero minutes after the hour. Look at how you write this time.

3:00

It is 30 minutes after the hour. Look at how you write this time.

3:30

Look at the clock hands. Write the time.

1.

2.

3.

4.

5.

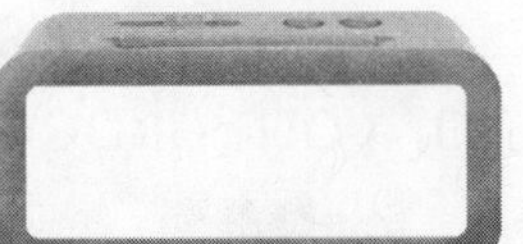

6.

Name ______________________

Time to the Hour and Half Hour

Look at the clock hands. Write the time.

1.

2.

3.

4.

5.

6.

PROBLEM SOLVING

7. Amy's music lesson begins at 4:00. Draw hands on the clock to show this time.

Name ________________________________

Lesson 82

COMMON CORE STANDARD CC.2.MD.7

Lesson Objective: Tell and write time to the nearest five minutes.

Time to 5 Minutes

The minute hand moves from one number to the next in 5 minutes.

Start at the 12. Count by fives.

Stop at the number the minute hand points to.

The hour is 8 o'clock.

It is 20 minutes after 8:00.

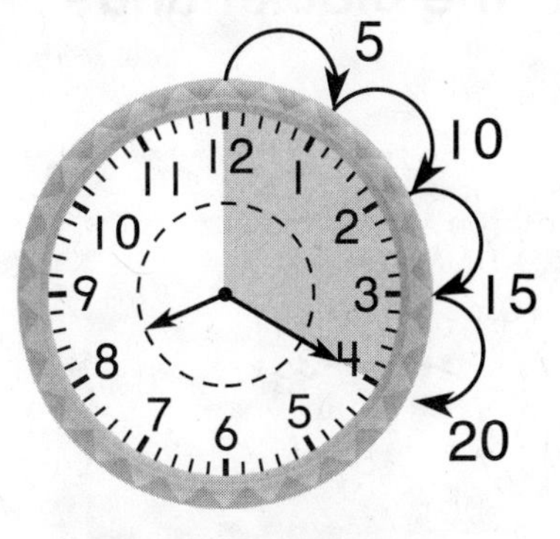

8:20

Look at the clock hands. Write the time.

1.

2.

3.

4.

5.

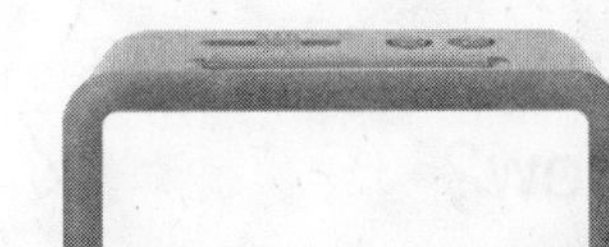

6.

Name ___________________________

Lesson 82
CC.2.MD.7

Time to 5 Minutes

Look at the clock hands. Write the time.

1.

2.

3.

4.

5.

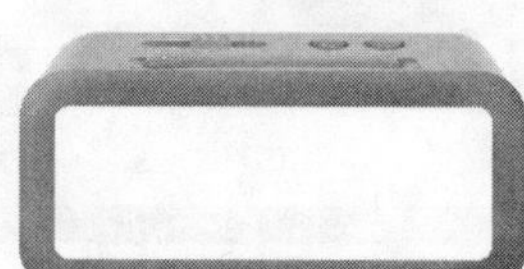

6.

PROBLEM SOLVING

Draw the minute hand to show the time. Then write the time.

7. My hour hand points between the 4 and the 5. My minute hand points to the 9. What time do I show?

Name ___________________________

Lesson 83

COMMON CORE STANDARD CC.2.MD.7

Lesson Objective: Practice telling time to the nearest five minutes.

Practice Telling Time

Use the clock hands to tell time.
First find the hour.

The hour is 11.

Now figure out minutes.
When the minute hand points to the 3 it is quarter past.

It is 15 minutes past 11.

The time is quarter past 11.

Draw the minute hand to show the time.
Write the time.

1. quarter past 9

2. 30 minutes after 11

3. half past 10

4. 15 minutes after 6

Name ____________________

Practice Telling Time

Lesson 83
CC.2.MD.7

Draw the minute hand to show the time. Write the time.

1. quarter past 7

2. half past 3

3. 50 minutes after 1

4. quarter past 11

5. 15 minutes after 8

6. 5 minutes after 6

PROBLEM SOLVING

Draw hands on the clock to solve.

7. Josh got to school at half past 8. Show this time on the clock.

Name ______________________

Lesson 84

COMMON CORE STANDARD CC.2.MD.7

Lesson Objective: Tell and write time using a.m. and p.m.

A.M. and P.M.

A.M. times *start* after midnight.
A.M. times *end* before noon.

get dressed for school

P.M. times *start* after noon.
P.M. times *end* before midnight.

tell a bedtime story

7:30

Write the time. Then circle A.M. or P.M.

1. finish homework

A.M.

P.M.

2. go to morning recess

A.M.

P.M.

3. eat breakfast

A.M.

P.M.

4. get ready for bed

A.M.

P.M.

Name ____________________

A.M. and P.M.

Write the time. Then circle A.M. or P.M.

1. walk the dog

A.M.

P.M.

2. finish breakfast

A.M.

P.M.

3. put on pajamas

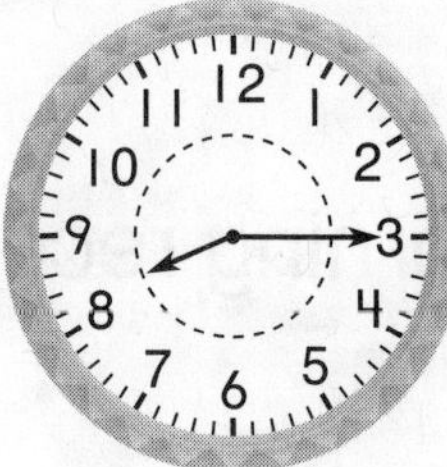

A.M.

P.M.

4. read a bedtime story

A.M.

P.M.

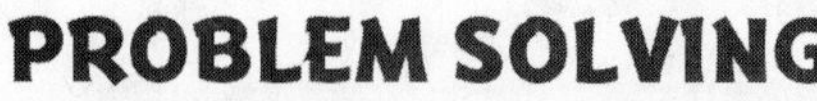

PROBLEM SOLVING

Use the list of times. Complete the story.

5. Jess woke up at ____________. She got on the bus at ____________ and went to school. She left school at ____________.

3:15 P.M.
8:30 A.M.
7:00 A.M.

Name ______________________________

Lesson 85

COMMON CORE STANDARD CC.2.MD.8

Lesson Objective: Find the total values of collections of dimes, nickels, and pennies.

Dimes, Nickels, and Pennies

1 dime
10¢

Count dimes by tens.

10¢, 20¢, 30¢

1 nickel
5¢

Count nickels by fives.

5¢, 10¢, 15¢

1 penny
1¢

Count pennies by ones.

1¢, 2¢, 3¢

Count on by tens.

Count on by fives.

Count on by ones.

10¢, 20¢, 25¢, 30¢, 31¢

31¢
total value

Count on to find the total value.

1. 

____

total value

2. 

____

total value

Name ______________________________

Lesson 85
CC.2.MD.8

Dimes, Nickels, and Pennies

Count on to find the total value.

1. 

____

total value

2. 

____

total value

3. 

total value

4. 

total value

PROBLEM SOLVING 

Solve. Write or draw to explain.

5. Aaron has 5 dimes and 2 nickels.
   How much money does Aaron have?

____

Name ______________________________

Lesson 86

COMMON CORE STANDARD CC.2.MD.8

Lesson Objective: Find the total values of collections of quarters, dimes, nickels, and pennies.

Quarters

I quarter
25¢

Count by twenty-fives.

25¢, 50¢, 75¢

Count by twenty-fives. Count by tens. Count by ones.

25¢, 50¢, 60¢, 61¢

61¢

total value

Count on to find the total value.

1.

____

total value

2.

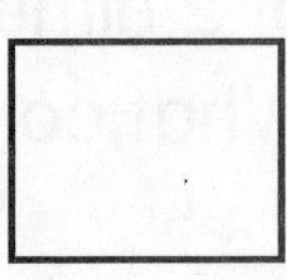

____

total value

Name ___________________________

Lesson 86

CC.2.MD.8

Quarters

Count on to find the total value.

1.

_______________________________________ [ ] total value

2.

_______________________________________ [ ] total value

3.

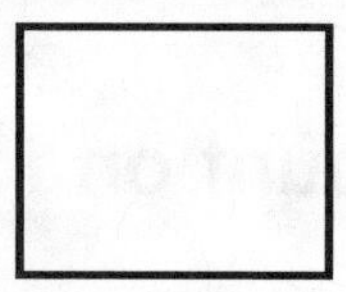

total value

PROBLEM SOLVING

Read the clue. Choose the name of a coin from the box to answer the question.

nickel	dime
quarter	penny

4. I have the same value as a group of 2 dimes and 1 nickel.
   What coin am I?

____

Name ____________________

COMMON CORE STANDARD CC.2.MD.8

Lesson Objective: Order coins in a collection by value and then find the total value.

Count Collections

Draw the coins in order by value. Start with the coin that has the greatest value.

25¢ 10¢ 5¢ 1¢

Start at 25¢. Count on.

25¢, 35¢, 40¢, 41¢ total value 41¢

Draw the coins in order. Find the total value.

1\. 

total value ____________

2\. 

total value ____________

3\. 

total value ____________

Name ______________________________

Count Collections

Draw and label the coins from greatest to least value. Find the total value.

1.

______

2.

______

3.

______

PROBLEM SOLVING

Solve. Write or draw to explain.

4. Rebecca has these coins. She spends 1 quarter. How much money does she have left?

______

Name ______________________________

Lesson 88

COMMON CORE STANDARD CC.2.MD.8

Lesson Objective: Represent money amounts less than a dollar using two different combinations of coins.

Show Amounts in Two Ways

You can show the same amount in different ways.

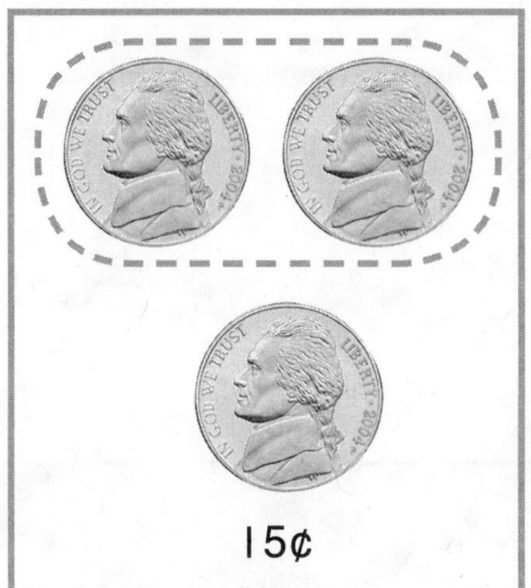

Trade 2 nickels for 1 dime.

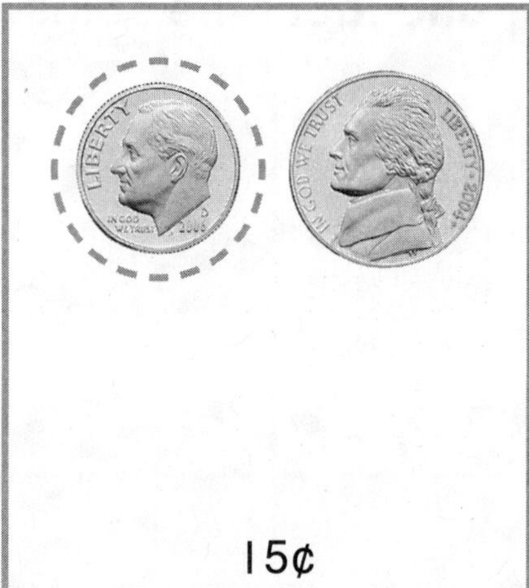

Count the coins.

5, 10, 15

Count the coins.

10, 15

Use coins. Show the amount in two ways. Draw and label the coins.

1.

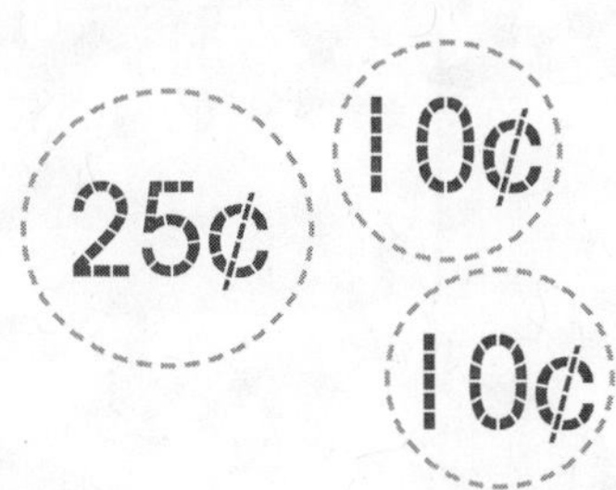

2.

Name ________________________________

Show Amounts in Two Ways

Use coins. Show the amounts in two ways. Draw and label the coins.

1. 39¢		
2. 70¢		
3. 57¢		

PROBLEM SOLVING

4. Madeline uses fewer than 5 coins to pay 60¢. Draw coins to show one way she could pay 60¢.

Name ____________________

COMMON CORE STANDARD CC.2.MD.8

Lesson Objective: Show one dollar in a variety of ways.

One Dollar

One dollar has the same value as 100 cents.

You can write one dollar like this: $1.00

Count on to 100¢ to show $1.00.

25¢, 50¢, 75¢, 100¢

$1.00
total value

Draw more coins to show $1.00. Write the total value.

1. dimes

____

2. nickels

____

Name ___________________________

Lesson 89
CC.2.MD.8

One Dollar

Circle coins to make $1.00.
Cross out the coins you do not use.

1.

2.

3.

PROBLEM SOLVING

4. Draw more coins to show $1.00 in all.

Name ______________________

COMMON CORE STANDARD CC.2.MD.8

Lesson Objective: Find and record the total value for money amounts greater than $1.

Amounts Greater Than $1

1. Count on and circle the coins that make one dollar.

2. Count on from 100¢ to find the total value for the whole group of coins.

110¢ 120¢

3. 120¢ is the same as 1 dollar and 20 cents.

Write $1.20.

Circle the money that makes $1. Then write the total value of the money shown.

1.

______

2.

______

Name ______________________

Amounts Greater Than $1

Circle the money that makes $1.00. Then write the total value of the money shown.

1\.

____

2\.

____

3\.

____

PROBLEM SOLVING

Solve. Write or draw to explain.

4\. Grace found 3 quarters, 3 dimes, and 1 nickel in her pocket. How much money did she find?

____

Name ______________________________

Lesson 91

COMMON CORE STANDARD CC.2.MD.8

Lesson Objective: Solve word problems involving money by using the strategy *act it out.*

Problem Solving • Money

Erin used one $1 bill and 3 nickels to buy a marker. How much money did Erin use to buy the marker?

Unlock the Problem

What do I need to find?	What information do I need to use?
how much money Erin used to buy the marker	Erin used one $1 bill and 3 nickels

Show how to solve the problem.

Draw to show the money that Erin used.

$1 5¢ 5¢ 5¢

Erin used $1.15 to buy the marker.

Use play coins and bills to solve. Draw to show what you did.

1. Zeke has one $1 bill, 2 dimes, and 1 nickel. How much money does Zeke have? __________

Name ______________________

Lesson 91
CC.2.MD.8

Problem Solving • Money

Use play coins and bills to solve.
Draw to show what you did.

1. Sara has 2 quarters, 1 nickel, and two $1 bills.
How much money does Sara have? ____________

2. Brad has one $1 bill, 4 dimes, and 2 nickels in his bank. How much money does Brad have in his bank? ____________

3. Mr. Morgan gives 1 quarter, 3 nickels, 4 pennies, and one $1 bill to the clerk. How much money does Mr. Morgan give the clerk? ____________

Name ______________________

Lesson 92

COMMON CORE STANDARD CC.2.MD.9

Lesson Objective: Measure the lengths of objects and use a line plot to display the measurement data.

Display Measurement Data

Each X on the line plot is for the length of one book.

5	6	7	8
X	X	X X	X

Lengths of Books in Inches

One book is 5 inches long.
One book is 6 inches long.
Two books are 7 inches long.
One book is 8 inches long.

1. Use an inch ruler. Measure and record the lengths of 4 pencils in inches.

1st pencil: ______ inches
2nd pencil: ______ inches
3rd pencil: ______ inches
4th pencil: ______ inches

2. Write the numbers and draw the Xs to complete the line plot.

______ ______ ______ ______

Lengths of Pencils in Inches

Name ______________________________

Display Measurement Data

1. Use an inch ruler. Measure and record the lengths of 4 different books in inches.

1st book: _____ inches
2nd book: _____ inches
3rd book: _____ inches
4th book: _____ inches

2. Make a line plot of the information above. Write a title for a line plot. Then write the numbers and draw the ***X***s.

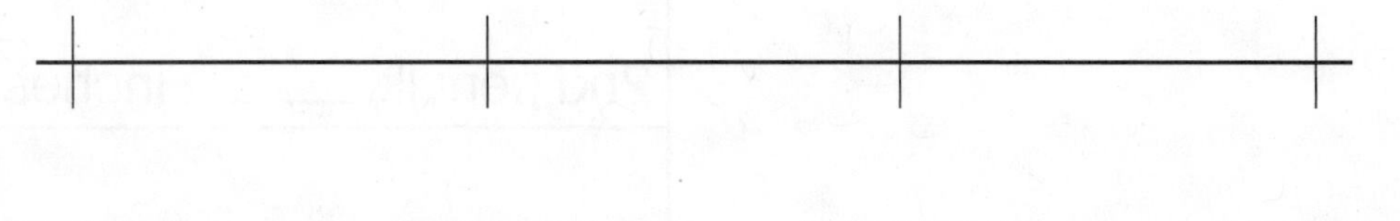

PROBLEM SOLVING

3. Jesse measured the lengths of some strings. Use his list to complete the line plot.

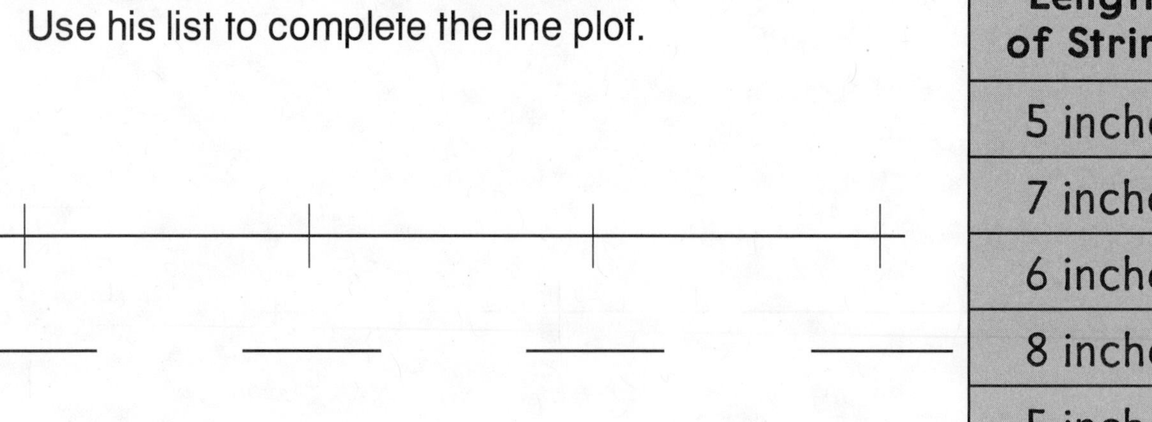

Lengths of Strings
5 inches
7 inches
6 inches
8 inches
5 inches

Name ______________________________

Lesson 93

COMMON CORE STANDARD CC.2.MD.10

Lesson Objective: Collect data in a survey and record that data in a tally chart.

Collect Data

You can take a survey to get information.

Which is your favorite sport?

Each tally mark stands for one person's answer. Count the tally marks.

Favorite Sport		
Sport	**Tally**	**Total**
soccer	IIII	4
basketball	~~IIII~~	5
football	III	3

Elijah asked his classmates to choose their favorite breakfast food. He made this chart.

1. Write numbers to complete the chart.

Favorite Breakfast Food		
Food	**Tally**	**Total**
cereal	~~IIII~~ III	8
pancakes	IIII	
toast	III	
eggs	~~IIII~~	

2. How many classmates chose pancakes?

_______ classmates

3. Which breakfast food did the fewest classmates choose?

____

Name ___________________________

Lesson 93
CC.2.MD.10

Collect Data

1. Take a survey. Ask 10 classmates how they got to school. Use tally marks to show their choices.

How We Got to School	
Way	**Tally**
walk	
bus	
car	
bike	

2. How many classmates rode in a bus to school?

_______ classmates

3. How many classmates rode in a car to school?

_______ classmates

4. In which way did the fewest classmates get to school?

____

5. In which way did the most classmates get to school?

____

6. Did more classmates get to school by walking or by riding in a car?

____

How many more? _______ more classmates

Name ______________________________

Lesson 94

COMMON CORE STANDARD CC.2.MD.10

Lesson Objective: Interpret data in picture graphs and use that information to solve problems.

Read Picture Graphs

A picture graph uses pictures to show information.

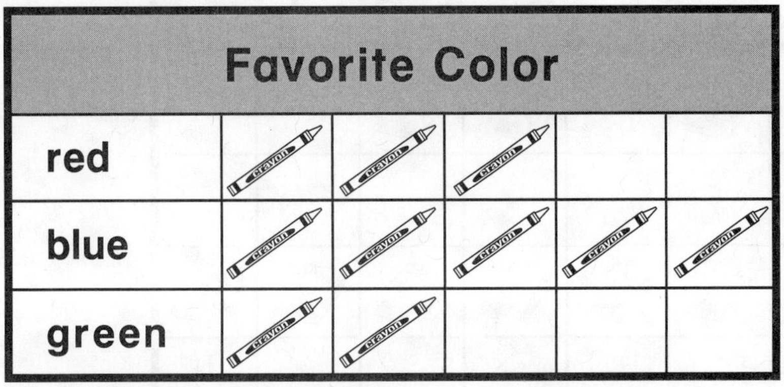

Favorite Color					
red	crayon	crayon	crayon		
blue	crayon	crayon	crayon	crayon	crayon
green	crayon	crayon			

Key: Each crayon stands for 1 child.

The row with __blue__ has 5 pictures.

So, __5__ children chose blue.

Use the picture graph to answer the questions.

1. How many children chose red? ______ children

2. Did more children choose green or choose red? ______________

3. Which color was chosen by the most children? ______________

4. How many children in all chose a favorite color? ______ children

Name ______________________________

Read Picture Graphs

Use the picture graph to answer the questions.

Number of Books Read						
Ryan	Math Grade 2	Math Grade 2	Math Grade 2	Math Grade 2		
Gwen	Math Grade 2	Math Grade 2				
Anna	Math Grade 2	Math Grade 2	Math Grade 2	Math Grade 2	Math Grade 2	Math Grade 2
Henry	Math Grade 2	Math Grade 2	Math Grade 2			

Key: Each Math Grade 2 stands for 1 book.

1. How many books in all did Henry and Anna read? _______ books

2. How many more books did Ryan read than Gwen? _______ more books

3. How many fewer books did Gwen read than Anna? _______ fewer books

4. How many books did the four children read in all? _______ books

PROBLEM SOLVING

Use the picture graph above. Write or draw to explain.

5. Carlos read 4 books. How many children read fewer books than Carlos?

_______ children

Name ______________________

Lesson 15

COMMON CORE STANDARD CC.2.MD.10

Lesson Objective: Make picture graphs to represent data.

Make Picture Graphs

This picture graph uses 1 picture for each animal.
Draw a △ for each tally mark.

Animals at the Pet Store	
Animal	**Tally**
fish	IIII
hamster	II
turtle	III

Animals at the Pet Store					
fish	△	△	△	△	
hamster	△	△			
turtle	△	△	△		

Key: Each △ stands for 1 animal.

How many turtles are at the pet store? 3 turtles

1. Use the tally chart to complete the picture graph.
Draw a ☺ for each child.

Favorite Color	
Color	**Tally**
pink	卌
yellow	III
blue	卌

Favorite Color					
pink	☺	☺	☺	☺	☺
yellow					
blue					

Key: Each ☺ stands for 1 child.

2. Which color did the fewest children choose? ______________

3. How many children chose pink? _____ children

4. How many more children chose blue than chose yellow? _____ more children

Name ____________________

Make Picture Graphs

1. Use the tally chart to complete the picture graph.
Draw a ☺ for each child.

Favorite Cookie	
Cookie	**Tally**
chocolate	III
oatmeal	I
peanut butter	~~IIII~~
shortbread	IIII

Favorite Cookie					
chocolate					
oatmeal					
peanut butter					
shortbread					

Key: Each ☺ stands for 1 child.

2. How many children chose chocolate? _______ children

3. How many fewer children chose oatmeal than peanut butter? _______ fewer children

4. Which cookie did the most children choose?

____

5. How many children in all chose a favorite cookie? _______ children

6. How many children chose oatmeal or shortbread? _______ children

Name ______________________________

Lesson 96

COMMON CORE STANDARD CC.2.MD.10

Lesson Objective: Interpret data in bar graphs and use that information to solve problems.

Read Bar Graphs

Look at the number below the right end of each bar.

This number tells how many of each model Max has.

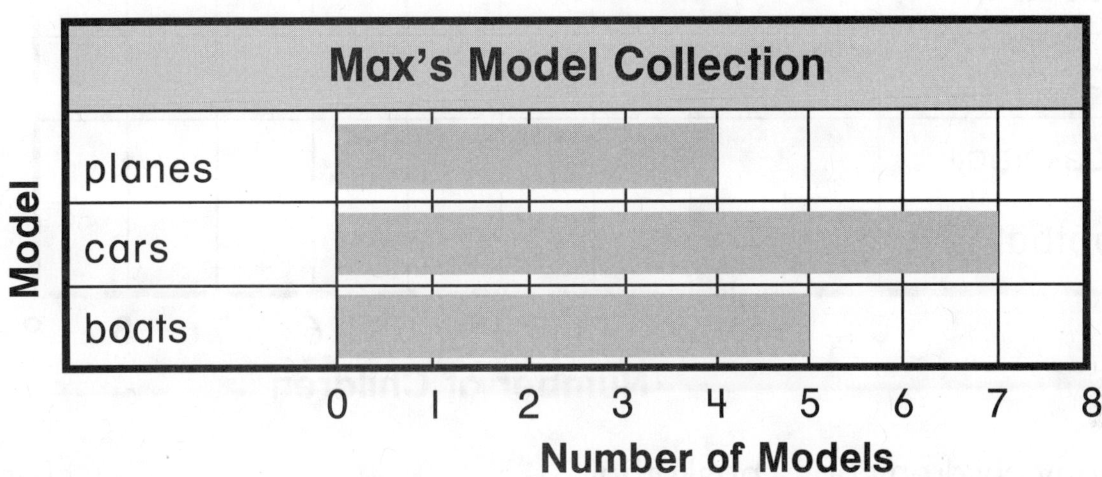

The bar for model cars ends at 7.

So, Max has __7__ car models.

Use the bar graph.

1. How many model planes does Max have? ______ model planes

2. Does Max have more model boats boats or model planes? more model ______________

3. How many models does Max have in all? ______ models

Name ______________________________

Read Bar Graphs

Use the bar graph.

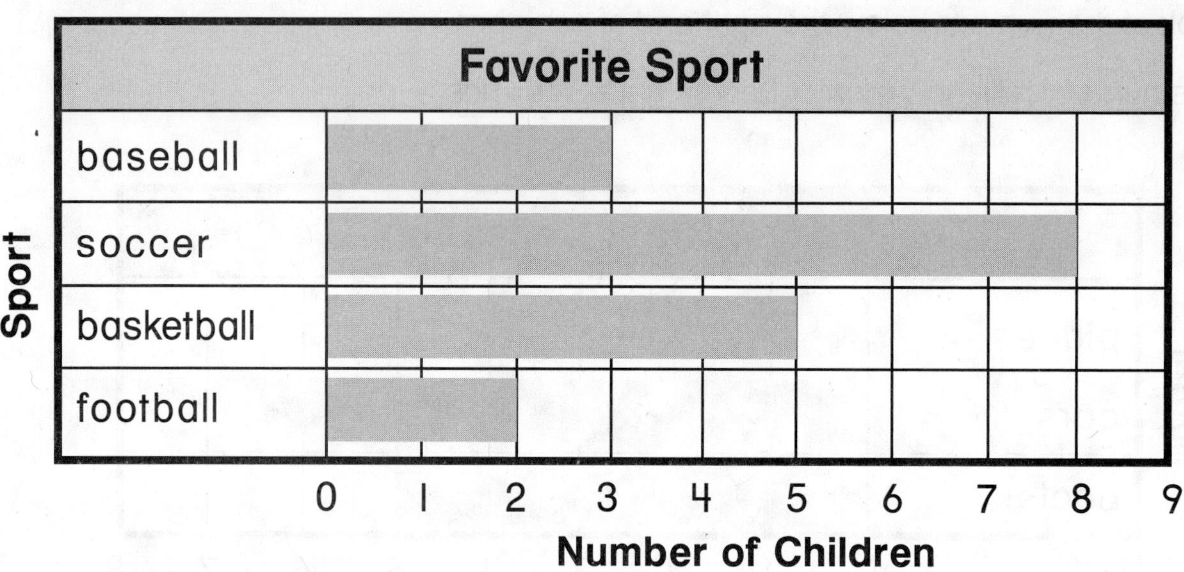

1. How many children chose basketball? _______ children

2. Which sport did the most children choose? ____________________

3. How many more children chose basketball than baseball? _______ more children

4. Which sport did the fewest children choose? ____________________

5. How many children chose a sport that was not soccer? _______ children

PROBLEM SOLVING REAL WORLD

6. How many children chose baseball or basketball? _______ children

Name ______________________________

COMMON CORE STANDARD CC.2.MD.10

Lesson Objective: Make bar graphs to represent data.

Make Bar Graphs

These bar graphs show how many games Alex, Sarah, and Tony played.

- Alex played 5 games.
- Sarah played 3 games.
- Tony played 4 games.

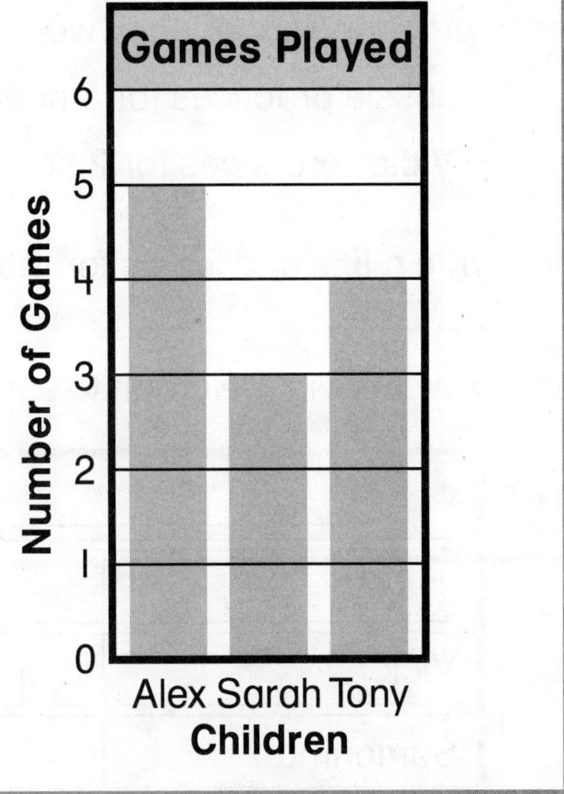

Jim is making a bar graph to show the number of markers his friends have.

- Adam has 4 markers.
- Clint has 3 markers.
- Erin has 2 markers.

1. Write labels for the graph.

2. Draw bars in the graph to show the number of markers that Clint and Erin have.

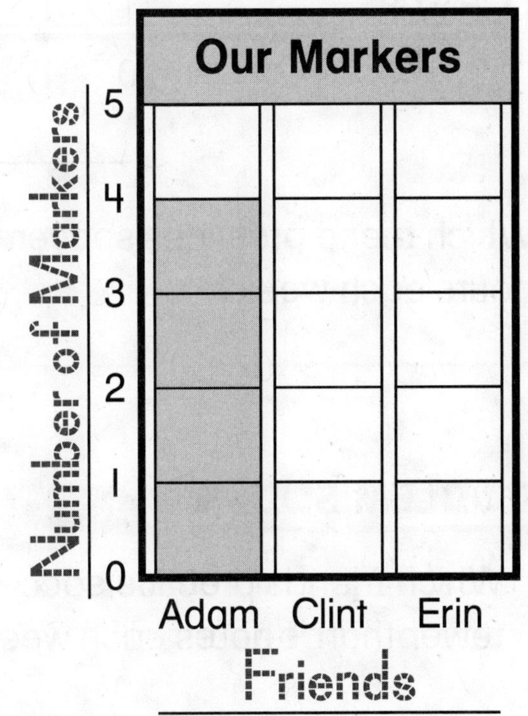

Name ______________________________

Make Bar Graphs

Maria asked her friends how many hours they practice soccer each week.

- Jessie practices for 3 hours.
- Victor practices for 2 hours.
- Samantha practices for 5 hours.
- David practices for 6 hours.

1. Write a title and labels for the bar graph.

____

2. Draw bars in the graph to show the data.

______________________________										
Jessie										
Victor										
Samantha										
David										
	0	1	2	3	4	5	6	7	8	9	10

____

3. Which friend practices soccer for the most hours each week?

____

PROBLEM SOLVING

4. Which friends practice soccer for fewer than 4 hours each week?

____

Name ______________________

Lesson 18
COMMON CORE STANDARD CC.2.MD.10
Lesson Objective: Solve problems involving data by using the strategy *make a graph.*

Problem Solving • Display Data

The list shows how many hours Morgan worked on her project. Describe how the number of hours changed from Week 1 to Week 4.

Week 1	1 hour
Week 2	2 hours
Week 3	3 hours
Week 4	4 hours

Unlock the Problem

What do I need to find?

how the number of hours changed from Week 1 to Week 4

What information do I need to use?

the number of hours Morgan worked on her project each week

Show how to solve the problem.

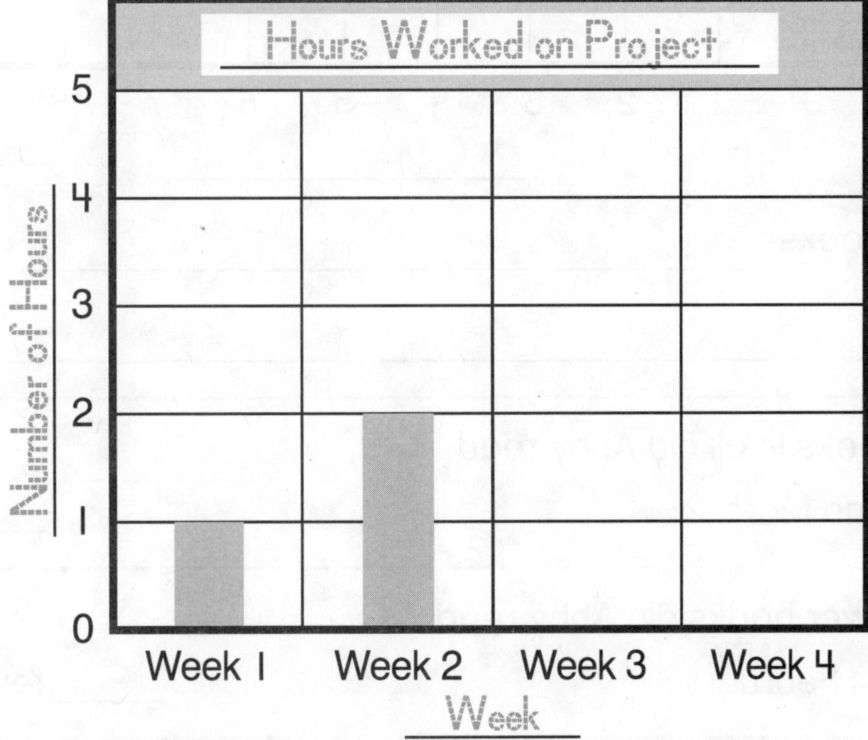

The number of hours ______________________

____

Name ______________________________

Lesson 98
CC.2.MD.10

Problem Solving • Display Data

Make a bar graph to solve the problem.

1. The list shows the number of books that Abby read each month. Describe how the number of books she read changed from February to May.

February	8 books
March	7 books
April	6 books
May	4 books

______________										
February										
March										
April										
May										
	0	1	2	3	4	5	6	7	8	9	10

____

The number of books ____

____

2. How many books in all did Abby read in February and March? _____ books

3. How many fewer books did Abby read in April than in February? _____ fewer books

4. In which months did Abby read fewer than 7 books? ______________________

Name ______________________________

COMMON CORE STANDARD CC.2.G.1

Lesson Objective: Identify three-dimensional shapes.

Three-Dimensional Shapes

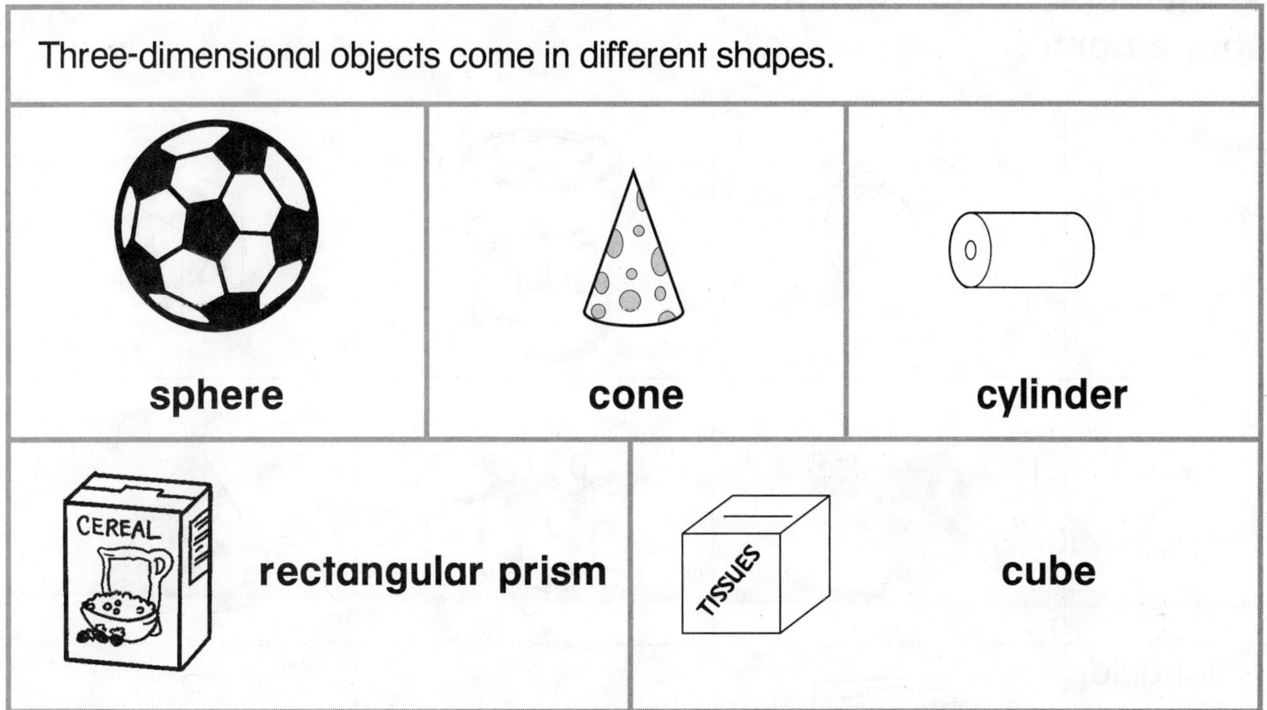

Circle the objects that match the shape name.

1. rectangular prism		Pasta 1 lb	
2. cylinder		Jelly	Soup
3. cone			

Name ______________________________

Lesson 99
CC.2.G.1

Three-Dimensional Shapes

Circle the objects that match the shape name.

1. cube			
2. cone			
3. rectangular prism			
4. cylinder			

PROBLEM SOLVING

5. Lisa draws a circle by tracing around the bottom of a block. Which could be the shape of Lisa's block? Circle the name of the shape.

cone   cube   rectangular prism

Name ___________________________

COMMON CORE STANDARD CC.2.G.1

Lesson Objective: Identify and describe three-dimensional shapes according to the number of faces, edges, and vertices.

Attributes of Three-Dimensional Shapes

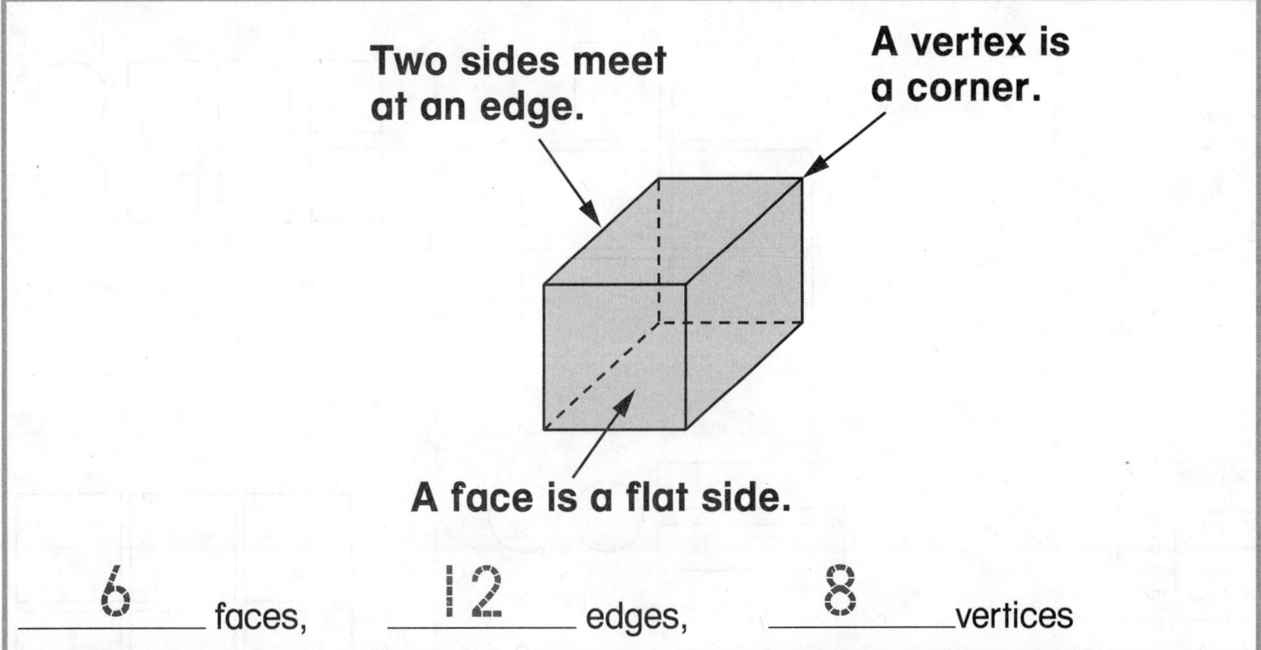

6 faces, 12 edges, 8 vertices

Write how many for each.

	faces	edges	vertices
1. cube	____	____	____
2. rectangular prism	____	____	____

Name ____________________

Attributes of Three-Dimensional Shapes

Circle the set of shapes that are the faces of the three-dimensional shape.

1.

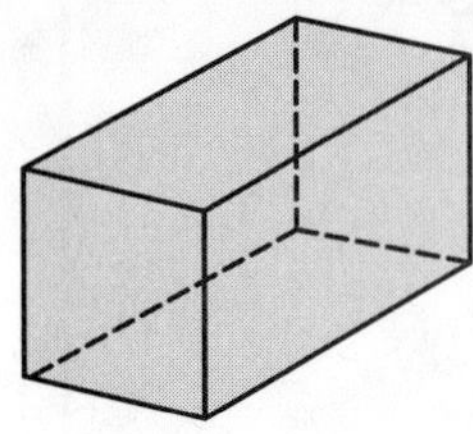

rectangular prism

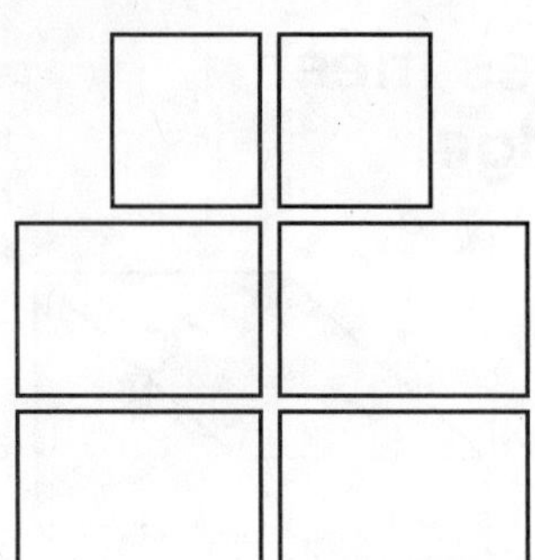

2.

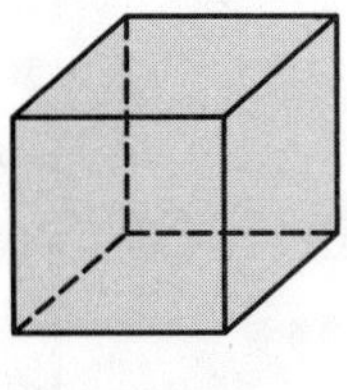

cube

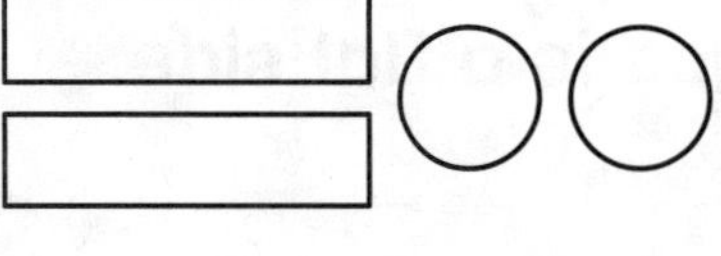

3.

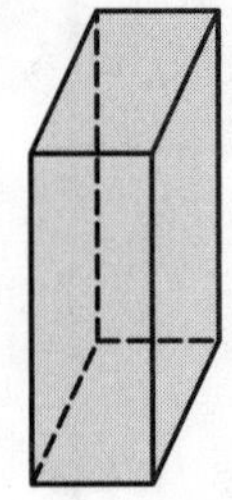

rectangular prism

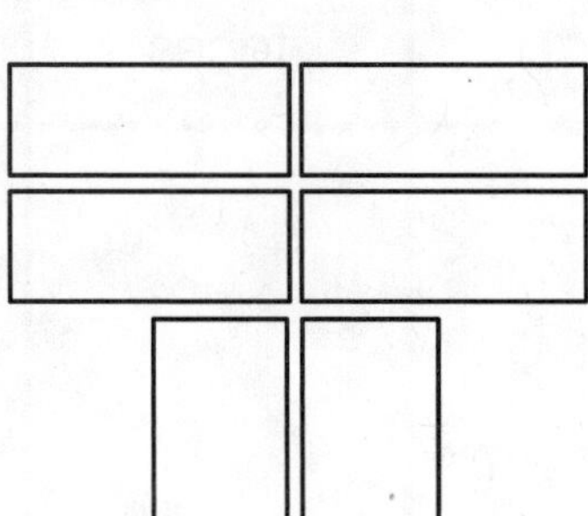

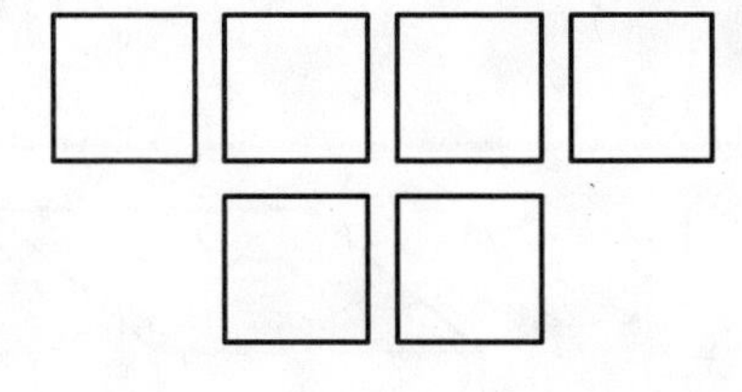

PROBLEM SOLVING

4. Kevin keeps his marbles in a container that has the shape of a cube. He wants to paint each face a different color. How many different paint colors does he need?

_____ different paint colors

Name ______________________________

Lesson 101

COMMON CORE STANDARD CC.2.G.1

Lesson Objective: Name 3-, 4-, 5-, and 6-sided shapes according to the number of sides and vertices.

Two-Dimensional Shapes

Count sides and vertices.

A pentagon has 5 sides.

1 2 5 3 4

pentagon

A hexagon has 6 vertices.

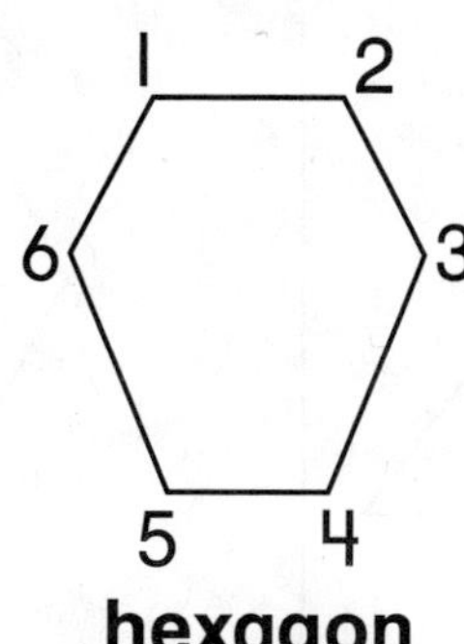

hexagon

Write the number of sides and the number of vertices.

1. triangle

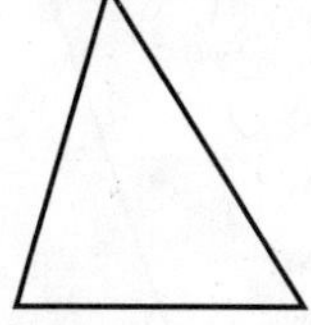

____ sides

____ vertices

2. rectangle

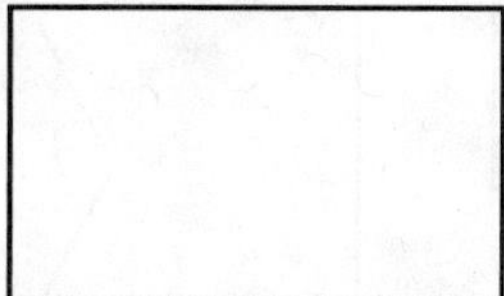

____ sides

____ vertices

3. quadrilateral

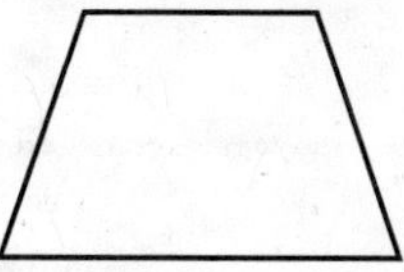

____ sides

____ vertices

4. pentagon

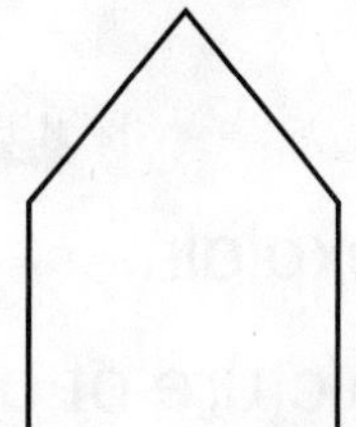

____ sides

____ vertices

Name ______________________________

Lesson 101
CC.2.G.1

Two-Dimensional Shapes

Write the number of sides and the number of vertices. Then write the name of the shape.

pentagon triangle hexagon quadrilateral

1.

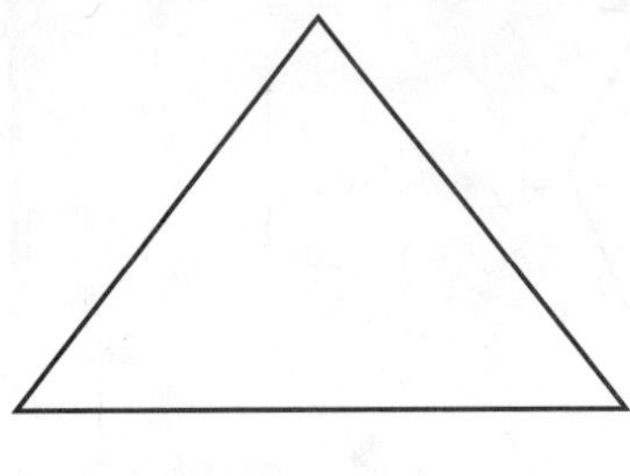

____ sides

____ vertices

____

2.

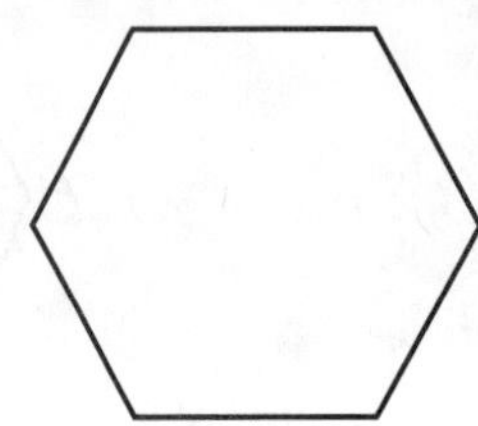

____ sides

____ vertices

____

3.

____ sides

____ vertices

____

4.

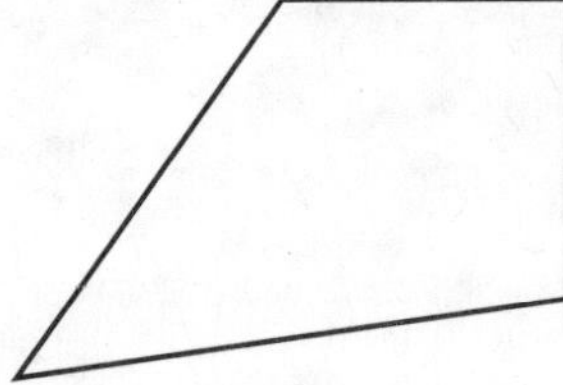

____ sides

____ vertices

____

5.

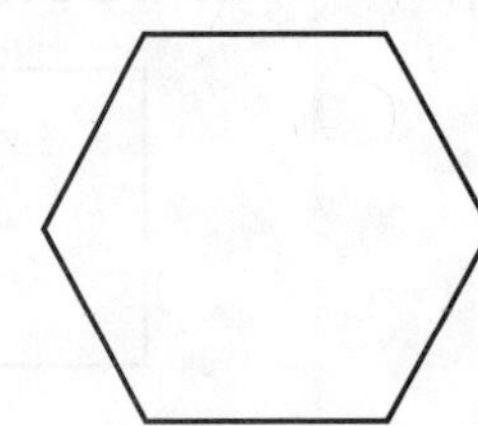

____ sides

____ vertices

____

6.

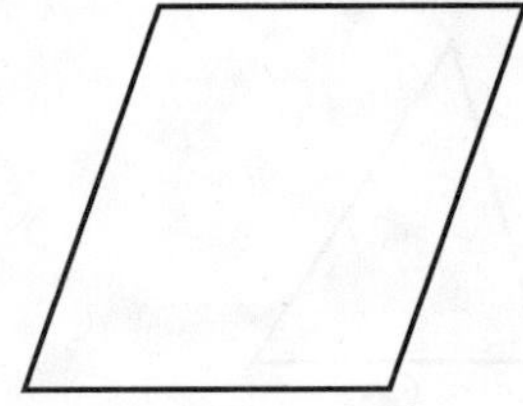

____ sides

____ vertices

____

PROBLEM SOLVING

Solve. Draw or write to explain.

7. Oscar is drawing a picture of a house. He draws a pentagon shape for a window. How many sides does his window have?

____ sides

Name ___________________________________

Lesson 102

COMMON CORE STANDARD CC.2.G.1

Lesson Objective: Identify angles in two-dimensional shapes.

Angles in Two-Dimensional Shapes

Two sides meet and form an angle.

There are  angles in a square.

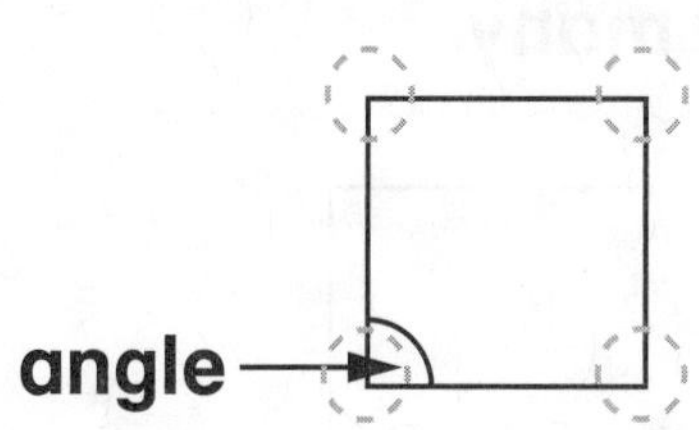

Circle the angles in each shape.
Write how many.

1.

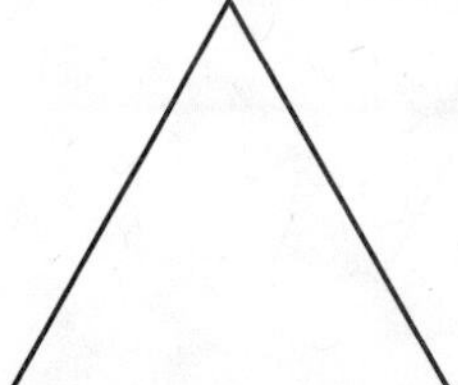

________ angles

2.

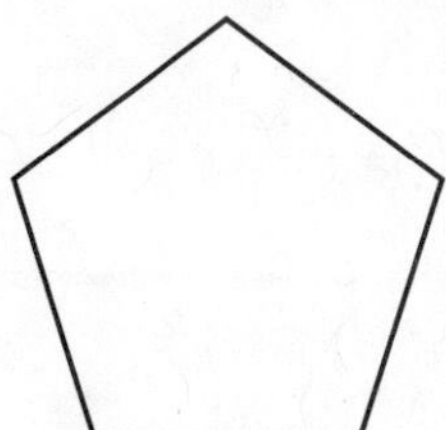

________ angles

3.

________ angles

Name ______________________

Angles in Two-Dimensional Shapes

Circle the angles in each shape.
Write how many.

1.

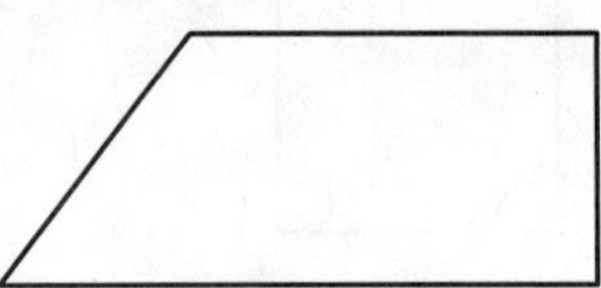

_____ **angles**

2.

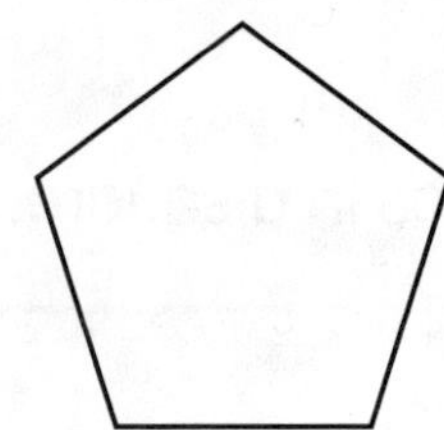

_____ **angles**

3.

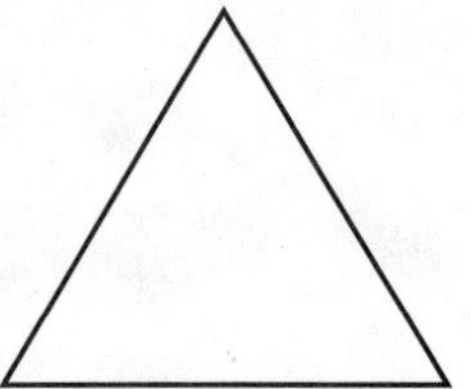

_____ **angles**

4.

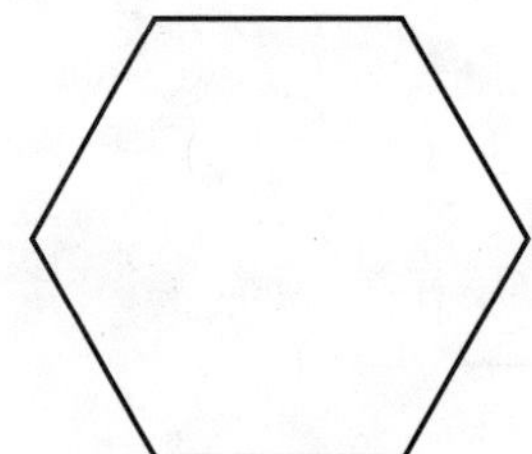

_____ **angles**

PROBLEM SOLVING

5. Logan drew 2 two-dimensional shapes that had 8 angles in all. Draw shapes Logan could have drawn.

Name ___________________________

Lesson 103

COMMON CORE STANDARD CC.2.G.1

Lesson Objective: Sort two-dimensional shapes according to their attributes.

Sort Two-Dimensional Shapes

Circle the shapes with 5 sides.

4 sides　3 sides　5 sides　6 sides

Circle the shapes with fewer than 5 angles.

3 angles　6 angles　4 angles　5 angles

Circle the shapes that match the rule.

1. Shapes with 4 sides

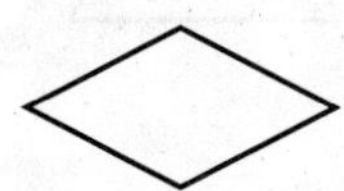
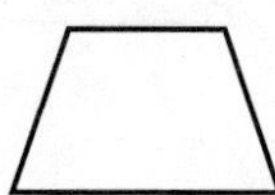
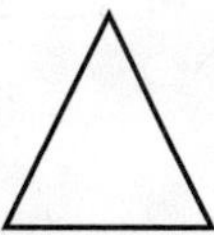
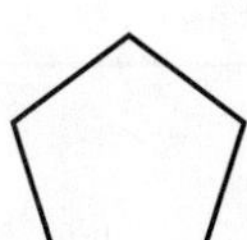

2. Shapes with more than 4 angles

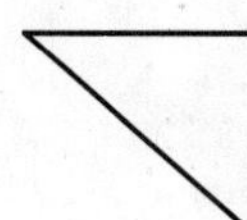
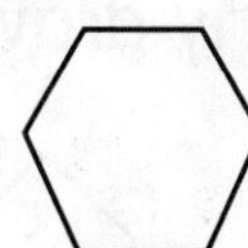
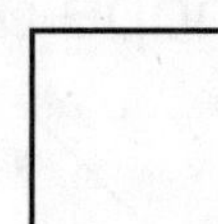
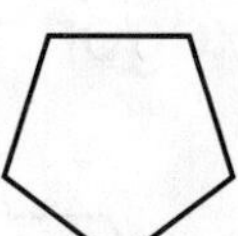

Name ____________________

Sort Two-Dimensional Shapes

Circle the shapes that match the rule.

1. Shapes with fewer than 5 sides

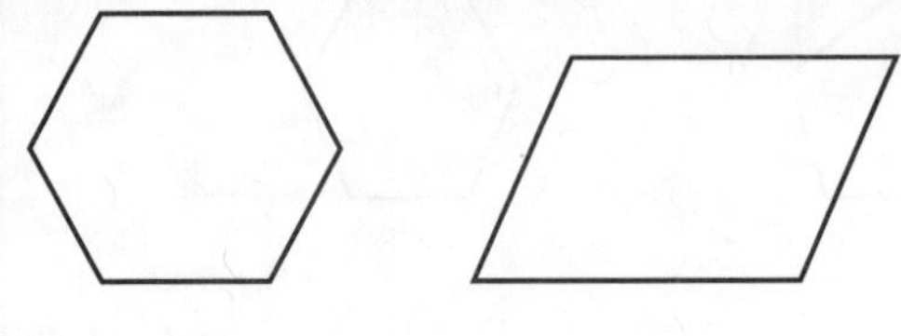
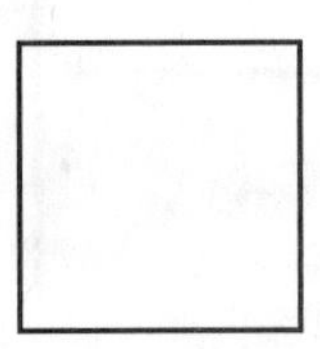
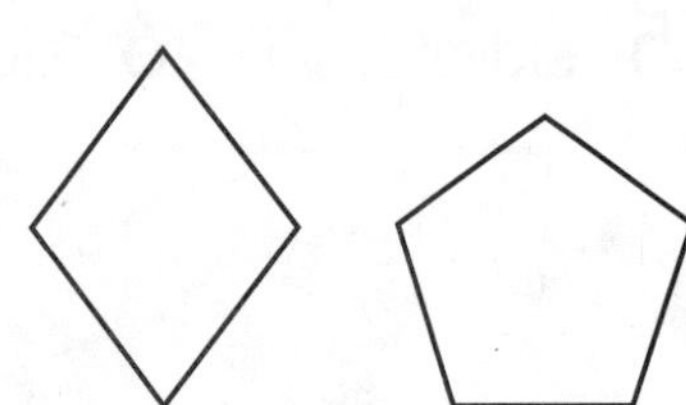

2. Shapes with more than 4 sides

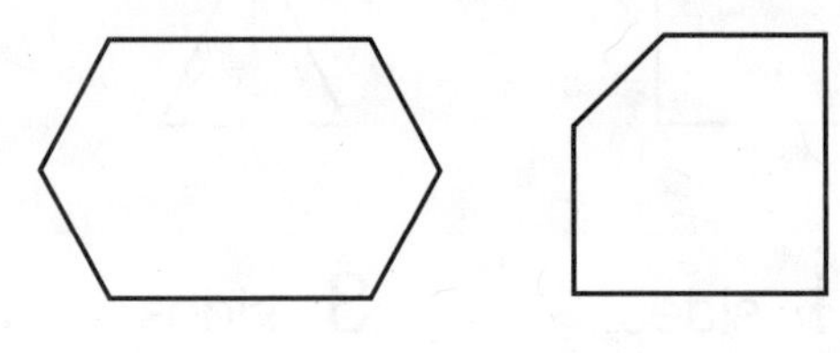
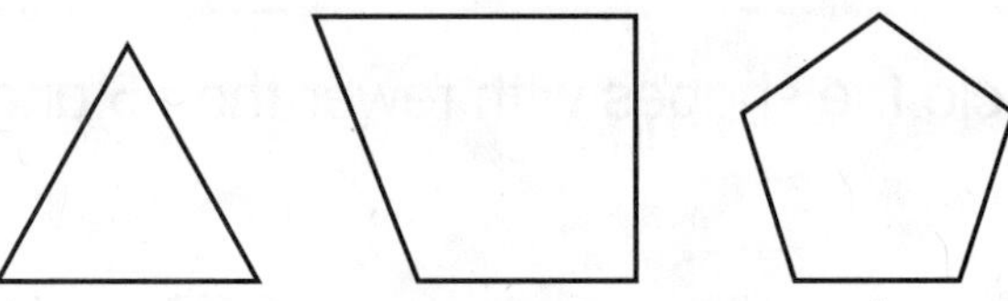

3. Shapes with 4 angles

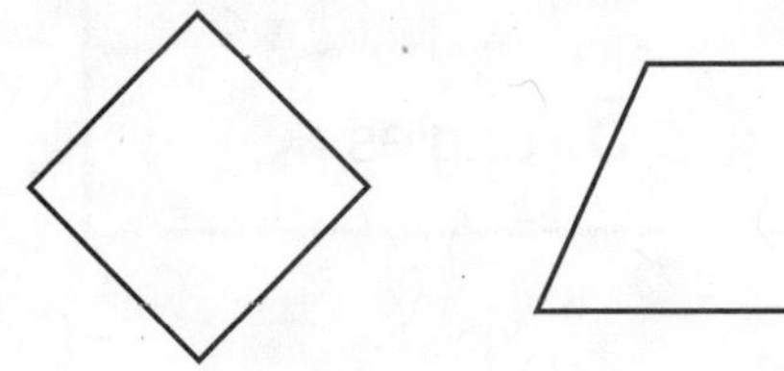
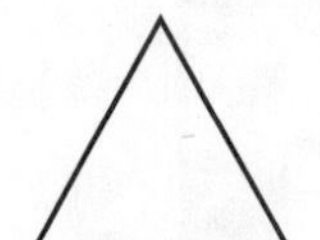
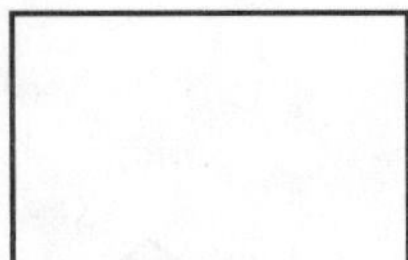

4. Shapes with fewer than 6 angles

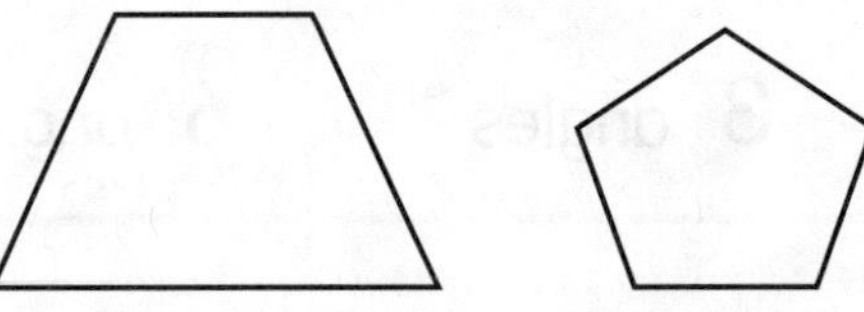
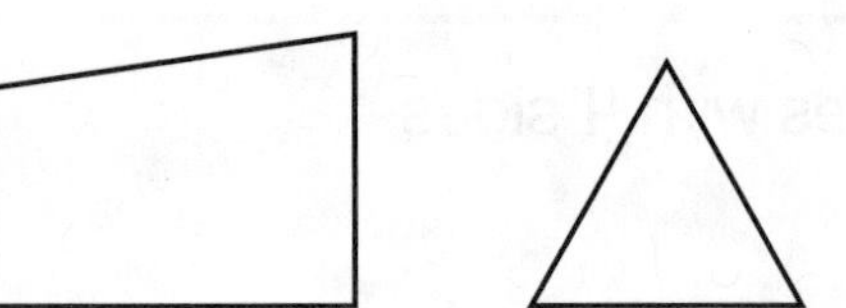

PROBLEM SOLVING

Circle the correct shape.

5. Tammy drew a shape with more than 3 angles.
It is not a hexagon. Which shape did Tammy draw?

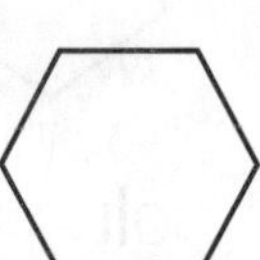
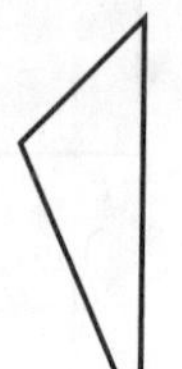
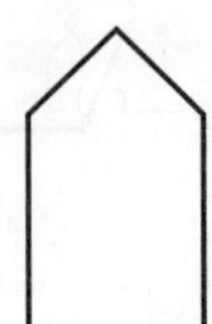

Name ___________________________

COMMON CORE STANDARD CC.2.G.2

Lesson Objective: Partition rectangles into equal-size squares and find the total number of these squares.

Partition Rectangles

How many color tiles cover this rectangle?

Make a row of color tiles on the rectangle. Trace around the square tiles.

How many squares? 3 squares

Use color tiles to cover the rectangle. Trace around the square tiles. Write how many.

1.

Number of rows: ________

Number of columns: ________

Total: ________ squares

2.

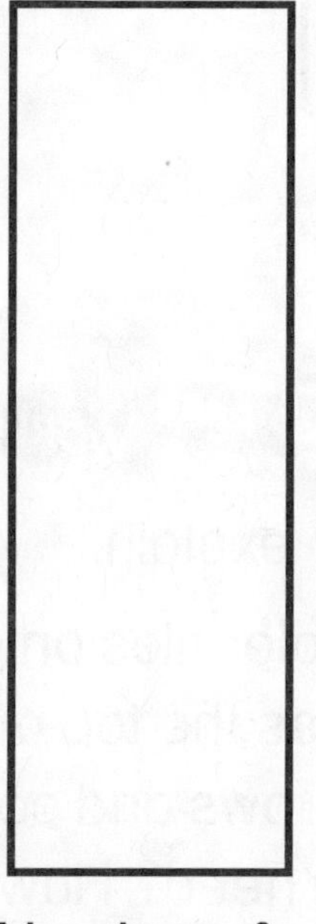

Number of rows: ________

Number of columns: ________

Total: ________ squares

Name ______________________

Partition Rectangles

Use color tiles to cover the rectangle.
Trace around the square tiles.
Write how many.

1.

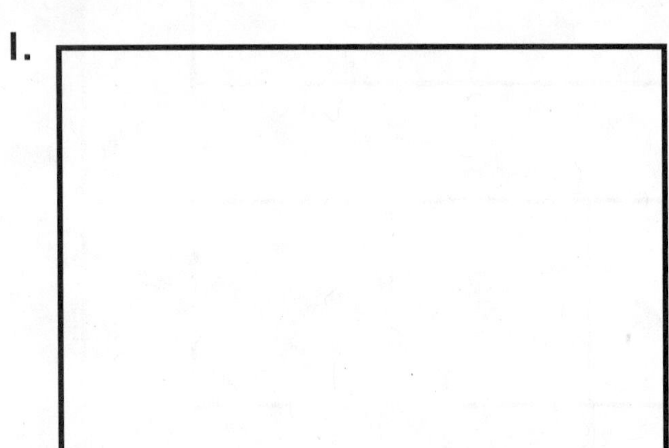

Number of rows: _____

Number of columns: _____

Total: _____ square tiles

2.

Number of rows: _____

Number of columns: _____

Total: _____ square tiles

PROBLEM SOLVING REAL WORLD

Solve. Write or draw to explain.

3. Nina wants to put color tiles on a square. 3 color tiles fit across the top of the square. How many rows and columns of of squares will Nina need? How many color tiles will she use in all?

Number of rows: _____

Number of columns: _____

Total: _____ square tiles

_____ tiles

Name ______________________________

Lesson 105

COMMON CORE STANDARD CC.2.G.3

Lesson Objective: Identify and name equal parts of circles and rectangles as halves, thirds, or fourths.

Equal Parts

You can divide a whole into equal parts.

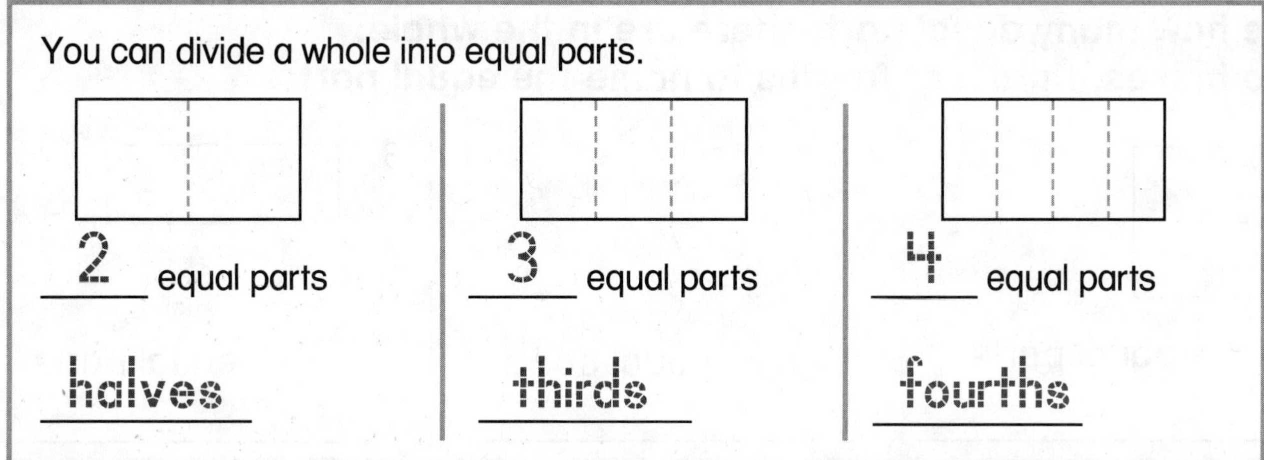

Write how many equal parts there are in the whole.
Write halves, thirds, or fourths to name the equal parts.

1. 

4 equal parts

fourths

2. 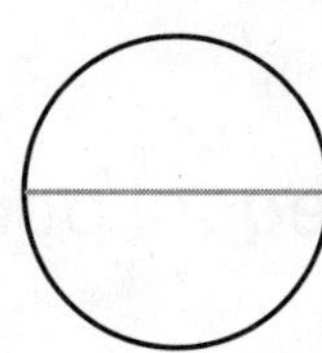

_____ equal parts

____

3. 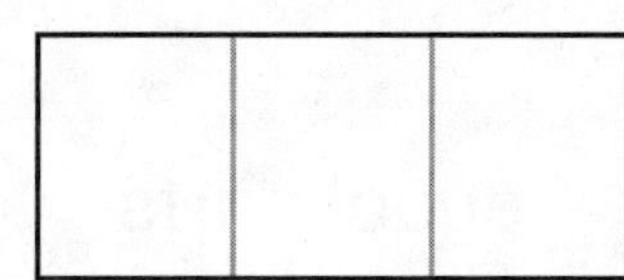

_____ equal parts

____

4. 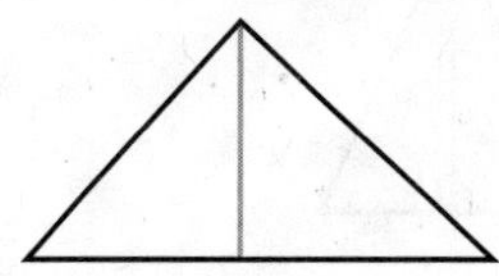

_____ equal parts

____

5. 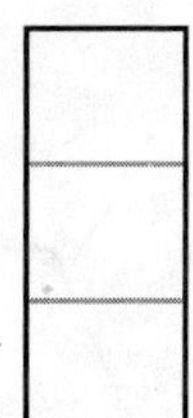

_____ equal parts

____

6. 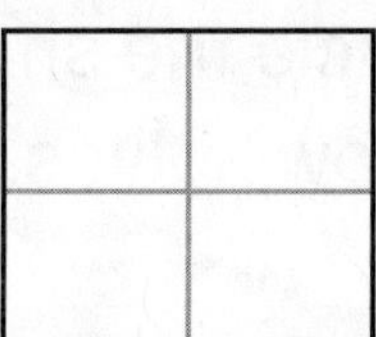

_____ equal parts

____

Name ________________________

Equal Parts

Write how many equal parts there are in the whole.
Write halves, thirds, or fourths to name the equal parts.

1. 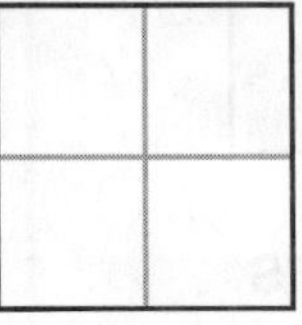

_____ equal parts

____

2. 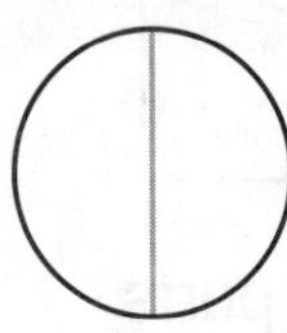

_____ equal parts

____

3. 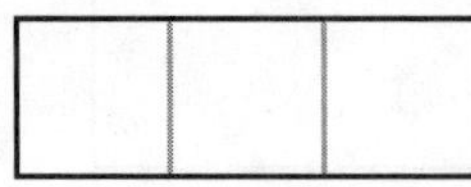

_____ equal parts

____

4. 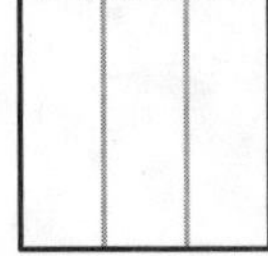

_____ equal parts

____

5. 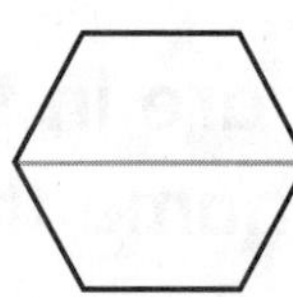

_____ equal parts

____

6. 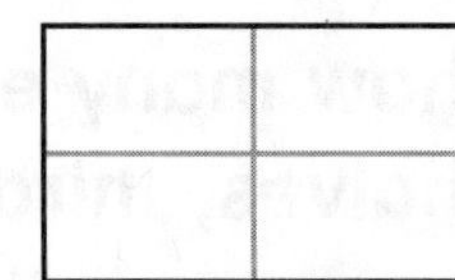

_____ equal parts

____

PROBLEM SOLVING

7. Sort the shapes.
   - Draw an X on the shapes that do not show equal parts.
   - Circle the shapes that show halves.

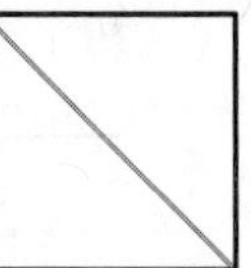
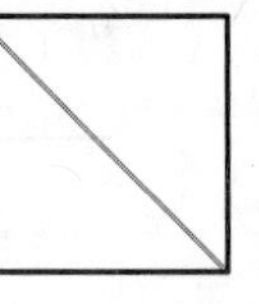
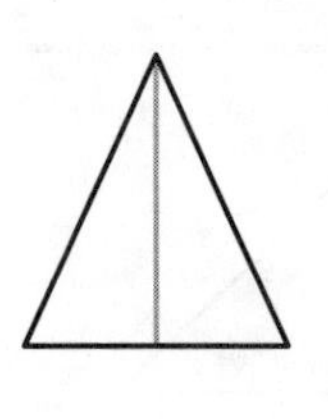
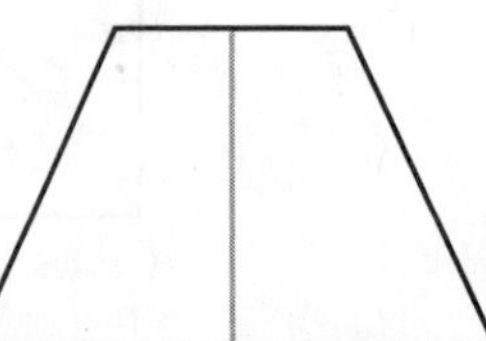
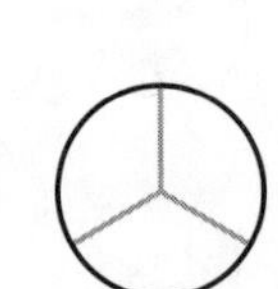
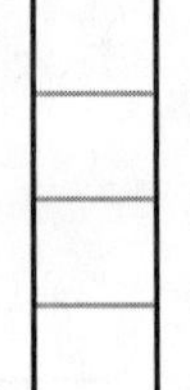

Name ________________________

Lesson 106

COMMON CORE STANDARD CC.2.G.3

Lesson Objective: Partition shapes to show halves, thirds, or fourths.

Show Equal Parts of a Whole

Trace to show the equal parts.

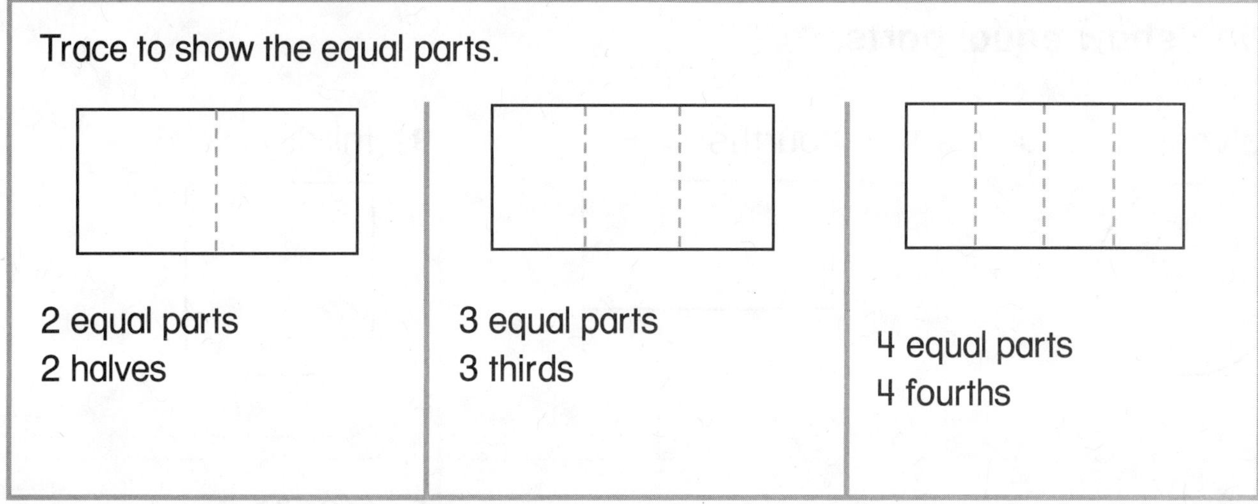

Draw to show equal parts.

1. halves

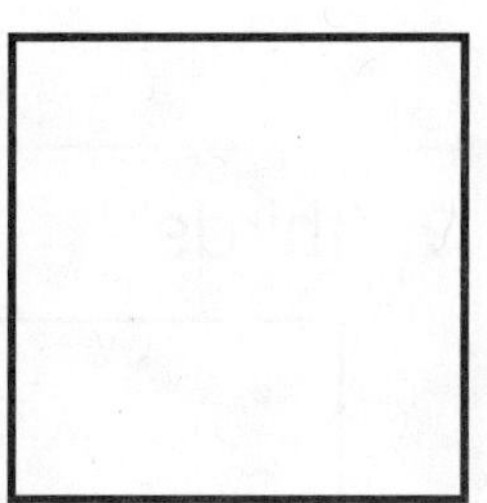

2. thirds

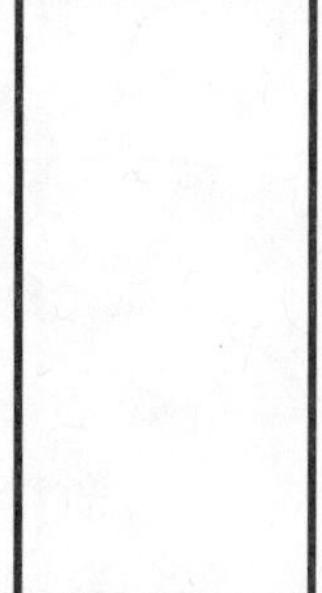

3. halves

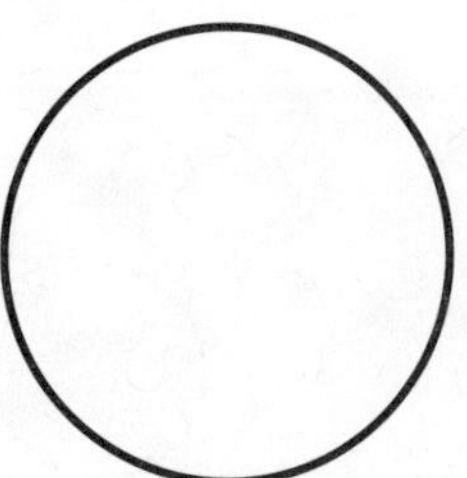

4. fourths

Name ____________________

Lesson 106
CC.2.G.3

Show Equal Parts of a Whole

Draw to show equal parts.

1. halves

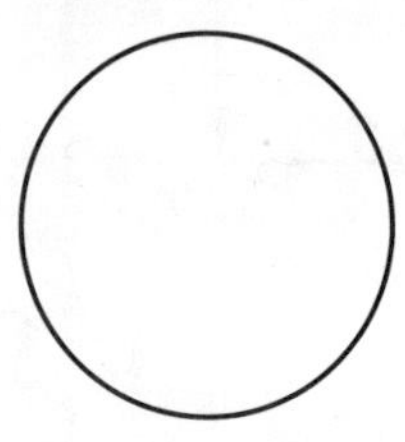

2. fourths

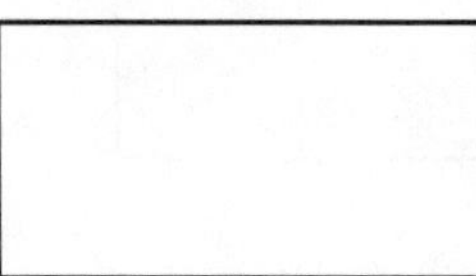

3. thirds

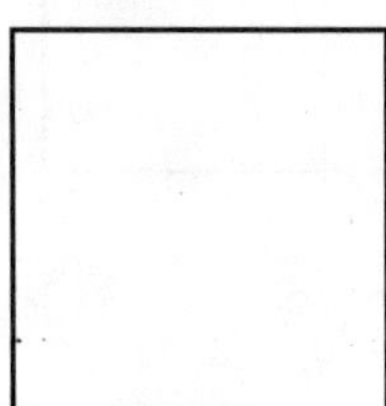

4. thirds

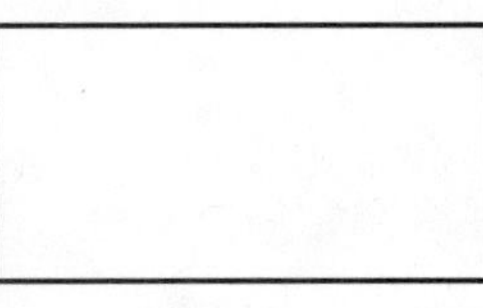

5. halves

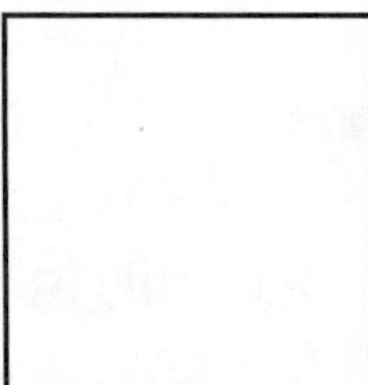

6. fourths

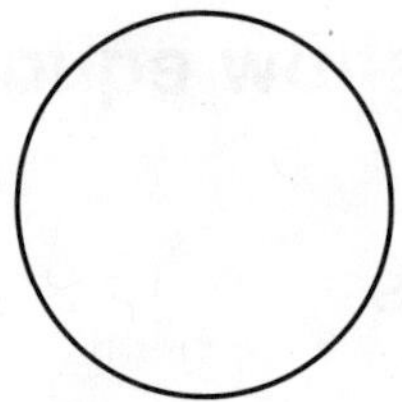

7. fourths

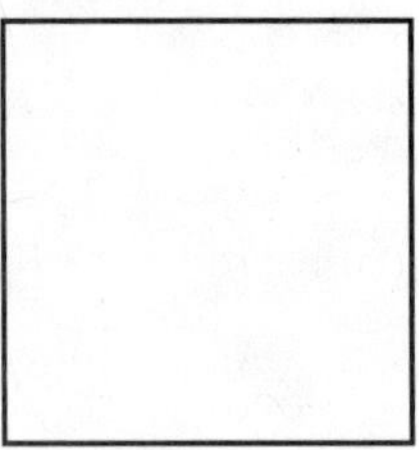

8. halves

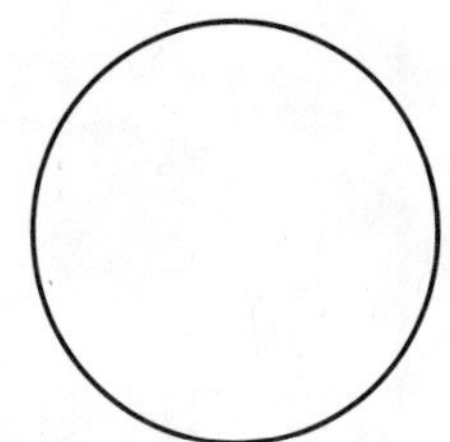

9. thirds

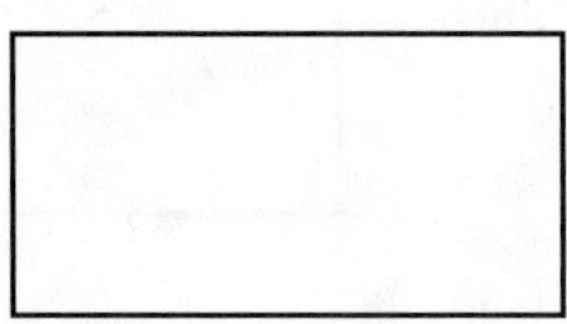

PROBLEM SOLVING

Solve. Write or draw to explain.

10. Joe has one sandwich. He cuts the sandwich into fourths. How many pieces of sandwich does he have?

_____ pieces

Name ___________________________

Lesson Objective: Identify and describe one equal part as a half of, a third of, or a fourth of a whole.

Describe Equal Parts

One equal part of each shape is shaded.

A half of the shape is shaded.	A third of the shape is shaded.	A fourth of the shape is shaded.

Draw to show halves.
Color a half of the shape.

1. 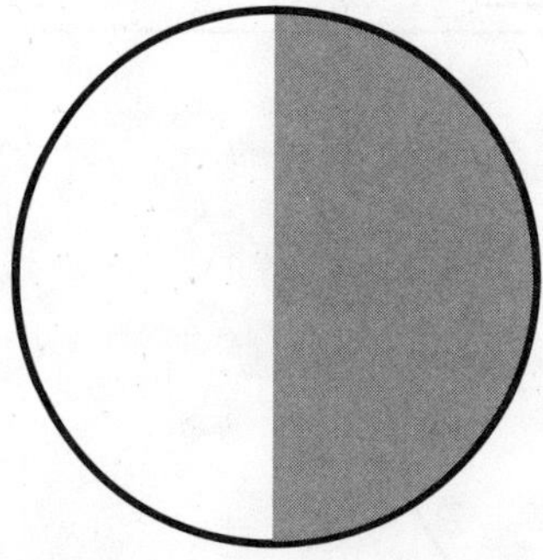

2. 

Draw to show fourths.
Color a fourth of the shape.

3. 

4. 

Name ___________________________

Lesson 107

CC.2.G.3

Describe Equal Parts

Draw to show halves.
Color a half of the shape.

1. 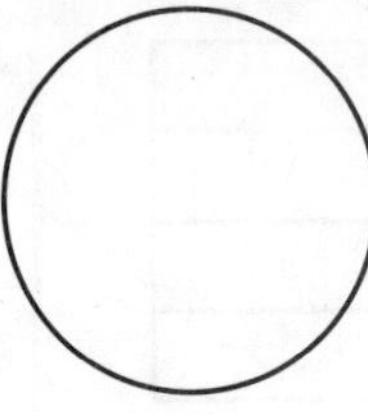

2. 

Draw to show thirds.
Color a third of the shape.

3. 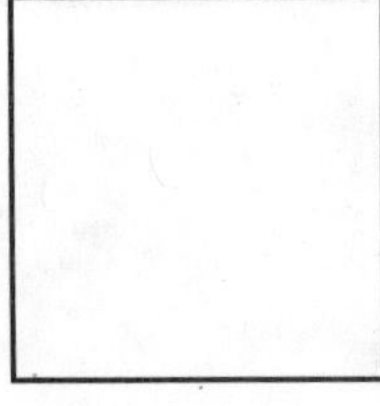

4. 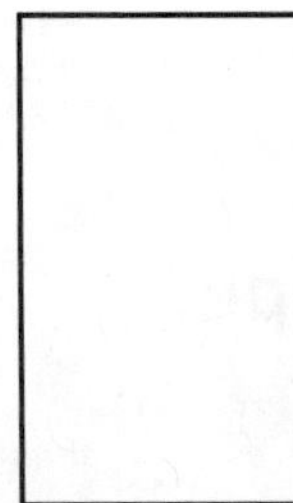

Draw to show fourths.
Color a fourth of the shape.

5. 

6. 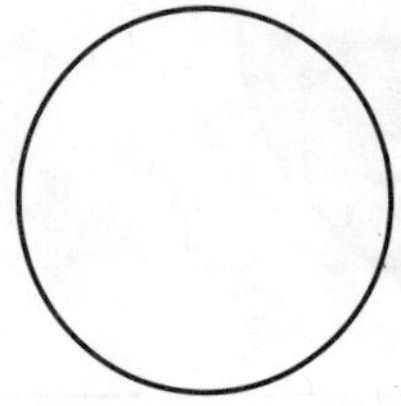

PROBLEM SOLVING

7. Circle all the shapes that have a third of the shape shaded.

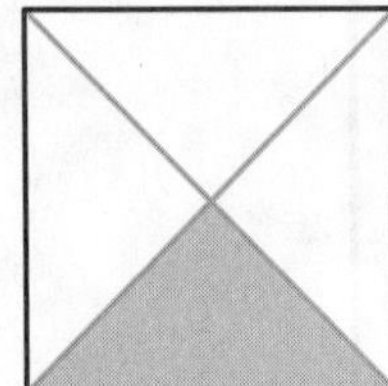 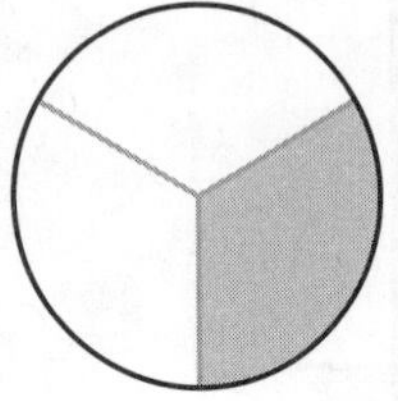 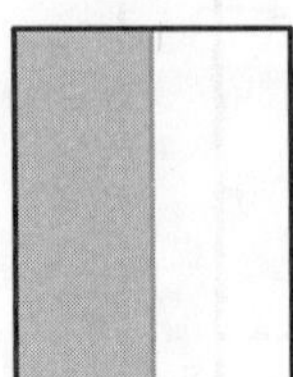 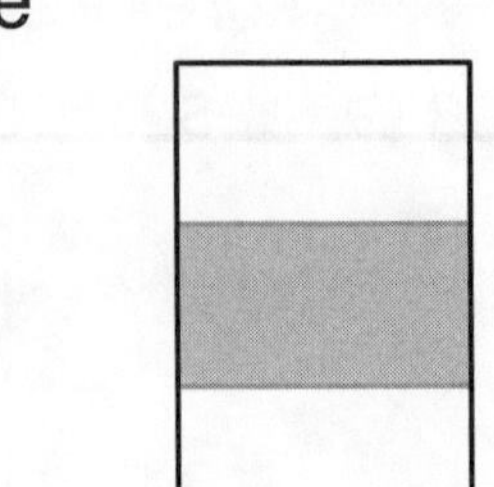 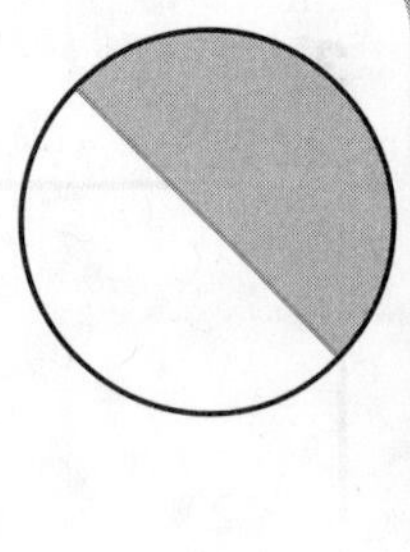

Name ________________________________

Lesson 108

COMMON CORE STANDARD CC.2.G.3

Lesson Objective: Solve problems involving wholes divided into equal shares by using the strategy *draw a diagram.*

Problem Solving • Equal Shares

Two gardens are the same size. Each garden is divided into halves, but the gardens are divided differently. How might the gardens be divided?

Unlock the Problem

What do I need to find?	**What information do I need to use?**
how the gardens are divided	There are 2 gardens. Each garden is divided into halves.

Show how to solve the problem.

Draw to show your answer.

1. Sophie has two pieces of paper that are the same size. She wants to divide each piece into fourths. What are two different ways she can divide the pieces of paper?

Name ____________________________

Problem Solving • Equal Shares

Draw to show your answer.

1. Max has square pizzas that are the same size. What are two different ways he can divide the pizzas into fourths?

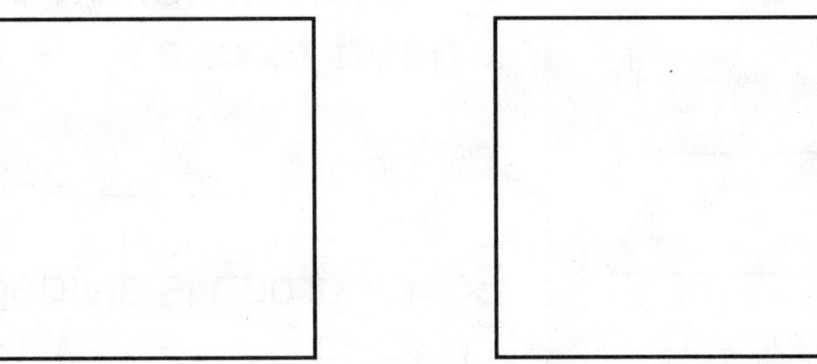

2. Lia has two pieces of paper that are the same size. What are two different ways she can divide the pieces of paper into halves?

3. Frank has two crackers that are the same size. What are two different ways he can divide the cracker into thirds?

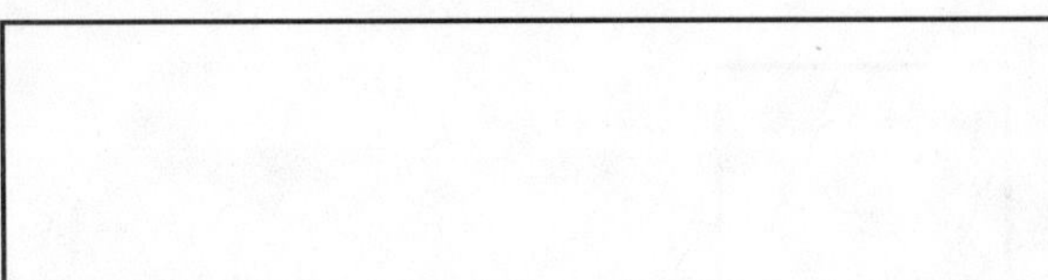